2021 中国 PPP 市场发展明度报告

上海财经大学 PPP 研究中心

上海财经大学出版社

图书在版编目(CIP)数据

2021中国PPP市场透明度报告/上海财经大学PPP研究中心著.—上海:上海财经大学出版社,2023.2
ISBN 978-7-5642-4123-0/F.4123

Ⅰ.①2… Ⅱ.①上… Ⅲ.①政府投资—合作—社会资本—研究报告—中国—2021 Ⅳ.①F832.48②F124.7

中国国家版本馆CIP数据核字(2023)第020025号

责任编辑 江 玉
封面设计 张克瑶

2021中国PPP市场透明度报告

著 作 者:	上海财经大学PPP研究中心
出版发行:	上海财经大学出版社有限公司
地　　址:	上海市中山北一路369号(邮编200083)
网　　址:	http://www.sufep.com
电子邮箱:	webmaster@sufep.com
经　　销:	全国新华书店
印刷装订:	江苏苏中印刷有限公司
开　　本:	787mm×1092mm　1/16
印　　张:	17.25
字　　数:	278千字
版　　次:	2023年2月第1版
印　　次:	2023年2月第1次印刷
定　　价:	128.00元

2021
中国PPP市场透明度报告

课题组

方 芳　　宗庆庆　　石 成

内 容 提 要

　　PPP是Public-Private Partnerships的英文首字母缩写,译为政府和社会资本合作。当前,中国的PPP模式已经不仅仅是政府的一种市场化投融资手段,更是一次全面的、系统的公共服务供给市场化社会化改革举措,因而各界对PPP的发展都寄予厚望,希望PPP能起到引领财政体制机制改革、助力公共事业全面深化改革的作用。在这一背景下,PPP项目的规范化管理就显得尤为重要,其中PPP项目及时、完善的信息公开又是PPP项目规范化管理的基础。2017年以来,财政部先后发布多份重要文件,不断强化PPP项目的信息公开管理工作:2017年初,财政部发布《政府和社会资本合作(PPP)综合信息平台信息公开管理暂行办法》,详细规定了PPP项目信息公开的各方面要求;2020年3月31日,财政部发布《政府与社会资本合作项目绩效管理操作指引》,全方位建立了完整的PPP绩效考核体系,明确了责任主体,将信息真实、公开、透明、质量纳入具体的考核细则;2021年12月16日,财政部修订发布《政府和社会资本合作(PPP)综合信息平台信息公开管理办法》,进一步拓展了责任主体,增加了信息公开内容,同时规范了信息公开的方式和时点,完善了监督机制和动态调整机制;2022年11月11日,财政部发布《关于进一步推动政府和社会资本合作(PPP)规范发展、阳光运行的通知》,从做好项目前期论证、推动项目规范运行、严防隐形债务风险以及保障项目阳光运行四个方面给出了PPP项目运行的具体指引。

　　在此背景下,上海财经大学PPP研究中心课题组继过去连续4年对PPP项目的信息公开工作进行评估后,又对截至2021年12月31日的中国PPP项目的最新信息公开状况进行了详细的评估。具体而言,课题组对2021年底财政部PPP管理库的10 175个项目的信息公开工作进行了详细评估,编制了一套"2021中国PPP市场透明度指数"。该指数囊括68个指标字段,并分为即时公开透明度指数、适时公开透明度指数,以及识别阶段、准备阶段、采购阶段和执行阶段等各阶段的透明度分指数。课题组采用层次分析法和专家打分法相结合的方法对指数进行合成:对于分指数下面的具体指标,按照专家对其重要程度的判定,设置不同的分值;而在分指数合成总指数时,则采用同类指数编制过程中常用的层次分析法,以保证指数编制方法的可靠性。最终,通过对指数具体结果的统计分析,课题组得到以下几个主要发现:

第一,2021年全国PPP市场透明度总指数为80.01,较2020年略有提高。这也是课题组评估中国PPP市场透明度以来,全国总指数首次达到80。进一步对PPP项目的异质性分析表明,PPP项目透明度指数没有明显的行业差异,示范项目和非示范项目的透明度指数差别也不大。

第二,省级层面的PPP市场透明度指数稳中有升,各省份PPP市场透明度指数进一步出现一定的分化趋势。前3名省份与后面省份的透明度指数表现出了不同的时间趋势:绝大多数省份2021年的透明度指数与2020年接近,有的甚至略有下降。但前3名省份的透明度指数出现了3~5不等的涨幅,逐渐拉开了与后面省份透明度指数的差距。云南(90.55)、河北(88.54)、山东(86.39)、湖南(81.43)和江苏(81.27)占据了省份榜单的前5名。

第三,多数城市PPP市场透明度指数较2020年有所提高。课题组挑选了53个PPP项目数量较多(入管理库的项目超50个)的城市,对其PPP信息公开工作进行了分析。通过和2020年PPP市场透明度指数对比可以发现,大部分地级以上城市2021年指数较2020年有所增长,尤其是山东日照,其2021年指数较2020年上升了21.79,紧随其后的是山东潍坊,较2020年上升了20.53。不过,同时也可以发现,少数地级以上城市2021年指数较2020年有所降低,降幅较大的是贵州贵阳和广西南宁,2021年指数较2020年分别下降了2.67和2.19。

第四,PPP信息透明度有助于提高地区社会资本参与热情和项目落地率。平均而言,PPP信息透明度越高的城市,社会资本出资比例越高,项目的开工间隔(使用合同签订时间与项目开工时间之间的差额来度量）也越短。

　　在指数的编制和分析过程中，课题组也提炼出了进一步改进PPP信息公开工作的一些政策建议，并对来年的报告提出了初步构想。我们希望通过进一步完善PPP信息公开和规范管理的制度来进一步提高PPP市场的信息透明度，进而助推整个PPP市场的规范化发展。

目 录

1 导论

1.1 PPP的概念内涵与操作流程 ········· 3

1.2 PPP市场透明度的概念内涵 ········· 5

1.3 PPP信息公开的必要性与意义 ········· 6

1.4 中国PPP信息公开实践历程 ········· 8

1.5 中国PPP市场发展基本概况 ········· 10

2 指标体系与计算方法

2.1 指标体系构建 ········· 21

2.2 指数计算方法 ········· 29

3 指数基本结果与总体分析

3.1 样本数据基本情况 ········· 41

3.2 全国总指数计算 ········· 43

3.3 全国总指数的异质性分析 ········· 47

4 省级指数的排名与分析

4.1 省级透明度总指数结果分析 ········· 53

4.2 分阶段省级透明度结果分析 ·· 58

4.3 "两评一案"省级结果分析 ·· 67

5 城市指数的排名与分析

5.1 城市PPP项目分布情况概述 ·· 73

5.2 重点城市指数的基本情况 ·· 74

5.3 主要城市"两评一案"结果 ·· 81

5.4 PPP信息透明度的社会经济效益分析 ································ 84

6 总结与展望

6.1 报告总结 ·· 89

6.2 政策建议 ·· 91

6.3 未来展望 ·· 92

附件一　专家判定矩阵调查表 ··· 95

附件二　PPP综合信息平台信息公开管理暂行办法 ···················· 97

附件三　政府和社会资本合作（PPP）综合信息平台信息公开
　　　　管理办法 ·· 107

附件四　PPP信息公开和规范管理制度目录 ······························ 112

附件五　项目数大于30的城市PPP市场透明度排名 ················ 114

后记 ·· 119

1 导论

1.1 PPP的概念内涵与操作流程

1.1.1 PPP含义

PPP是Public Private Partnerships的英文首字母缩写,直译为政府和社会资本合作。PPP是社会资本参与基础设施和公用事业项目投资运营的一种制度创新,不同的国际组织对其均有自己不尽相同的定义。例如,亚洲开发银行认为PPP是指为开展基础设施建设和提供公共服务,公共部门和私营部门之间可能建立的一系列合作伙伴关系。联合国发展计划署认为PPP是指政府、营利性企业和非营利性组织基于某个项目而形成的相互合作关系,在这种关系中,政府并不是把项目的责任全部转移给私营部门,而是由参与合作的各方共同承担责任和融资风险。欧盟委员会认为PPP是公共部门和私人部门之间的一种合作关系,其目的是为了提供传统上由公共部门提供的公共项目或服务。世界银行则认为PPP是私营部门和政府机构间就提供公共资产和公共服务签订的长期合同,而私营部门须承担重大风险和管理责任。根据中国政府的定义,政府和社会资本合作模式是指政府通过特许经营权、合理定价、财政补贴等事先公开的收益约定规则,引入社会资本参与城市基础设施等公益性事业投资和运营,以利益共享和风险共担为特征,发挥双方优势,提高公共产品或服务的质量和供给效率。中国政府对PPP模式的定义与其他国际组织定义的差异主要体现在"社会资本"和"私人资本"上,在中国,社会资本覆盖范围更广,除了私人资本、境外资本等之外,还包括国有企业资本等。

综合上述几个定义,可以认为,广义上,PPP就是指政府和社会资本充分发挥各自优势,为提供公共产品或服务而建立的合作伙伴关系,这些合作通常集中于基础设施及公共服务领域。在PPP模式的合作中,政府一般采取竞争性方式选择具有投融资、运营管理能力的社会资本,双方按照平等协商原则订立合同,由社会资本提供公共服务,政府依据公共服务绩效评价结果向社会资本支付对价。具体而言,PPP通常模式是由社会资本主要负责基础设施和公用事业的项目设计、建设、运营和维护工作,承担商业和财务风险,通过政府购买、使用者付费或其他回报机制获得合理投资回报;政府主要负责公共服务及基础设施质量和价格监管,保护消费者利益,以保证公共利益最大化,并承担政策法律风险。PPP最初主要是在基础设施领域产生的制度创新,随后逐渐发展并覆盖大多数公共产品或服务领域,包括交通、能源、水利、水务等经济基础设施和科技、环保、教育、文化、体育、卫生、旅游、社会福利等社会基础设施。

1.1.2 PPP操作流程

财政部于2014年11月下发《政府和社会资本合作操作指南》,对PPP项目的全生命周期的操作规范进行了规定,对PPP项目的设计、融资、建造、运营、维护至终止移交的各环节操作流程进行了全方位规范。PPP项目操作流程可分为项目识别、项目准备、项目采购、项目执行和项目移交五个阶段(如图1-1所示)。区分这五个阶段,是PPP市场透明度指数编制工作的重要中间步骤。

图1-1 PPP项目操作流程

此外,2017年11月,财政部印发《关于规范政府和社会资本合作(PPP)综合信息平台项目库管理的通知》(财办金〔2017〕92号),对PPP项目的流程管理进一步优化,实行分类管理,将PPP项目按阶段分为项目储备清单和项目管理库。项目储备清单内的项目重点用于孵化和推介,项目管理库内的项目则要接受严格监管,确保全生命周期规范运作。对照之前的五阶段划分,储备清单主要对应识别阶段,是地方政府部门有意愿采用PPP模式的备选项目,但由于尚未完成物有所值评价和财政承受能力论证等的审核,严格而言还不能称之为PPP项目,因而属于储备库;管理库则囊括准备阶段、采购阶段、执行阶段和移交阶段,是严格按照相关管理办法进行全生命周期管理的PPP项目。

1.2 PPP市场透明度的概念内涵

就字面上的理解，信息透明度是指一个市场、公司或项目的信息公开程度。不过具体到本报告所聚焦的PPP市场透明度，则特指各责任主体（主管部门、政府授权合作方、社会资本方、中介机构等）对PPP项目信息公开的程度。从理论上讲，整个PPP市场的信息公开程度还包括项目管理方式的公开、政策文件的公开、项目各参与方的信息公开，如目前已有的PPP专家库、机构库等包含的丰富的信息，但限于数据可得性等原因，本报告中的PPP市场透明度主要指PPP项目的信息公开程度，并在此基础上汇总形成各类透明度指数。从横向看，我们主要构建了省份、城市以及行业等透明度指数。从纵向看，我们主要构建了透明度总指数、即时公开透明度指数、适时公开透明度指数以及分阶段指数。除了PPP项目信息公开程度外，本报告还专门构建分析了PPP中介机构信息透明度，将其作为专门的一章。

PPP是一个市场化的公共服务供给机制，需要与市场化相适应的管理手段和服务能力，提升PPP市场透明度就是其中重要一环。经过三年多的系统推进，PPP信息公开工作取得积极成效。全国PPP综合信息平台已成为各地强化项目管理、推进项目对接、推动项目落地的重要工具。当前，我国正加速推进PPP项目信息和政务服务信息公开，不断提升PPP管理透明度。

2017年1月，财政部金融司发布《关于印发〈政府和社会资本合作（PPP）综合信息平台信息公开管理暂行办法〉的通知》（财金〔2017〕1号，后文简称1号文），明确PPP项目信息公开的责任主体，细化公开内容、时点和方式，确保及时充分披露入库PPP项目的基本情况、实施方案、评价论证报告、采购文件、项目合同等关键信息，并要求示范项目率先公开，确保项目在阳光下运作，强化政府监管和社会监督，推动项目规范实施。因此，该文件也是本报告评估中国PPP市场透明度的主要依据：达到该文件各项信息公开要求的PPP项目，即为信息透明度高的项目，反之，若对于该文件要求披露的信息，PPP项目没有披露，则为信息透明度低的项目。而且为了保证评估的客观、公平，凡不在该文件要求范围内的相关信息，课题组均暂不将其纳入评估范围。这是因为课题组的数据也来自财政部政府和社会资本合作中心的信息平台，而该信息平台的设计依据主要就是1号文。

1.3 PPP信息公开的必要性与意义

第一，改善营商环境，鼓励社会资本参与公共事业。通常而言，在政府和社会资本的合作中，政府天然处于强势地位，因此，社会资本往往对与政府的合作有顾虑。PPP更是一种社会资本先期投入、分期收回的长期投资模式，诚信政府对社会资本的参与至关重要。因此，提高PPP市场透明度，有助于打消社会资本方参与PPP项目的顾虑，营造公平、公正的市场环境。同时，提高PPP市场透明度，也有助于强化政府和企业的契约精神，铲除腐败土壤，维护廉洁高效的政府形象。

第二，促进社会和谐，增强民众的关注与信心。作为一项公共事业，而不是商业项目，PPP与民众的切身利益密切相关。一方面，PPP项目一般是为普通民众提供的公共产品与服务，建设和运行的质量直接关系到民众的切身利益；另一方面，PPP项目要么最终需要纳税人的税收来买单，要么需要使用者来付费，因而也直接关系到民众利益。因此，加大PPP信息公开力度，有助于社会公众更方便地关注、监督PPP市场和PPP项目，促进社会公众的理解和配合，也为相关工作的推进营造和谐氛围。

第三，提升供给效率，增强公共产品绩效管理。PPP项目主要应用于基础设施等公共产品与服务中，这些项目一般具有信息不对称性强、定价难等特征，因此，加强PPP项目信息公开工作，有助于各领域的专业人士科学严谨地评估PPP项目中的定价基准、财政承受能力和收费标准等问题，有助于公共产品与服务的科学定价。同时，PPP市场透明度的提高也有助于缓解公共产品建设和运行中的信息不对称问题，铲除内幕交易的土壤，实现国有资产的保值增值，维护纳税人和消费者的权益。最后，完善的信息公开也有助于化解地方债务风险和金融风险。

第四，提升治理水平，构建新型公共管理模式。PPP是一种市场化、社会化的公共产品与服务的供给管理模式,旨在通过改革创新,打破垄断,引入竞争机制,利用市场的专业化和创新能力,丰富公共产品与服务的供给,提高公共产品与服务的供给质量,满足人们不断增长的多样化的公共产品与服务的需求。因此,加强PPP项目信息公开对提升治理水平和构建新型公共管理模式具有重要的现实意义。早在20世纪八九十年代,我国在基础设施建设领域就开始尝试公私合作模式,但由于制度建设缺位,导致项目"异化变形"。为了解决这些问题,在本轮推广PPP的过程中,行业主管部门从制度建设入手,按照"顶层设计+配套政策+操作指引"三位一体的思路,制定了覆盖PPP全生命周期的制度体系。完善的信息公开就是这一制度体系中不可或缺的一部分,主管部门可以以PPP信息披露为抓手,敦促地方政府以及PPP项目各个参与方更规范地参与PPP项目,进而共同促进这一新型公共管理模式的不断完善。

第五,促进PPP发展,推动全面深化改革进程。在公共服务领域推广运用PPP,是全面深化改革的一项重要任务,是推进供给侧结构性改革的一个重要举措,是实施创新驱动、发展新经济的一种重要手段。推动PPP市场发展,充分体现了依法治国和发挥市场在资源配置中的决定性作用以及更好发挥政府作用的核心精神。PPP市场的发展,推动了整个行政体制、财政体制和投融资体制的改革。因此,通过提高PPP市场透明度带来的PPP市场规范化发展,对于其他改革事业也有很大的借鉴价值。当前,中国PPP市场的信息披露工作在同类政府事务中处于领先地位,甚至在全球都处于领先地位。深入评估分析和总结PPP市场信息公开工作取得的成绩和经验,可以为其他改革事业提供有益借鉴。

第六,营造国家形象,展示中国制度自信。PPP项目各国都有所涉历,多个国际组织也非常关注各国的PPP市场。中国的PPP项目在经过多年探索之后,形成了自己的模式和风格,在很多方面都有所创新。总结分析PPP市场透明度,对于塑造中国政府开放、高效的形象,提高中国在国际PPP市场上的影响力和话语权,具有很大的帮助。此外,基础设施也是"一带一路"倡议中的重要组成部分,通过信息公开推动PPP规范化,有助于PPP的中国模式在"一带一路"国家和地区的推广,在输出产品和技术的同时,也输出中国的软实力。

1.4 中国PPP信息公开实践历程

自2013年我国大力推广PPP项目以来,根据党中央、国务院的部署,财政部先后出台了1号文、《关于规范政府和社会资本合作(PPP)综合信息平台项目库管理的通知》(财办金〔2017〕92号)、《关于进一步规范全国PPP综合信息平台项目信息管理工作的通知》(财政企函〔2018〕2号)、《关于修订发布〈政府和社会资本合作(PPP)综合信息平台信息公开管理办法〉的通知》(财金〔2021〕110号,后文简称110号文)以及《关于进一步推动政府和社会资本合作(PPP)规范发展、阳光运行的通知》(财金〔2022〕119号)等文件。此外,财政部统筹推进PPP改革,推进PPP项目信息公开的工作。

第一,建立全国政府和社会资本合作(PPP)综合信息平台。2015年,财政部在国家"互联网+"行动计划指导下,构建了一个覆盖全国各地区、涉及19大领域、贯穿项目实施全过程、服务主体全覆盖的PPP综合信息平台。首先,建立了贯通"中央—省—市—县"各级财政部门的PPP项目信息采集和管理的一条通道。其次,设置信息披露和线上管理两大平台,用来发布PPP政策法规、工作动态、项目合作、知识分享以及信息跟踪管理等,而且还满足了项目管理、交易撮合、信息服务三大功能。最后,涵盖了项目库、专家库、机构库和资料库四大核心应用数据库,其中,项目库用于收集和管理全国PPP项目的关键信息和资料,专家库和机构库用于收集和管理专家、咨询机构、社会资本、金融机构等各参与方信息,资料库用于收集和管理PPP相关政策法规、工作动态、指南手册、培训材料和经典案例等信息。

第二,建立信息披露机制。明确了PPP项目信息公开的责任主体、各阶段公开信息内容和具体要求,制定了专家库、机构库管理的规定,明确了PPP专家、咨询机构信息公开的要求。

第三,创新PPP信息披露制度。按月披露PPP项目入库和退库的信息,按季度开展PPP项目信息统计和发布。通过财政部门户网站"PPP专栏",财政部政府和社会资本合作中心中、英文网站及微信公众号"道PPP""中国PPP地图"手机客户端等网络媒介,实现PPP政策文件和工作动态的多点发布。目前,我国已经形成定期披露、全面披露、多方式披露的PPP项目信息公开格局。在各方面的关心支持和共同努力下，PPP信息公开工作取得积极成效。项目库、机构库、专家库的社会影响力和认可度不断提高，已成为各地强化项目管理、推进项目对接、推动项目落地的重要抓手。项目库季报被视为PPP市场的"沪深指数"。金融机构甚至为信息公开程度更高的示范项目开辟了信贷支持的"绿色通道"。据统计，截至2021年12月末，PPP综合信息平台收录的累计在库项目10 239个，PPP中介机构360家。网站、微信公众号等已成为PPP信息的权威发布平台。

第四，建立完善PPP信息公开管理办法。2017年1月，财政部金融司印发1号文，明确PPP项目信息公开的责任主体，细化公开内容、时点和方式，确保及时充分披露入库PPP项目的基本情况、实施方案、评价论证报告、采购文件、项目合同等关键信息，推动项目规范实施。2020年3月31日，财政部发布《政府与社会资本合作项目绩效管理操作指引》，全方位建立了完整的PPP绩效考核体系，明确了责任主体，将信息真实、公开、透明、质量纳入具体的考核细则。这意味着PPP绩效管理政策的实施将更加精准有效地提升信息公开的质量。2021年12月16日，财政部发布110号文，与先前相比，这一PPP信息公开管理办法进一步拓展了责任主体，增加了信息公开内容，同时规范了信息公开的方式（从即时公开和适时公开变成主动公开和依申请公开）和时点，并建立完善监督机制和动态调整机制。这对于进一步提升PPP项目规范管理以及促进PPP项目高质量发展有着重要意义。2022年11月11日，财政部发布《关于进一步推动政府和社会资本合作（PPP）规范发展、阳光运行的通知》，从做好项目前期论证、推动项目规范运行、严防隐形债务风险以及保障项目阳光运行四个方面给出了具体指引，该文对推动PPP模式逐步迈向高质量发展、更好地撬动社会资本、建设全国统一大市场和构建双循环新发展格局都具有重要意义。

PPP信息公开对中国PPP发展产生了积极作用。世界银行发布的2020年度《基础设施发展基准报告》从PPP准备、采购、合同管理和民间自提项目四个维度，对140个经济体的PPP政策法规建设进行了打分评价。报告指出，中国搭建了PPP基础制度框架，规范了物有所值评价、财政承受能力论证等关键环节的操作方法，制定了采购文件、工程进度等重要信息的公示制度，营造了良好的政策环境。在分数构成上，中国PPP采购得分80分（高收入经济体平均得分73分，中上收入经济体平均得分62分），位居全球前列；合同管理得分81分（高收入经济体平均得分64分，中上收入经济体平均得分64分);PPP准备得分54分(高收入经济体平均得分50分,中上收入经济体平均得分44分);民间自提项目得分50分(高收入经济体平均得分63分,中上收入经济体平均得分60分)。信息公开是完善国家治理体系和提高治理能力现代化的重要抓手,同时也是提高政府管理水平的有效措施。加强PPP信息公开是贯彻落实新发展理念、全面深化改革以及提高国家治理能力现代化的重要举措,同时有利于推动PPP模式制度化、规范化、标准化,逐步迈向高质量发展。

PPP市场信息公开工作取得的成绩和经验需要总结,同时也要深入剖析有待进一步完善的内容。本评估报告旨在通过编制指数的方式,对PPP市场的透明度工作进行经验总结,分析其成绩和不足。而严谨、公正的市场透明度评估,有赖于评估方法的科学性,具体到本报告,就体现在PPP市场透明度指标体系和指数编制方法的设计上,这将是我们在第2章讨论的重点。

1.5　中国PPP市场发展基本概况

按照《关于规范政府和社会资本合作综合信息平台运行的通知》(财金〔2015〕166号)要求,财政部建立了全国政府和社会资本合作(PPP)综合信息平台及项目库。本报告对PPP项目信息公开的评估就是基于该信息平台上所能获取的数据,因此,在本节,我们首先根据该平台上的数据,对中国PPP市场的基本情况进行简述。

1.5.1　全国管理库PPP项目情况和阶段分布

截至2021年末,管理库项目累计10 175个,同比增加251个,增长2.5%;累计投资额16.0万亿元,同比增加0.8万亿元,增长5.3%,覆盖31个省份及新疆生产建设兵团、19个行业领域;落地项目累计7 683个,投资额12.8万亿元,落地率75.5%,比2020年末上升4.0个百分点;开工项目累计4 804个,投资额7.65万亿元,开工率62.5%,比2020年末上升2.3个百分点;管理库准备、采购、执行阶段项目数分别为460个、2 032个、7 683个,投资额分别为5 550亿元、2.7万亿元、12.8万亿元(如图1-2所示),目前无移交阶段项目。

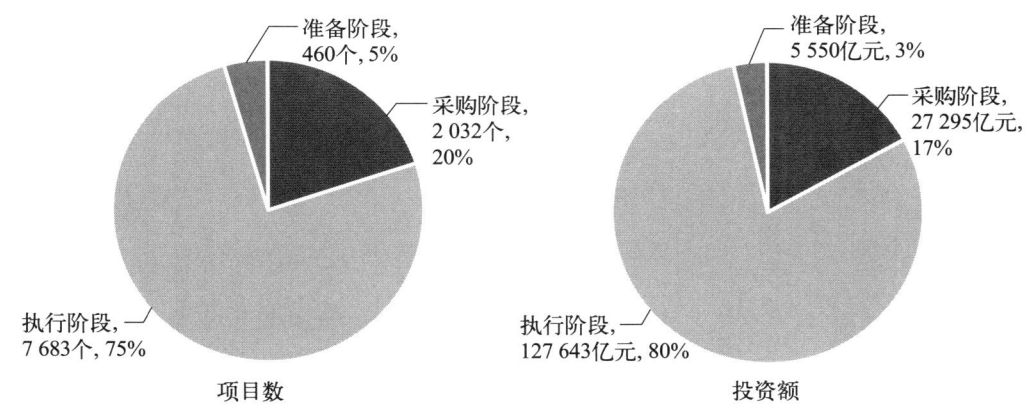

图1-2 2021年末管理库各阶段项目情况

2021年，PPP市场由过去的重数量和速度向重质量转变。全年新入管理库项目674个，同比减少324个，下降32.5%；新入库项目投资额1.3万亿元，同比减少0.3万亿元，下降18.8%。由于管理库内存量项目结构调整导致投资额变化，因而新入库项目投资额减去退库项目投资额与净入库项目投资额不一致。

全年净入库项目（即2021年末比2020年末新增在库项目）251个，同比减少233个，下降48.1%。

1.5.2 管理库项目地区分布情况

2021年各地新入库项目数排名前5位的是广西81个、贵州72个、江西69个、河南58个、山西41个；新入库项目投资额排名前5位的是广西2 875亿元、贵州1 025亿元、四川917亿元、重庆833亿元、江西729亿元。2021年新入库项目数、投资额地区分布如图1-3所示。

截至2021年末，按累计项目数排序，管理库前5位是河南838个、山东（含青岛）760个、贵州571个、广东559个、四川559个，合计占入库项目总数的32.3%。按累计投资额排序，管理库前5位是云南1.3万亿元、贵州1.2万亿元、四川1.2万亿元、河南1.1万亿元、浙江1.0万亿元，合计占入库项目总投资额的36.0%。截至2021年末，管理库各地项目数、投资额情况分别如图1-4和图1-5所示。

12 | 2021 中国 PPP 市场透明度报告

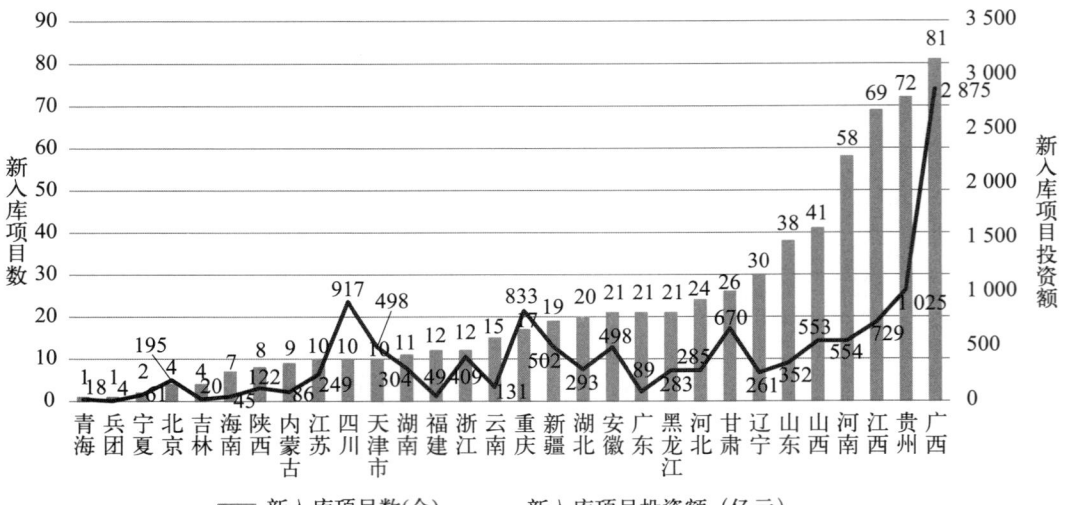

注："兵团"是指新疆生产建设兵团，下同。

图 1-3　2021 年新入库项目数、投资额地区分布

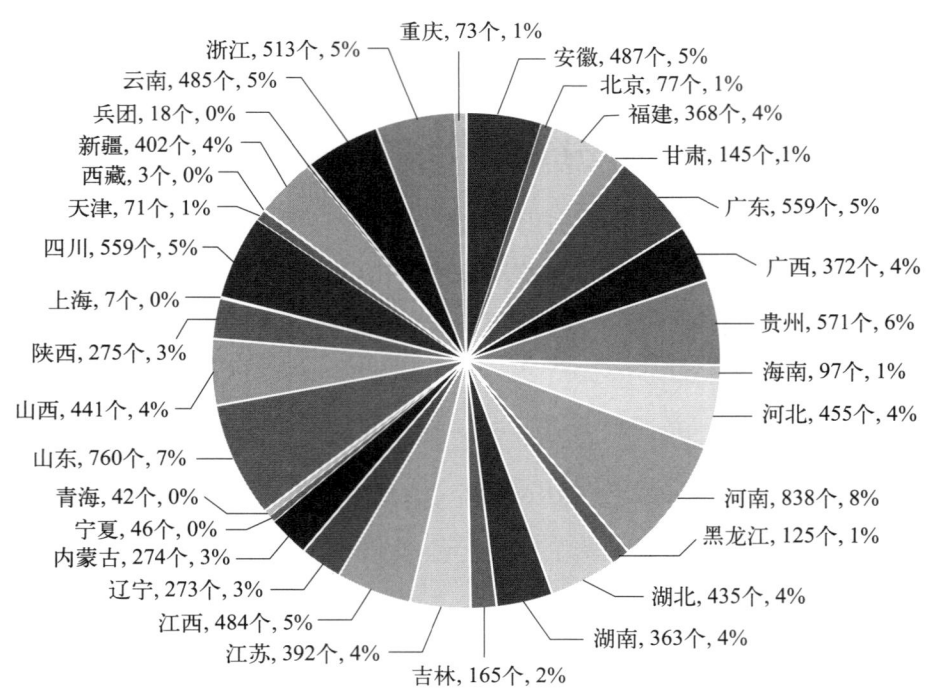

图 1-4　截至 2021 年末各地管理库项目数

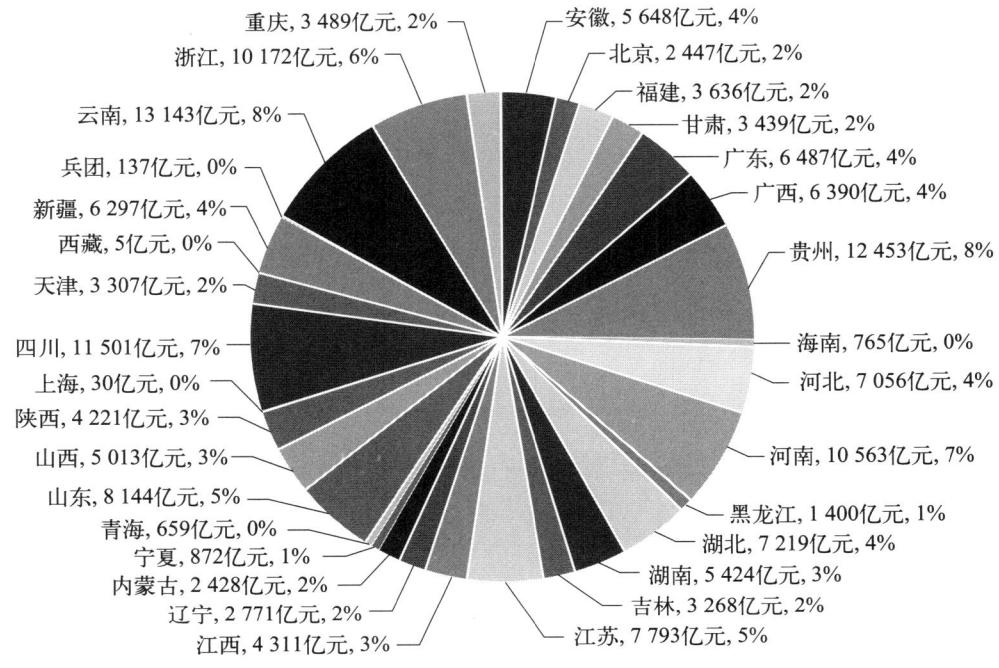

图1-5 截至2021年末各地管理库项目投资额

1.5.3 管理库项目行业分布情况

2021年管理库新入库项目数前5位是市政工程258个、交通运输98个、生态建设和环境保护49个、教育43个、城镇综合开发38个；新入库项目投资额前5位是交通运输7 009亿元、市政工程2 533亿元、城镇综合开发767亿元、生态建设和环境保护548亿元、保障性安居工程353亿元。2021年新入库项目数、投资额行业分布如图1-6所示。

截至2021年末，管理库各行业累计PPP项目数、投资额如图1-7和图1-8所示。其中，项目数前5位是市政工程4 169个、交通运输1 424个、生态建设和环境保护957个、城镇综合开发610个、教育508个，合计占管理库项目总数的75.4%；项目投资额前5位是交通运输5.6万亿元、市政工程4.6万亿元、城镇综合开发1.9万亿元、生态建设和环境保护1.1万亿元、水利建设3 924亿元，合计占管理库总投资额的84.7%。

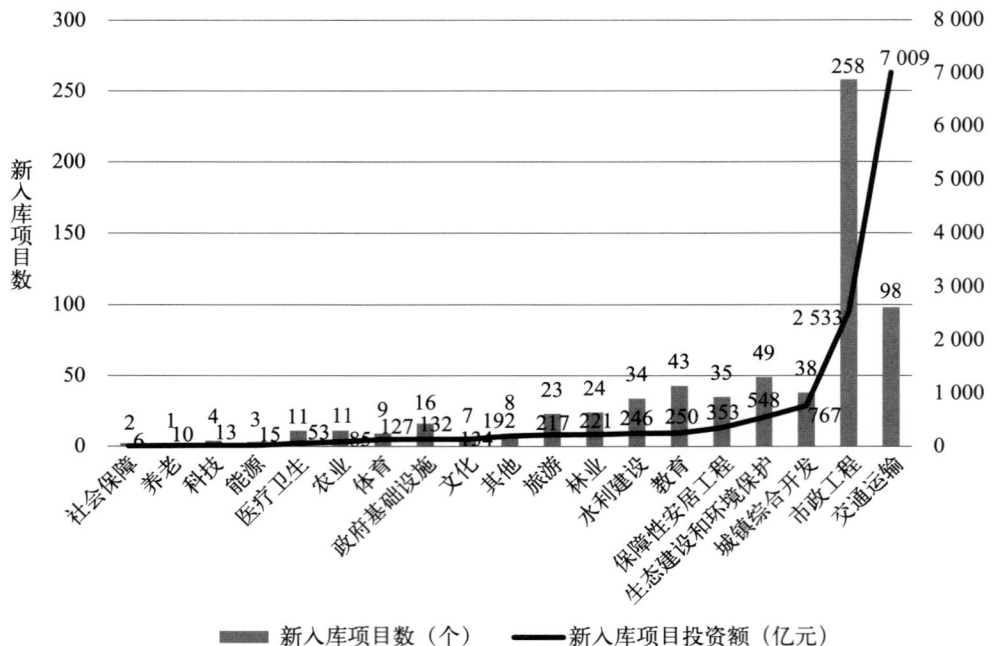

图1-6 2021年新入库项目数、投资额行业分布

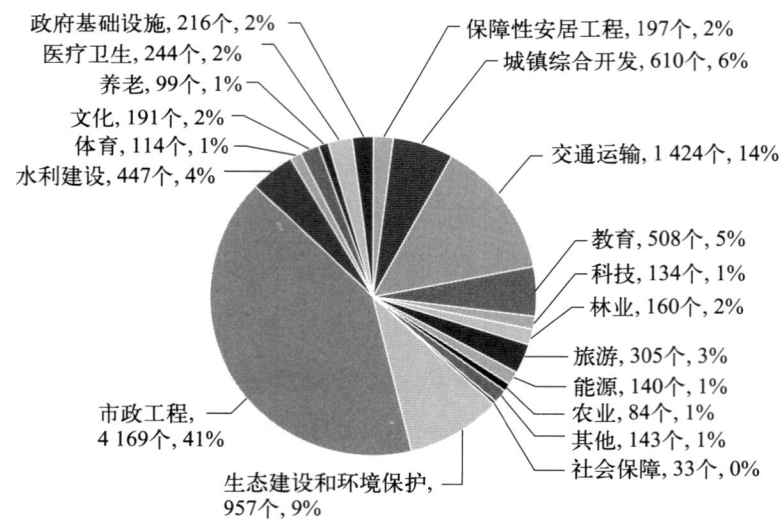

图1-7 截至2021年末管理库项目数行业分布

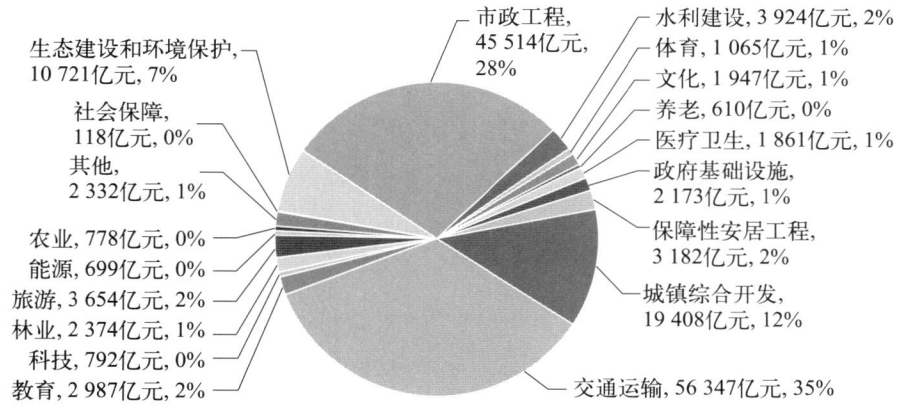

图 1-8 截至 2021 年末管理库项目投资额行业分布

1.5.4 管理库项目按回报机制分布情况

按照三种回报机制统计，2021 年使用者付费类项目新入库 44 个，投资额 2 088 亿元，占净入库项目投资额的 16.2%；可行性缺口补助（即政府市场混合付费）类项目新入库 467 个，投资额 9 453 亿元，占净入库项目投资额的 73.2%；政府付费类项目净入库 163 个，投资额 1 369 亿元，占净入库项目投资额的 10.6%。

截至 2021 年末，累计使用者付费类项目 607 个，投资额 1.6 万亿元，分别占管理库的 6.0% 和 9.7%；累计可行性缺口补助类项目 5 982 个，投资额 11.0 万亿元，分别占管理库的 58.8% 和 68.9%；累计政府付费类项目 3 586 个，投资额 3.4 万亿元，分别占管理库的 35.2% 和 21.5%（如图 1-9 所示）。

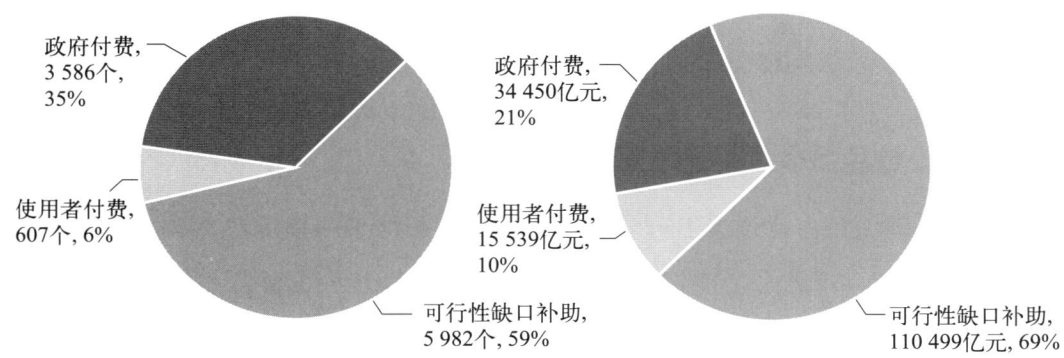

图 1-9 2021 年末管理库项目数和投资额按回报机制分布

1.5.5 管理库项目按运作方式分布情况

2021年管理库新入库项目数前3位是BOT 526个、其他67个以及TOT 33个，投资额前3位是BOT 11 208亿元、其他910亿元以及TOT+BOT 306亿元。2021年新入库项目数、投资额按运作方式分布如图1-10所示。

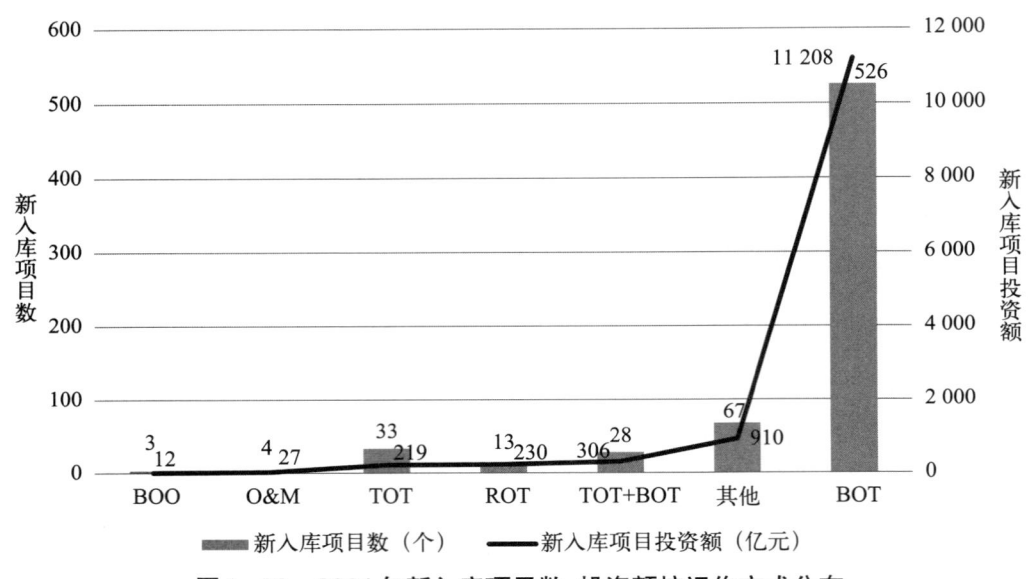

图1-10　2021年新入库项目数、投资额按运作方式分布

按照累计项目数排序，管理库前3位是BOT 7 995个、其他997个以及TOT+BOT 399个，合计占项目库项目数的92.3%。按累计投资额排序，管理库前3位是BOT 13.0万亿元、其他2.0万亿元以及TOT+BOT 4 076亿元。截至2021年末管理库各运作方式项目数、投资额情况如图1-11所示。

1.5.6 绿色低碳项目占比情况

绿色低碳项目占比逐步上升。2021年项目库新增项目中绿色低碳项目373个，项目投资额为3 457亿元，分别占比55.3%与26.8%，其中已落地项目数53个，落地率为14.2%。截至2021年末，项目库中绿色低碳项目累计5 881个，占比为57.8%，累计投资金额5.7万亿元，占比为35.4%，其中已经落地4 315个，落地率为73.4%。

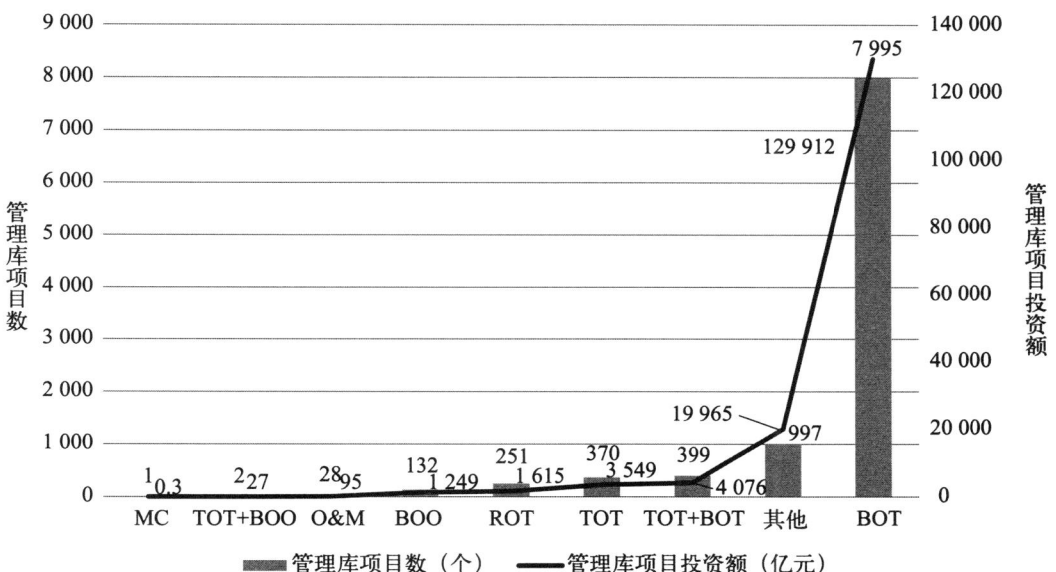

图1-11 截至2021年末管理库项目数、投资额按运作方式分布

2

指标体系与计算方法

2.1 指标体系构建

2.1.1 指标体系基本原则

指标体系是否科学、合理,直接关系到指数编制的质量和结果评估的可靠性。为此,设定的指标体系必须客观合理地、尽可能全面地反映影响PPP信息透明度的所有因素,同时也要考虑到数据的可获得性、可靠性等。要建立一套既科学又可执行的PPP市场透明度评价指标体系,必须遵照一定的原则。因此,课题组首先明确了PPP透明度评价指标体系构建中应该坚持的几个原则,主要包括层次性原则、共通性原则、连续性原则等。

(1) **层次性原则**。层次性指的是指标体系自身的多重性。由于PPP信息内容涵盖的多层次性,指标体系也必须由多层次结构组成,才能反映出各层次的特征。同时,各个要素相互联系构成一个有机整体,能从项目的不同阶段、不同层次反映PPP市场透明度的总体情况。具体而言,参考PPP相关信息公开管理办法的精神,PPP市场透明度的指标体系可以分为总指数、分阶段二级指标和底层具体指标三个层次,由此透明度指数可以分为总指数,以及识别阶段、准备阶段、采购阶段、执行阶段和移交阶段五个阶段的分指数等。当然,考虑到不同项目可能处于不同的阶段,因而并不是每一个项目的透明度指数都完整囊括这五个阶段。

(2) **共通性原则**。课题组评价的是每一个PPP项目的信息公开透明度,由于项目会存在一些特有的信息,因而基于可比性的考虑,课题组主要选取那些适用于全体项目样本的指标。那些不是对所有项目均适用的指标,如"设计文件及批复文件""项目采购阶段调整、更新的政府方授权文件""增减资情况"等,课题组暂时没有将其纳入指标体系,但会在报告末尾对完善该类指标信息披露工作的管理办法提供一些政策建议。

（3）连续性原则。本次编制的指数是课题组第四次评估PPP市场的透明度，因而指标体系不仅要反映2021年我国PPP项目信息披露的实际情况，而且要考虑到其与前面三年的衔接，保持指数的连续性，当然也要考虑到未来可能的变更。换言之，指标体系应具备较强的动态适应性。课题组希望可以通过长期追踪的方式，对我国PPP市场的信息公开状况进行持续性评估。

（4）突出性原则。指标的选择要尽量全面，但同时也应该区别主次和轻重，要突出重点。对于某些特别重要的指标，要尽量多地选择相关字段。同时，课题组通过专家问卷调查的方式，对比较重要的指标设置高分，对不太重要的信息设置低分。例如物有所值评价方面、财政承受能力论证方面，可以赋予比那些基本项目信息等更重要的分数值。

（5）公正性原则。作为一个政策效果评估的报告，PPP市场透明度报告发布后，预期会对不同的地区和项目产生一定的影响。因此，透明度指数报告必须坚持公平、公正的原则，做到一视同仁，坚持成绩和问题都点到、都说透。既要如实展示不同地区、不同类型的PPP项目信息公开的客观状况，同时也要尽可能讲清楚导致各地区和行业等PPP市场透明度指数结果出现差异的各类原因，特别是那些客观、外生的原因，要尽量做到公正公允。

（6）时点性原则。本次评估的是截止到2021年12月31日财政部PPP综合信息平台管理库里所有的项目信息披露情况，属于存量概念，即评估的对象是截至这个时点所有PPP项目历史累加的信息披露情况。囿于数据的可获得性，课题组的评估没有涉及这些信息披露的具体时间等动态特征，例如，部分指标作为适时公开指标，理论上课题组除了可以评估其是否披露外，还可以评估其披露的及时性，这也是信息披露工作的重要评价方面，然而课题组无法获得相关指标披露具体时点等细节信息，因而这方面的信息就暂时无法纳入课题组的指标体系。

2.1.2 指标体系设计依据

（1）设计依据。评估PPP市场的信息公开现状，首要的依据就是相关政策文件。2017年1月23日，财政部正式发布1号文，这是主管部门对PPP项目信息披露工作的主要操作指南。各地的PPP项目信息披露工作均是按照该文件执行的。因此，1号文的政策细则便是课题组设计PPP市场透明度指标体系时最主要的依据。课题组设计的指标体系主要来自该1号文的要求,1号文中没有要求的信息,原则上就不进入课题组的指标体系,这样处理是为了使指标体系对不同地区而言是公平公正的。

必须说明的是,正如我们在第1章说明的那样,2021年12月16日,财政部发布110号文。与先前相比,这一PPP信息公开管理办法进一步拓展了责任主体,增加了信息公开内容,同时规范了信息公开的方式(从即时公开和适时公开变成主动公开和依申请公开)和时点,并建立了完善监督机制和动态调整机制。但考虑到该办法开始实施的时间为2022年1月1日,而课题组本次评估的是截止到2021年12月31日财政部PPP综合信息平台管理库里所有的项目,因而在本年度的报告中,课题组仍采用2017年的1号文作为指标体系设计的主要依据。课题组将在来年的报告中使用110号文及其相应的附件作为评估依据。

(2)**数据来源**。根据主管部门财政部政府和社会资本合作中心的规定,各地的PPP项目均要在财政部政府和社会资本合作中心网站首页开设的PPP综合信息平台系统中进行入库和公布。考虑到数据来源的一致性,课题组选择该PPP综合信息平台系统作为主要数据来源。因此,本报告中指标设置的主要依据是1号文,数据来源则主要为财政部PPP综合信息平台系统。

(3)**评估对象**。财政部办公厅于2017年11月10日发布《关于规范政府和社会资本合作(PPP)综合信息平台项目库管理的通知》,要求在全国PPP综合信息平台项目库基础上构建储备库和管理库。该文认为:"储备库是指识别阶段项目,是地方政府部门有意愿采用PPP模式的备选项目,但尚未完成物有所值评价和财政承受能力论证的审核。管理库是指准备、采购、执行和移交阶段项目。"结合PPP主管部门的政策意见,课题组将分析对象限定在至少已经进入准备阶段的项目,即已经进入管理库中的项目。最终纳入课题组分析对象的样本共计10 175个,与上一年度的相比有一定的增加。

(4)**获取方式**。课题组以政府和社会资本合作中心网站可获取数据为基础[①],同时参考2017年1号文中的要求来筛选及获取指标,并对其进行归类。经过课题组的整理,指标体系共包含68个指标字段,课题组对其进行了逐个提取,包括网站直接阅

---

① 财政部政府和社会资本合作中心也向课题组直接提供了部分数据。课题组对这一支持表示感谢。

读提取和下载PDF文件阅读提取等方式。

在68个字段中，部分指标的信息需要阅读相应PDF文件后方可提取，然而课题组在人工阅读后发现，其中存在"伪造"的样本：一些项目显示某个指标上传了PDF附件，但实际上只是一个空白文件或虚假文件，这是因为依据系统规定，该PDF文件是必填项，如不上传，整个项目就无法上网入库，也无法进行下一步操作，因此，为了整个项目信息的入库工作，一些项目选择了上传一个虚假的或空白的PDF文件。为了甄别并在未来减少这些"虚假上传"的行为，保障评估工作的科学和公平，课题组对所有项目的所有PDF文件进行了细致的人工核实，并对这些"虚假上传"行为进行"惩罚"。具体而言，对于PDF文件指标，课题组设置的得分细则为：上传文件且为真，可以赋值为1；没有上传文件，赋值为0；上传文件但为假文件，则赋值为-1。此外，还有部分文件字段上传不够全面，对于这种情形，课题组将其赋值为0.5。

2.1.3 指标体系具体构建

根据1号文的要求，PPP项目的有些信息应该即时公开，而有些信息则可以适时公开。其中，即时公开的指标很容易处理，但适时公开指标则比较棘手，原因是课题组需要界定什么时候公开算是"适时"，而课题组无法获得项目进入某个阶段的具体时间或该信息何时就应该被披露等信息。不过，按照1号文的规定，多数适时公开都是指"进入执行阶段的6个月内公开"，因此，为了克服这一难题，课题组延续前面几年的惯用做法，决定选择2021年6月底进入执行阶段的项目作为适时公开的分析对象，这样对于在2021年6月底之前已经进入执行阶段的项目，如果截至2021年12月31日仍未公开对应的信息，课题组就可以判定该项目没有"适时"公开相应信息，换句话说，适时公开的工作做得不到位。

这样处理后，即时公开信息对应的研究样本和适时公开信息对应的研究样本就存在差异了。具体而言，截至2021年12月底进入管理库的总样本有10 175个，这些样本都可以作为即时公开透明度的评估样本；但在2021年6月底以前进入执行阶段的样本只有7 598个，这些样本将作为适时公开透明度的评估样本。对于单个项目而言，有些项目同时包含了即时公开和适时公开的信息，有些项目则仅包含即时公开的信息，无法放在一个框架下来评估。因此，对于单个项目的信息透明度而言，PPP信息透明度指数就包含两个独立的指标,一个是即时公开透明度指数,另一个是适时公开透明度指数。不过考虑到最终主要在地区和行业领域等类别层面上对PPP市场透明度进行评估分析,因此,在总指数计算上,课题组将通过层次分析法对即时公开透明度指数和适时公开透明度指数进行赋权,在省份、行业等层面上合成一个PPP市场透明度的总指数。

即时公开透明度指数和适时公开透明度指数下面均包括分阶段指数和具体指标两个层次。PPP项目一般分为五个阶段:识别阶段、准备阶段、采购阶段、执行阶段和移交阶段,但我国目前还没有进入移交阶段的PPP项目,因此,无论是即时公开透明度指数还是适时公开透明度指数,都暂不包含这一阶段。此外,由于对适时公开的指标,执行阶段也缺少合适的指标字段,因而适时公开透明度指数也不包含执行阶段的信息。由此,最终即时公开透明度指数包含识别阶段、准备阶段、采购阶段和执行阶段四个阶段,适时公开透明度指数则包含识别阶段、准备阶段和采购阶段三个阶段。

最终的指标体系层级如图2-1所示,即时公开透明度指数和适时公开透明度指数的具体指标体系则分别如表2-1和表2-2所示。

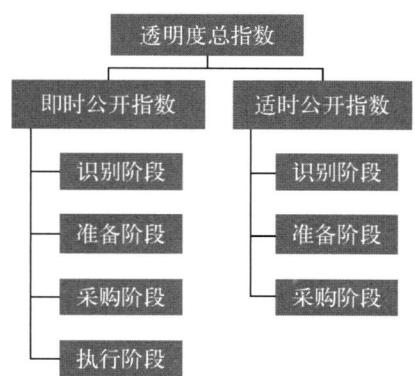

图2-1　PPP透明度指标体系层级

表2-1　PPP即时公开信息透明度指数指标体系

一级指标	具 体 指 标	备注
识别阶段	项目总投资	
	拟合作期限	
	二级行业	

(续表)

一级指标	具体指标	备注
识别阶段	项目运作方式	
	回报机制	
	项目发起时间	
	发起类型	
	发起人名称	
	项目概况	
	项目联系人	
	项目联系电话	
	财政联系人	
	财政联系电话	
	项目用地总面积	
	计划开发年度	
	采购社会资本方式的选择	
	实施方案描述	
	项目合作范围（识别）	
	物有所值定性评价指标及权重、评分标准、评分结果	
	物有所值评价通过与否的评价结论（含财政部门对报告的审核意见）	
	本项目以及年度全部已实施和拟实施的PPP项目财政支出责任数额及年度预算安排情况，以及每一年度全部PPP项目从预算中安排的支出责任占一般公共预算支出比例情况	
	通过财政承受能力论证与否的结论	
准备阶段	拟引入社会资本投资额	
	政府拟出资额	
	审核通过实施方案的政府名称	
	本级政府对实施方案审核通过时间	
	本级人民政府对实施机构即PPP项目合同的政府方签约主体的授权文件	
	政府对实施方案的审核通过文件	

一级指标	具 体 指 标	备注
采购阶段	项目资格预审公告(含资格预审申请文件)	
	预中标及成交结果公告；中标、成交结果公告及中标通知书	
	项目本级行业主管部门对拟签署PPP合同的审核意见	
	项目本级财政部门对拟签署PPP合同的审核意见	
	项目本级法制部门对拟签署PPP合同的审核意见	
	项目本级人民政府是否批准了拟签署的PPP合同	
	批准日期	
	项目本级人民政府对PPP项目合同中约定的政府跨年度财政支出责任纳入中期财政规划的审核意见	
	审核日期	
执行阶段	项目公司名称	
	项目公司成立时间	
	项目公司注册资金	
	项目公司经济性质	
	股东认缴	
	本级人民政府对政府方出资代表的授权	

表2-2　PPP适时公开信息透明度指数指标体系

一级指标	具 体 指 标	备注
识别阶段	物有所值评价报告及批复附件	
	财政承受能力论证报告及批复附件	
	新建或改扩建项目建议书及批复文件	
	可行性研究报告	
	设计文件及批复文件	
	存量公共资产或权益的资产评估报告	
准备阶段	物有所值评价完成时间	
	财政承受能力论证完成时间	
	审核通过的项目实施方案及修正案	

(续表)

一级指标	具体指标	备注
采购阶段	资格预审：公告时间	
	资格预审：预审时间	
	项目采购：公告时间	
	采购结果：响应文件评审时间	
	采购结果：结果确认谈判时间	
	采购结果：政府审核时间	
	采购结果：合同签署时间	
	采购结果：合同公布时间	
	采购结果：合同公布媒体	
	合同签订的项目投资额	
	采购文件	
	资格预审专家评审结论性意见及资格预审专家名单	
	响应文件专家评审结论性意见及评审专家名单	
	确认谈判工作组成员名单	
	已签署的PPP项目合同	
	本项目政府支出责任确认文件或更新调整文件，以及同级人大（或人大常委会）将本项目财政支出责任纳入跨年度预算的批复文件	

2.1.4 其他核心问题说明

本报告主要评估是否进行了信息披露，而不是信息披露内容的"质量"。本报告评估的主要内容是PPP项目的信息披露工作，包括这些信息披露的完整程度、重要程度等的区分，但除了明显造假外，课题组的评估不涉及其披露的具体内容的"质量"和"优劣"。具体而言，对于一项指标，一个项目公开披露了其相关信息，在课题组的评估中就是得分的，但该信息中反映的具体工作可能做得很好，也可能做得很差，这暂时不在课题组的评估范围内。例如，对于财政承受能力论证报告的PDF文件，作为一个非常重要的信息，课题组通过人工核查的方法，一一核实其披露情况，同时专家打分中也可能对其赋予较高的分值，这些都是评估中要考虑的因素。至于财政承受能力论证报告做得是否规范、科学,论证是否充分,结论是否可靠等内容,则不在课题组的评估范围内。因为从逻辑上讲,即便这份财政承受能力论证报告不太规范,或者质量不高,但只要有关责任方选择了真实公开披露该报告,那在信息披露工作上就是得分的。当然,未来课题组会考虑超越"信息透明度评估"的范畴,对这些重点报告中所反映的某地或某领域PPP工作的规范性进行重点的专题评估。

2.2 指数计算方法

2.2.1 计算方法简介

在多指标综合评价中,权重确定直接影响评价的结果。确定权重的方法有很多,根据计算权重时原始数据的来源不同,大体上可分为主观赋权法和客观赋权法两大类。主观赋权法主要是由专家根据经验主观判断而得到,如Delphi法、层次分析法(The Analytic Hierarchy Process, AHP)、专家打分法等,这类方法能纳入权威专家对不同指标之间的相对重要程度的考量,但客观性稍差。客观赋权法主要是依据各指标的具体数值计算而得到,它不依赖于人的主观判断,因而客观性较强,但不一定能科学反映不同指标之间的相对重要程度,也不一定能满足决策者的主观要求。客观赋权法这类方法的代表有主成分分析法和变异系数法等。主观赋权法和客观赋权法各有优劣,本项目最终选择的是主观赋权法。具体而言,在计算各准则层指标对上层目标的权重时,课题组使用层次分析法;而在计算各具体指标对上一层准则层的权重时,课题组则选择了专家打分法。①

2.2.2 层次分析法

层次分析法是一种系统分析与决策的综合评价方法,它可以较合理地解决定性

---

① 课题组在计算各具体指标对上一层准则层的权重时,还使用了变异系数法,结果发现变异系数法与专家打分法得出的结果非常一致。最终选择专家打分法是因为这一方法更能够体现包括行业主管部门、高校学者、社会资本方在内的社会各界对不同指标重要性的看法与态度,而不是仅仅依赖于不同指标之间的统计特征,更有利于各个地区发现PPP信息披露工作中存在的问题并有针对性地改进。

问题定量化的处理过程。层次分析法的主要特点是通过建立层次结构，把人们的判断转化为若干因素两两之间重要性的比较，从而把难以量化的定性判断转化为可操作的定量判断。

在所构建的层次分析模型中，通过调查判断，形成判定矩阵。当检验判定矩阵通过一致性检验时，则可以接受判定矩阵，并计算得出各指标的权重值；若该一致性检验未通过，则意味着判定矩阵的元素值需要调整，直至通过一致性检验为止。具体地，层次分析法的实施步骤如下：

第一步，建立层次结构模型。通过对影响PPP信息透明度各因素的深入分析，将有关各因素按从属关系分解成若干层次，最上层为目标层，中间层为准则层，具体的指标在最下层。本报告的层级结构模型如图2-1所示。

第二步，构建判定矩阵。构建判定矩阵，比较两两具体指标之间的相对重要性。根据本项目构建的PPP项目透明度层级示意图，共涉及两个分类指数，因而涉及三个判定矩阵，分别是总指数判定矩阵（判定即时公开透明度指数和适时公开透明度指数在合成PPP市场透明度总指数时的相对重要性）、即时公开透明度指数判定矩阵（判定识别阶段、准备阶段、采购阶段和执行阶段的分指数在合成即时公开透明度指数时的相对重要性）和适时公开透明度指数判定矩阵（判定识别阶段、准备阶段和采购阶段的分指数在合成适时公开透明度指数时的相对重要性）。

一般地，假设比较n个因素$c_1, c_2, \cdots, c_n$对上一层因素的影响，判定矩阵要求每次两两比较两个因素对上一层因素的相对重要性，这一相对重要性通常用数值1～9来体现，以构成判定矩阵的每个元素赋值c_{ij}（数值的含义如表2-3所示，一般由具备丰富经验的专家来选择）。全部比较结果构成"成对比较矩阵"，也称为"正互反矩阵"。

表2-3 判定矩阵标度含义

标度c_{ij}	定 义	含 义
1	同等重要	c_i和c_j的影响相同
3	稍微重要	c_i比c_j的影响稍强
5	较强重要	c_i比c_j的影响强
7	强烈重要	c_i比c_j的影响明显地强

(续表)

标度 c_{ij}	定义	含义
9	极端重要	c_i 比 c_j 的影响绝对地强
2,4,6,8	两相邻判断的中间值	c_i 与 c_j 的影响之比在上述两个相邻等级之间
$1/2,\cdots,1/9$	倒数	c_i 与 c_j 的影响之比为上面 a_{ij} 的互反数

$$C = \begin{pmatrix} c_{11} & c_{12} & \cdots & c_{1n} \\ c_{21} & c_{22} & \cdots & c_{2n} \\ \vdots & \vdots & \vdots & \vdots \\ c_{n1} & c_{n2} & \cdots & c_{nn} \end{pmatrix}$$

$C = (c_{ij})_{n \times n}, c_{ij} > 0, c_{ji} = \dfrac{1}{c_{ij}}, c_{ii} = 1$。

若正互反矩阵 C 满足 $c_{ij} \times c_{jk} = c_{ik}$，则称 C 为完全一致性矩阵。

第三步，计算判定矩阵的最大特征值及其特征向量。在运用判定矩阵确定各指标权重时，实际上就是求解判定矩阵的特征向量。通过解正互反矩阵的最大特征值，可求得相应的特征向量，经归一化后即为权重向量。

$$CW = \lambda_{\max} W$$

第四步，一致性检验。首先，计算该 n 阶判定矩阵的一致性指标值 CI。

$$CI = \frac{\lambda_{\max} - n}{n - 1}$$

其次，计算平均随机一致性指标 RI。从 1～9 及其倒数中随机抽取数字构成 n 阶正互反矩阵，计算其最大特征值；重复 1 000 次，得到 1 000 个随机正互反矩阵的最大特征值，再计算 1 000 个最大特征值的均值；计算平均随机一致性指标 RI。

$$RI = \frac{k - n}{n - 1}$$

最后，计算一致性比率 CR，并验证是否一致。

$$CR = \frac{CI}{RI}$$

当 $CR < 0.1$ 时，一般认为矩阵 A 的不一致程度在容许范围之内，可以用其特征向量作为权向量，否则需对判定矩阵进行修正（重复第二步和第三步），直至 CR 小于 0.1 为止。

第五步，计算权重向量。将通过一致性检验的判定矩阵最大特征值所对应的特征向量进行归一化即可得到该层各因素对上层因素的权重大小。

根据这一方法，课题组邀请了包括高校学者代表（3位）、政府主管部门代表（3位）、社会资本方代表（3位）以及中介咨询机构代表（2位）在内的共11位业内权威专家进行三个判定矩阵的填写，并随后通过前文所述的层次分析法计算出各阶段的具体权重，最后求得不同专家所赋权重的平均数。附件一给出了专家判定矩阵调查表。表2-4则给出了根据专家判定矩阵计算出的权重表。其中，在即时公开透明度指数方面，识别阶段、准备阶段、采购阶段和执行阶段的分指数在合成即时公开透明度指数时的权重分别为0.19、0.19、0.40和0.22；在适时公开透明度指数方面，识别阶段、准备阶段和采购阶段的分指数在合成适时公开透明度指数时的权重分别为0.25、0.30和0.45；而在将适时公开透明度指数和即时公开透明度指数加总合成PPP市场透明度总指数时，根据专家填写的判定矩阵计算出两者的权重分别是0.61和0.39。

表2-4 透明度指数专家判定矩阵权重表

即时公开透明度指数		适时公开透明度指数		总指数权重	
阶段	权重	阶段	权重	分指数	权重
识别阶段	0.19	识别阶段	0.25	适时公开	0.39
准备阶段	0.19	准备阶段	0.30	即时公开	0.61
采购阶段	0.40	采购阶段	0.45	—	—
执行阶段	0.22	—	—	—	—

2.2.3 具体指标权重计算方法

以上AHP层次分析法确定了中间各层级相对其上一层级的权重大小，还需要确定最下层（即各具体指标）对其上一层的权重大小，对此，课题组使用了专家打分法。

具体而言，根据上文所讨论的内容，特别是其中的"突出性原则"，课题组将通过专家打分的方法，对其中的具体指标进行打分。经过专家打分后，不同的具体指标就相当于包含了一定的权重。课题组将不同的具体指标划分为"一般""重要"和"特别重要"三种程度，分别用1分、2分和3分来表示，然后交由专家对不同的指标进行赋分。数值越高，代表该具体指标相对越重要。课题组同样邀请了包括高校学者代表、政府主管部门代表、社会资本方代表以及中介咨询机构代表在内的共11位专家进行打分。表2-5和表2-6给出了专家打分的具体结果。需要进一步说明的是，上述不同指标的具体得分都是在某阶段内相互对比的，而不是直接进行全部指标间的对比。为清晰展示这一点，我们在表2-5和表2-6中列出了得分所对应的在本阶段内的具体权重。

表2-5 即时公开透明度指数具体指标专家打分结果

所属阶段	具 体 指 标	得分	权重
识别阶段	项目总投资	2.455	5.52
	拟合作期限	2.273	5.11
	二级行业	1.091	2.45
	项目运作方式	2.182	4.91
	回报机制	2.909	6.54
	项目发起时间	1.636	3.68
	发起类型	1.455	3.27
	发起人名称	1.182	2.66
	项目概况	2.000	4.50
	项目联系人	1.455	3.27
	项目联系电话	1.455	3.27
	财政联系人	1.455	3.27
	财政联系电话	1.455	3.27
	项目用地总面积	2.000	4.50

（续表）

所属阶段	具 体 指 标	得分	权重
识别阶段	计划开发年度	2.000	4.50
	采购社会资本方式的选择	2.455	5.52
	实施方案描述	2.364	5.32
	项目合作范围（识别）	2.182	4.91
	物有所值定性评价指标及权重、评分标准、评分结果	2.545	5.72
	物有所值评价通过与否的评价结论（含财政部门对报告的审核意见）	2.636	5.93
	本项目以及年度全部已实施和拟实施的PPP项目财政支出责任数额及年度预算安排情况，以及每一年度全部PPP项目从预算中安排的支出责任占一般公共预算支出比例情况	2.818	6.34
	通过财政承受能力论证与否的结论	2.455	5.52
准备阶段	拟引入社会资本投资额	2.182	18.2
	政府拟出资额	2.273	18.9
	审核通过实施方案的政府名称	1.727	14.4
	本级政府对实施方案审核通过时间	1.727	14.4
	本级人民政府对实施机构即PPP项目合同的政府方签约主体的授权文件	2.000	16.7
	政府对实施方案的审核通过文件	2.091	17.4
采购阶段	项目资格预审公告（含资格预审申请文件）	2.364	11.2
	预中标及成交结果公告；中标、成交结果公告及中标通知书	2.545	12.1
	项目本级行业主管部门对拟签署PPP合同的审核意见	1.909	9.1
	项目本级财政部门对拟签署PPP合同的审核意见	2.000	9.5
	项目本级法制部门对拟签署PPP合同的审核意见	1.909	9.1
	项目本级人民政府是否批准了拟签署的PPP合同	2.455	11.6
	批准日期	2.455	11.6
	项目本级人民政府对PPP项目合同中约定的政府跨年度财政支出责任纳入中期财政规划的审核意见	2.727	12.9
	审核日期	2.727	12.9
执行阶段	项目公司名称	1.636	15.6
	项目公司成立时间	1.545	14.8

（续表）

所属阶段	具体指标	得分	权重
执行阶段	项目公司注册资金	1.818	17.4
	项目公司经济性质	1.455	13.9
	股东认缴	2.000	19.1
	本级人民政府对政府方出资代表的授权	2.000	19.1

表2-6 适时公开透明度指数具体指标专家打分结果

一级指标	具体指标	得分	权重
识别阶段	物有所值评价报告及批复附件	3.000	18.0
	财政承受能力论证报告及批复附件	3.000	18.0
	新建或改扩建项目建议书及批复文件	2.333	14.0
	可行性研究报告	2.667	16.0
	设计文件及批复文件	2.677	16.1
	存量公共资产或权益的资产评估报告	3.000	18.0
准备阶段	物有所值评价完成时间	1.556	33.3
	财政承受能力论证完成时间	1.556	33.3
	审核通过的项目实施方案及修正案	1.556	33.3
采购阶段	资格预审：公告时间	1.778	5.5
	资格预审：预审时间	1.667	5.2
	项目采购：公告时间	1.889	5.9
	采购结果：响应文件评审时间	1.556	4.8
	采购结果：结果确认谈判时间	1.889	5.9
	采购结果：政府审核时间	1.778	5.5
	采购结果：合同签署时间	1.778	5.5
	采购结果：合同公布时间	1.889	5.9
	采购结果：合同公布媒体	1.444	4.5
	合同签订的项目投资额	2.556	8.0

(续表)

一级指标	具 体 指 标	得分	权重
采购阶段	采购文件	2.889	9.0
	资格预审专家评审结论性意见及资格预审专家名单	2.111	6.6
	响应文件专家评审结论性意见及评审专家名单	2.111	6.6
	确认谈判工作组成员名单	1.222	3.8
	PPP项目合同附件	2.556	8.0
	本级政府支出责任确认文件	3.000	9.3

2.2.4 指数合成计算过程

在多指标体系综合评价中，合成是指通过一定的算式将多个指标对事物不同方面的评价值综合在一起，以得到一个整体性的评价。可用于合成的数学方法很多，常见的合成模型有加权算术平均合成模型、加权几何平均合成模型、加权算术平均和加权几何平均联合使用的混合合成模型。三种模型有各自的特点和适用场合，并没有优劣之分。在综合比较了三种合成方法之后，课题组选用了加权算术平均合成模型。加权算术平均合成模型的公式如下：

$$d = \sum_{i=1}^{n} w_i d_i$$

其中，d为综合指数，w_i为各评价指标归一化后的权重，d_i为单个指标的评价得分，n为评价指标的个数。具体指数合成时，是由下往上逐层汇总而成，先计算各层分组指数，然后由各层分组指数加权汇总得到综合指数（逐层级的计算过程详见第4章）。

具体而言，课题组首先通过网站读取方式获取各个具体指标的披露情况并赋值（共四种可能的取值，分别是：1代表公开且无明显造假行为，0代表没有公开，0.5代表部分公开，−1代表"虚假"公开）。之后根据专家打分法再将这些具体指标的得分加总，计算出某个阶段（比如适时公开的识别阶段等）的得分率（百分制）。随后，在此基础上再根据用层次分析法得出的权重，将不同阶段的分指数合成为即时公开透明度指数或适时公开透明度指数。最后，对即时公开透明度指数和适时公开透明度指数按照层次分析法得出的权重进行加权，计算出PPP市场透明度总指数。

根据课题组的指标体系设计和指数计算方法，理论上某项目的透明度总指数（或者分阶段指数）的满分可以达到100分，表示课题组设计的指标均得到了正确、完整的公开。最低分可以少于0分，即出现负分，表示该项目公布的信息中存在较多的虚假信息。0分则表示课题组设计的指标在该项目中均没有得到公开，也可能表示该项目公开了一些指标但同时也虚假公开了另外一些指标，导致成绩被"抹杀"了，经过课题组"惩罚"后，近似等于所有指标均没有公开，当然这一情况也很不容易出现，特别是对于很多指标合成后的总指数。

需要强调的是，在计算总指数时，由于有些项目没有完整的五个业务阶段，因此，为保证指数的稳定性，课题组通过权重归一化使得相对权重保持一致。例如，在即时公开透明度指数的计算中，识别、准备、采购和执行四个阶段的权重分别为0.19、0.19、0.40和0.22，但某个项目只有前三个阶段，那么这三个阶段的权重就分别为：

识别阶段=0.19/(0.19+0.19+0.40)=0.244

准备阶段=0.19/(0.19+0.19+0.40)=0.244

采购阶段=0.40/(0.19+0.19+0.40)=0.512

3

指数基本结果与总体分析

3.1 样本数据基本情况

3.1.1 样本概况

根据前文的介绍,课题组将PPP市场透明度指数编制分为即时公开透明度指数和适时公开透明度指数两部分。其中,即时公开透明度指数涉及10 175个项目样本,较2020年增加了213个,变化不大;适时公开透明度指数则涉及7 598个项目,较2020年增加了1 797个。此外,在2021年的10 175个总样本中,处于准备阶段、采购阶段和执行阶段的项目分别有460个、2 032个和7 683个。从图3-1中可以看出,相对于2020年而言,2021年的项目样本中进入执行阶段的样本占比略微上升,处于准备阶段的样本占比则略有下降。

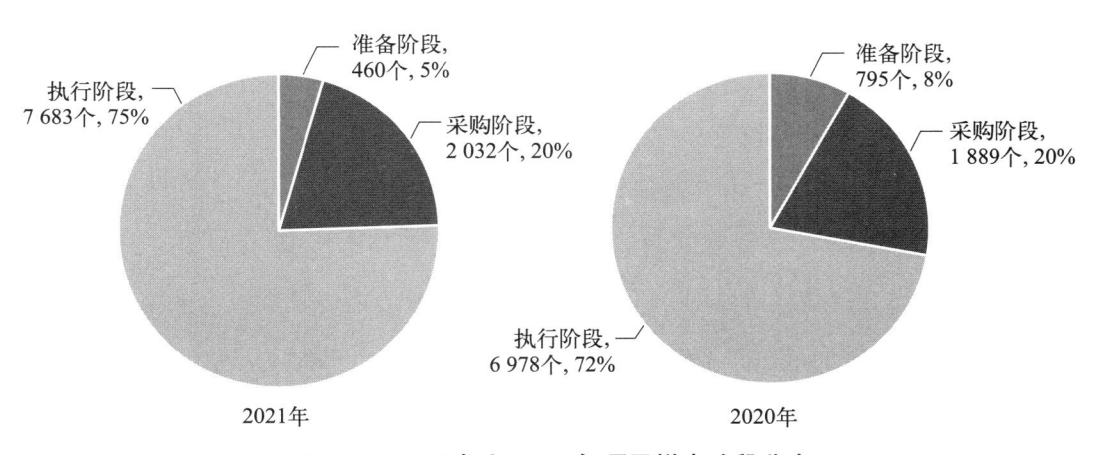

图3-1 2020年和2021年项目样本阶段分布

3.1.2 指标构建

在第2章有关指标体系的介绍中,我们已经知道,本指数共包含68个指标字段,基本来自政府和社会资本合作中心网站,对于其中的31个指标字段,课题组需要从政府和社会资本合作中心网站上进行人工读取，主要目的是核实其真实性。在这些指标的构建中，对37个直接从网站或政府和社会资本合作中心获取的数据，课题组直接对其进行0和1的赋值，即某项目公布了该项指标，就赋1分，没有公布这些指标，就赋0分。而对于从政府和社会资本合作中心网站人工采集的指标，课题组对其打分更加细化：完整公布该指标信息，赋1分；部分公布，为0.5分；没有公布，为0分；显示公开了该信息（如有PDF附件）但为假文件或错误文件，则设为−1分，以示惩戒。

对部分公开和错误公开的样本，这里需要再稍作解释。所谓部分公布，主要是指该指标信息实际上包含了多个信息，但只公布了其中的一部分。例如，对于"物有所值定性评价指标及权重、评分标准、评分结果"，如果只公布了评分标准，或者只公布了评分结果，就只给0.5分。再如，对于物有所值评价报告、财政承受能力论证报告，文件要求是公布"物有所值评价报告及本级行业主管部门会同财政部门的审核通过意见"以及"财政承受能力论证报告及本级财政部门的审核通过意见"等，有些项目只公布其中的物有所值评价报告或财政承受能力论证报告，没有公布批复文件，或者情况相反，对这类情况，课题组也给0.5分。而赋值为−1分的所谓错误公开，主要情形为上传的PDF附件是空白文档、错误文档，以及信息的张冠李戴等情形。不过，对于极少一部分附件，虽然没有实质内容，但对为什么没有这些内容进行了合理化解释，例如，项目在政策要求之前就已经运行，根据不溯及既往的原则，课题组不认定这种解释文件为错误公开，以免产生"误伤"。

这里以适时公开的"物有所值评价报告及本级行业主管部门会同财政部门的审核通过意见"为例，来说明课题组手工数据采集的基本情况。如图3-2所示，在7 598个适时公开评估样本中，完整公开"物有所值评价报告及本级行业主管部门会同财政部门的审核通过意见"的样本有6 553个，部分公开的有1 024个，没有公开的有9个，公开但文件为假文件、错误文件的样本有12个。与2020年相比，该指标完整公开率从83%上升到2021年的86%，虚假公开比率从1%降到到0.16%，未公开比率从0.26%下降至0.12%。

最后，这些具体指标的公开程度得分再乘以上一章关于具体指标相对重要程度的专家评分，即可得到该指标的具体分数，进而可以逐级计算得到全国或某地区的PPP市场透明度指数。

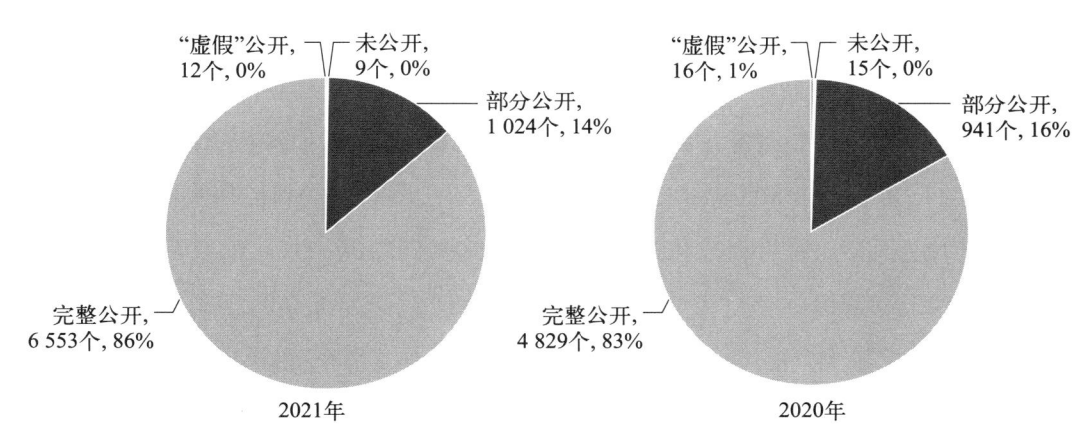

图3-2 物有所值评价报告及附件披露情况

3.2 全国总指数计算

3.2.1 指数合成

计算得到各指标的具体得分后,就可以计算出某个PPP项目在某阶段的得分率(标准化为100),这也就是透明度指数在该阶段的分指数。我们首先以适时公开透明度指数中的识别阶段为例进行说明,这个阶段包含6个信息,分别为"物有所值评价报告及本级行业主管部门会同财政部门的审核通过意见""财政承受能力论证报告及本级财政部门的审核通过意见""新建或改扩建项目建议书及批复文件""可行性研究报告或资金申请报告或申请核准项目的报告,及相关主管部门对上述报告的批复、批准或核准等文件;存量公共资产的资产评估报告""设计文件及批复文件"和"存量公共资产或权益的资产评估报告及存量资产或权益转让时所可能涉及到的各类方案等"。这6个指标在专家评分过程中的得分分别为3分、3分、2.333分、2.667分、2.667分和3分,这样,在适时公开的识别阶段总分就是16.667分。假如某个项目在识别阶段6个指标的信息公开中分别被判定为1(完全公开)、1(完全公开)、0.5(部分公开)、0.5(部分公开)、0(未公开)和-1("虚假"公开),那么该项目在识别阶段的得分率就为[1×3+1×3+0.5×2.333+0.5×2.667+0×2.667+(-1)×3]/16.667×100=33。这个33即为该项目在适时公开阶段的透明度分指数。同理,可得到即时公开和适时公开各个阶段的透明度分指数。

表3-1给出了不同阶段的即时公开透明度指数,从中我们可以看出,在10 175个即时公开透明度评估对象中,识别阶段、准备阶段、采购阶段和执行阶段的平均指数分别为95.30、92.00、80.24和65.63。相对而言,在识别阶段和准备阶段,PPP项目信息披露较为理想,采购阶段和执行阶段的信息公开则差一些。从管理机制而言,识别阶段和准备阶段的信息大多是PPP项目入库时就必须提交的相关信息,由于入库时主管部门审查较严,因而指数普遍较高,但进入采购阶段和执行阶段后的项目,信息是否按照要求及时上传到PPP综合信息平台,并不妨碍项目工作往前推进,信息公开的监管工作缺乏强硬抓手,从而导致采购阶段和执行阶段的指数较低。此外,与2020年比较,准备阶段、采购阶段和执行阶段的指数均有上升,识别阶段指数基本维持不变。

表3-1 不同阶段的即时公开透明度指数

阶 段	2021年			2020年		
	样本量	均 值	标准差	样本量	均 值	标准差
识别阶段	10 175	95.30	3.70	9 662	95.58	3.30
准备阶段	10 175	92.00	13.22	9 662	90.41	16.61
采购阶段	9 715	80.24	18.28	8 866	78.85	23.24
执行阶段	7 683	65.63	26.50	6 978	64.85	32.15

表3-2给出了即时公开各个阶段透明度指数的具体分布,从中可以看出一些信息公开较好的项目在某些阶段指数可以达到100,但一些信息公开工作不到位的项目在某阶段的指数可能出现负值。我们在前文已经多次介绍过,这是因为部分项目上传的PDF文件附件中有假文件、错误文件等,而被课题组进行了"扣分"惩罚。我们关注这些"异常"项目,对其进行特别处理,是希望这样能够敦促相关责任部门尽快改进这些方面的工作,补齐短板,推动PPP项目规范化管理。不过,相对而言,我们更关注大多数项目的信息公开情况,因为大多数项目的信息透明度指数结果才能代表整个PPP市场的信息透明程度。因此,我们在表3-2中也给出了不同阶段透明

度分指数的25%和75%两个分位数对应的具体数值。对比2021年和2020年即时公开各阶段透明度指数分布可以看出：2021年的识别阶段即时公开信息工作与2020年相比差别不大，2021年即时公开识别阶段的25分位数和75分位数分别为94.28和97.13，2020年则分别为94.27和100；从准备阶段和采购阶段看，2021年的即时公开信息工作相比2020年有明显改善，2021年即时公开准备阶段和采购阶段的25分位数分别为91.67和80.10，高于2020年的83.33和76.71；最后我们考察执行阶段，2021年即时公开执行阶段的25分位数为61.74，高于2020年的53.91，这表明在那些指数较低的项目上，与2020年相比，2021年执行阶段的即时公开信息工作更为出色。在即时公开执行阶段75分位数上，2021和2020年的数据差不多。总体来看，细致考察指数分布得到的结论与表3-1基本一致，在即时公开方面，2021年识别阶段和准备阶段的信息公开工作略优于2020年。

表3-2 即时公开各阶段透明度指数的分布

阶段	2021年				2020年			
	最小值	25分位	75分位	最大值	最小值	25分位	75分位	最大值
识别阶段	57.00	94.28	97.13	100	66.26	94.27	100	100
准备阶段	−16.67	91.67	100	100	−17.43	83.33	100	100
采购阶段	0	80.10	89.07	100	0	76.71	88.36	100
执行阶段	0	61.74	88.87	100	0	53.91	90.43	100

表3-3给出了不同阶段的适时公开透明度指数，从中我们可以看出，在7 598个适时公开透明度评估对象中，识别阶段、准备阶段、采购阶段的平均指数分别为55.13、97.15和76.80。在不同阶段的比较上，相对而言，识别阶段较差，而准备阶段的信息公开工作较为理想，我们判断这主要是因为在识别阶段的适时公开信息中，需要公开的主要信息包括物有所值评价报告、财政承受能力论证报告等几个核心文件，对于这些文件，一些项目的信息公开工作做得不太理想。对比2020年的各阶段适时公开透明度指数可以发现，准备阶段这两年的平均指数差别不大，识别阶段和采购阶段2021年平均指数均高于2020年。

表3-3 不同阶段的适时公开透明度指数

阶 段	2021年 样本量	2021年 均值	2021年 标准差	2020年 样本量	2020年 均值	2020年 标准差
识别阶段	7 598	55.13	14.97	5 801	50.50	13.71
准备阶段	7 598	97.15	5.66	5 801	97.83	6.86
采购阶段	7 598	76.80	9.61	5 801	74.80	11.01

表3-4给出了适时公开各阶段透明度指数的具体分布，包括最小值、最大值、上四分位数和下四分位数。从中我们可以看到，在适时公开的信息中，准备阶段和采购阶段的大部分项目的信息公开工作都较好，而识别阶段则较差。因此，如果想提高PPP项目适时公开信息的整体透明度，可以将焦点集中于物有所值评价报告、财政承受能力论证报告等几个核心报告的规范、完整披露上，相信补齐短板后能让适时公开透明度指数大幅上升。与2020年适时公开各阶段透明度指数对比，总体看2021年适时公开识别阶段、准备阶段和采购阶段信息披露工作要略优于2020年。

表3-4 适时公开各阶段透明度指数的分布

阶 段	2021年 最小值	2021年 25分位	2021年 75分位	2021年 最大值	2020年 最小值	2020年 25分位	2020年 75分位	2020年 最大值
识别阶段	−51.97	51.97	69.10	100	−51.97	43.97	54.97	100
准备阶段	0	98.50	100	100	0	100	100	100
采购阶段	3.81	72.70	84.80	94.16	0	70.42	84.78	94.12

3.2.2 总指数结果

在得到各阶段的透明度分指数后，我们就可以按照第2章介绍的用层次分析法得到的各阶段分指数的权重来合成即时公开透明度指数和适时公开透明度指数。表3-5即为即时公开透明度指数和适时公开透明度指数的总体情况。从中可以看出，即时公开透明度指数和适时公开透明度指数平均数值分别为83.27和74.90。与2020年相比，2021年的这两项指标基本保持平稳，数值上略有提高，不过幅度都不大。

表3-5 即时公开和适时公开透明度指数

指数	2021年 样本量	2021年 均值	2021年 标准差	2020年 样本量	2020年 均值	2020年 标准差
即时公开透明度指数	10 175	83.27	10.72	9 962	80.37	8.57
适时公开透明度指数	7 598	74.90	7.38	5 801	74.67	3.02

最后，在得到即时公开透明度指数和适时公开透明度指数之后，在全国平均意义上，我们还可以按照用层次分析法计算得到的将即时公开透明度指数和适时公开透明度指数合成总指数时的权重，合成全国PPP市场透明度总指数。结论是：**截至2021年12月底，全国PPP市场透明度总指数为80.01（83.27×0.61+74.9×0.39），略高于2020年的78.15**。这也是课题组评估中国PPP市场透明度以来，全国总指数首次达到80。图3-3显示了全国PPP市场透明度总指数、即时公开透明度指数、适时公开透明度指数，以及各阶段透明度分指数的平均结果分布。

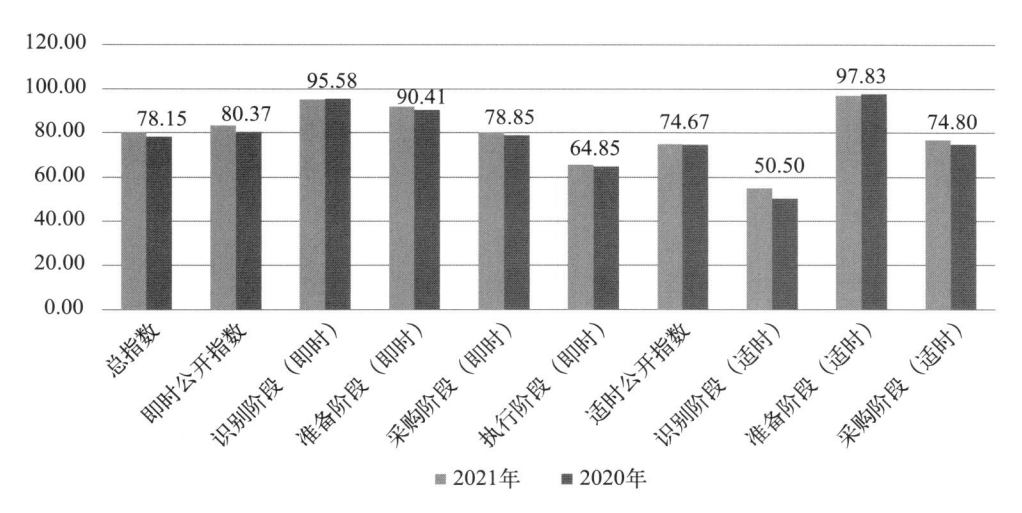

图3-3 全国PPP市场透明度总指数及各阶段指数

3.3 全国总指数的异质性分析

根据上文的分析，全国PPP市场透明度指数实际上是由全国约10 200个PPP项目的透明度指数平均而得到的。正如在上一节我们所看到的,全国PPP项目透明度平均结果可能掩盖了不同项目的异质性。因此,为了对全国的PPP市场透明度有更深入和直观的展示,在本节,我们主要从不同行业、不同类型等角度,对全国PPP市场透明度进行一些总体层面的分析。在后面的两章里,我们还将从省份和城市层面对各地PPP市场透明度进行更详细的讨论。

3.3.1 不同行业的PPP市场透明度指数

我们首先来看不同行业的PPP市场透明度指数。从图3-4中我们可以发现,不同行业的PPP市场透明度指数虽然存在一定的差异,但差异数值并不大。分行业透明度总指数最高的为水利建设行业81.7,最低的是社会保障行业78.4,最高和最低仅相差3.3。观察不同行业的即时公开透明度指数和适时公开透明度指数,以及不同阶段的分指数,也有类似发现。因此,总体而言,不同行业PPP项目在信息公开上没有呈现出明显的异质性。这表明现存的PPP项目信息公开的制度规范具有一定的行业普适性。由于不同行业领域的PPP项目往往由不同的行业主管部门来负责具体的运行管理和监督,因而上述结果也说明不同行业主管部门在PPP项目信息公开的管理上并没有很明显的勤懒之分。此外,从图3-4中还可以观察到,各个行业2021年的PPP市场透明度指数相比2020年均有所提高。

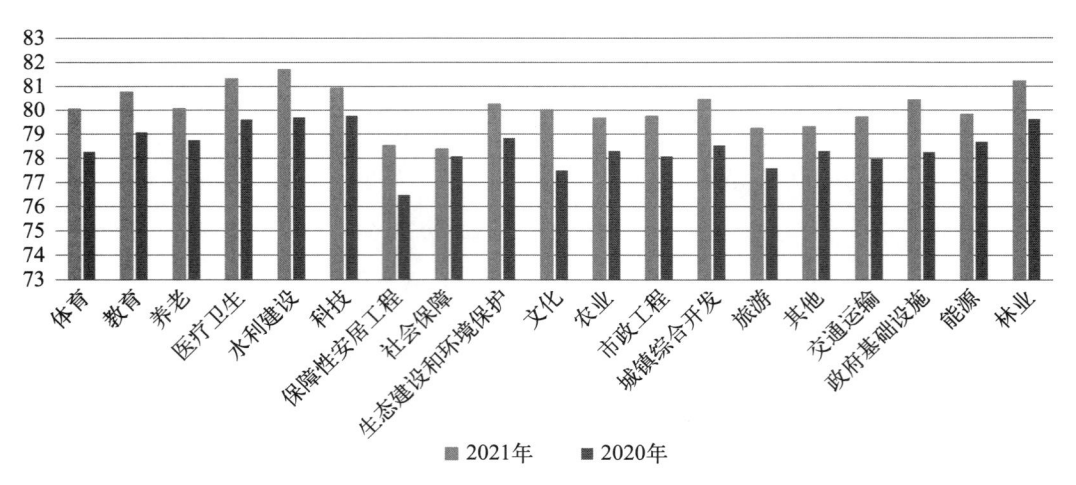

图3-4 分行业PPP市场透明度总指数

3.3.2 示范项目和非示范项目的透明度指数

现在我们来分析示范项目和非示范项目在信息公开方面的差异。如图3-5所示,2021年的示范项目和非示范项目的透明度指数相差不大,示范项目的总体信息公开程度略高于非示范项目,这一结论与前几年报告中得到的结论很类似。总结我们近三年的评估结果,示范项目的透明度指数从2019年的77.19提高到2020年的78.9,再提高到2021年的79.92,增长幅度并不大;同样,非示范项目的透明度指数从2019年的76.01增长到2020年的78.23,2021年的这一数值为80.34,增长幅度也不大。这些结果说明,"是否示范项目"这一变量随着时间的推移,越来越不能解释项目间透明度指数的差异。

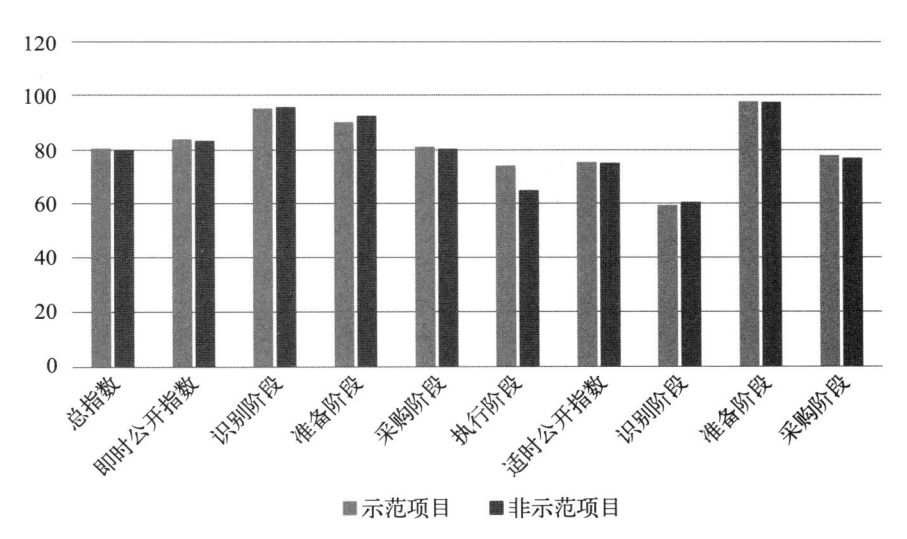

图3-5 2021年示范项目与非示范项目的透明度指数

# 4

省级指数的排名与分析

4.1 省级透明度总指数结果分析

4.1.1 省级指数总体排名

上一章介绍了全国层面的2021年PPP市场透明度指数的基本情况，本章主要介绍分省份的分析结果。为了得到各省份PPP市场透明度指数，课题组首先基于各个项目的透明度指数计算了各省份即时公开透明度指数和适时公开透明度指数，计算方法是先算出各省份所有项目的即时公开透明度指数和适时公开透明度指数的算术平均，然后按照第2章计算出来的权重合成得出各省份PPP市场透明度指数（即时公开权重为0.61，适时公开权重为0.39）。表4-1给出了2021年32个省级单位（省、直辖市、自治区、新疆生产建设兵团，下同）PPP项目的数量及透明度总指数的具体结果。从中我们可以得到以下几个结论：

第一，总体上看，2021年省级层面的PPP市场透明度指数相比2020年稳中有升。绝大多数省份的透明度指数在70以上，有9个省份的透明度指数超过了80，云南的透明度指数甚至达到了90，这是课题组评估中国PPP市场透明度5年来首次有省份的透明度总指数达到90。

第二，与2020年相比，各省份PPP市场透明度指数进一步出现一定的分化趋势。我们可以很明显地看到，前3名省份与后面省份的透明度指数表现出了不同的时间趋势：绝大多数省份2021年的透明度指数与2020年接近，其中有的略有下降；而前3名省份的透明度指数出现了3~5不等的涨幅，逐渐拉开了与后面省份透明度指数的差距。

第三，具体排名而言，透明度排名第一的省份仍是云南（90.55），排名第二的是河北（88.54），排名第三的是山东（86.39），排名第四的是湖南（81.43），排名第五的是江苏（81.27）。而西藏、宁夏、海南、北京、上海则表现相对较差，它们占据了这份榜单的最后5名。对比2020年的排行榜可以发现，PPP项目信息透明度工作进步最大的省份是浙江(79.94)，其在全国的排名较上一年上升了10位，挤进全国前十。PPP市场透明度指数排名下降较多的省份有陕西、内蒙古、广东、山西、湖北、福建，都下降了3位。其指数分别从2020年的81.25、80.61、79.30、78.47、78.22、77.35下降到了2021年的79.78、79.46、78.15、77.60、77.11、76.15，虽然下降幅度不大，但由于省份之间指数差距本就很小，因而这些省份在2021年全国PPP市场透明度指数排名中分别仅列第十一、十二、十六、二十一、二十五位。四川、广西、甘肃等省份排名相较上一年均有较大幅度的上升。

表4-1　2021年省级PPP市场透明度总指数与排名

省份	2021年项目数量	2021年透明度指数	2021年排名	较上一年排名变化	2020年项目数量	2020年透明度指数
云南	485	90.55	1	0	495	84.98
河北	455	88.54	2	+1	734	82.99
山东	760	86.39	3	−1	434	83.72
湖南	363	81.43	4	0	160	82.69
江苏	392	81.27	5	0	386	82.63
吉林	165	80.54	6	0	376	81.82
甘肃	145	80.39	7	+3	786	80.52
新疆	402	80.24	8	−1	389	81.71
四川	559	80.07	9	+6	552	78.99
浙江	513	79.94	10	+10	359	77.60
陕西	275	79.78	11	−3	278	81.25
内蒙古	274	79.46	12	−3	123	80.61
河南	838	78.76	13	−2	42	79.91
安徽	487	78.39	14	−2	474	79.65
青海	42	78.29	15	−1	262	79.22
广东	559	78.15	16	−3	551	79.30
辽宁	273	77.97	17	0	406	78.22

(续表)

省份	2021年项目数量	2021年透明度指数	2021年排名	较上一年排名变化	2020年项目数量	2020年透明度指数
黑龙江	125	77.67	18	+1	293	78.17
山西	441	77.60	19	−3	103	78.47
天津	71	77.48	20	+1	55	77.45
湖北	435	77.11	21	−3	419	78.22
贵州	571	76.90	22	+1	507	77.17
广西	372	76.89	23	+4	57	76.40
江西	484	76.70	24	+1	529	76.91
福建	368	76.15	25	−3	241	77.35
兵团	18	76.13	26	−2	418	77.05
重庆	73	75.05	27	−1	16	76.56
上海	7	71.60	28	+2	7	72.40
北京	77	70.92	29	−1	69	74.73
海南	98	68.16	30	+1	95	69.76
宁夏	46	64.82	31	−2	43	73.83
西藏	3	56.02	32	0	3	56.45

注：① 本报告表格所涉及的项目数量总体指的是即时公开透明度指数所涉及的10 175个PPP项目，适时公开透明度指数所涉及的7 598个PPP项目是它的一个子集；② "+"表示排名上升，"−"表示排名下降，下同。

4.1.2 即时公开和适时公开省级排名

图4-1和图4-2分别给出了各省份2020年和2021年PPP项目即时公开透明度指数和适时公开透明度指数的分布图。从中我们可以发现：

第一，各省份即时公开透明度指数基本要高于适时公开透明度指数，这一发现与第3章的描述是一致的，再次表明全国各省份PPP项目对适时指标的信息披露工作做得不如即时公开理想。

第二，各省级行政区的透明度总指数、适时公开透明度指数与即时公开透明度指数的省份排名总体是一致的，但也不是完全相同。由于即时公开指数的权重为0.61，而适时公开指数的权重为0.39，不出意外，那些在即时公开透明度方面做得较好的省份会在总指数上获得一个较好的排名，比如除西藏外即时公开前5名的省份实际上就是总指数榜单上的前5名。尽管如此，即时公开透明度指数和适时公开透明度指数的省份排名之间还存在一定的差异。即时公开透明度指数排名第四位的湖南，适时公开透明度指数排名第十四位，说明湖南在相关信息即时公开方面的工作开展确实较好，但是在适时公开方面的工作较差。而即时公开透明度指数排名最末的海南，适时公开透明度指数排在倒数第二位，说明海南需要同时加强即时公开和适时公开两方面的工作。两份榜单的差异进一步表明各地区在PPP项目信息公开方面各有优劣，需要取长补短，才能提升整体的透明度，推动PPP项目信息更好地公开。

通过2021年和2020年数据对比可以发现，各省份即时公开透明度指数和适时公开透明度指数的跨期变动没有呈现出显性的规律，表现为较平稳且有小幅度增减。从即时公开透明度指数变化情况看，有17个省份的指数上升，15个省份的指数下降。即时公开透明度指数上升幅度最大的是宁夏，从2020年的66.33上升至2021年的88.14，其次是甘肃、江苏和湖南；而即时公开透明度指数下降幅度最大的是安徽，从2020年的82.31下降至2021年的78.42。从适时公开透明度指数变化情况看，有27个省份的指数上升，4个省份的指数下降。适时公开透明度指数上升幅度最大的是宁

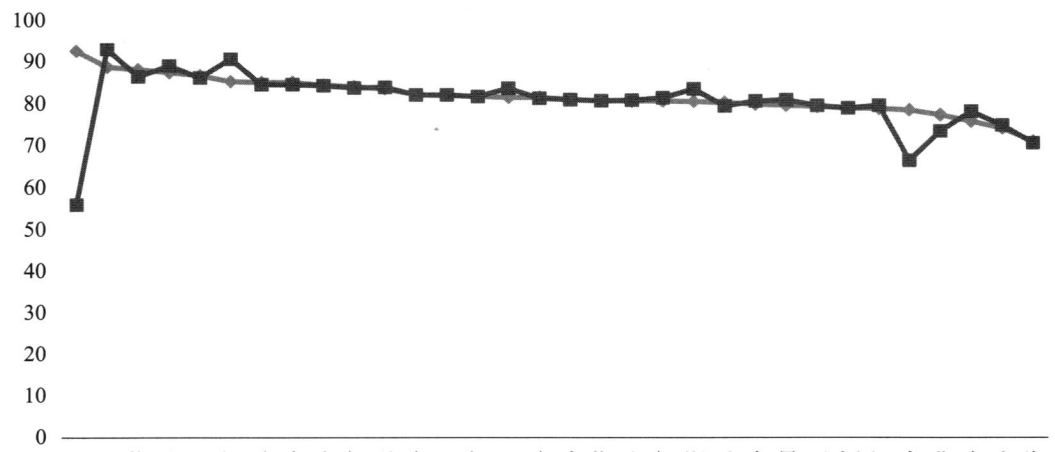

图4-1　2020年和2021年各省份PPP即时公开透明度指数

图 4-2　2020 年和 2021 年各省份 PPP 适时公开透明度指数

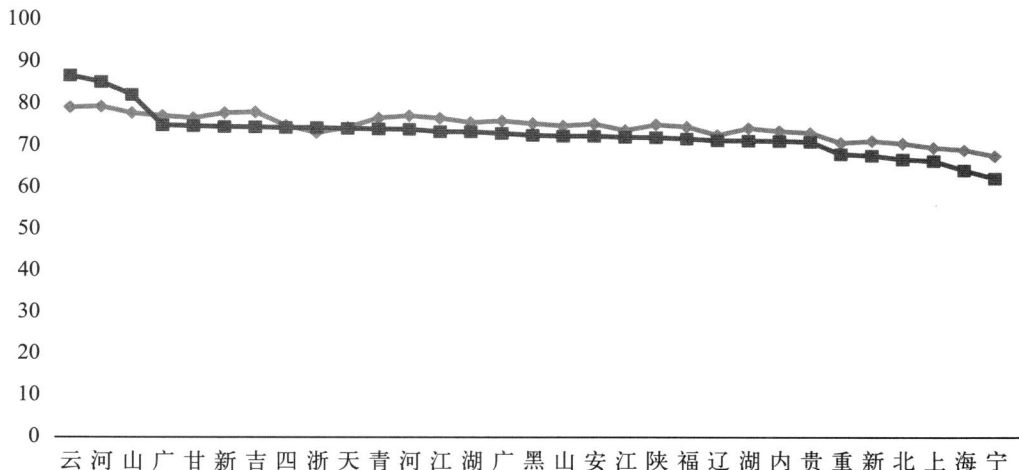

夏,从 2020 年的 62.45 上升到 2021 年的 67.82,适时公开透明度指数上升幅度最小的是天津,从 2020 年的 74.30 上升到 2021 年的 74.54,仅上涨 0.24;适时公开透明度指数下降幅度最大的是云南,从 2020 年的 86.80 下降到 2021 年的 79.267。总体看,多数省份适时公开透明度指数呈现上升趋势,表明它们在 PPP 项目信息适时公开方面的管理工作不断加强。

4.1.3　透明度指数与项目数量关系

在指数编制过程中,有部分专家以及地方财政部门代表人员曾建议我们将各地区管理的 PPP 数量因素考虑在内,原因是部分省份需要管理的 PPP 数量较多,可能增大了其监管和督促信息公开的难度,从而拉低了 PPP 市场透明度指数。因此,为了具体考察各地管理的 PPP 项目数量与该地区 PPP 市场透明度指数的对应关系,我们使用省份的 PPP 市场透明度总指数和项目数量作散点图并进行线性拟合,结果如图 4-3 所示。结果表明,省份需要监管的 PPP 项目数量与该省份 PPP 市场透明度指数不仅没有明显的负向关系,反而呈现出一定的正相关关系。从统计学意义上讲,"由

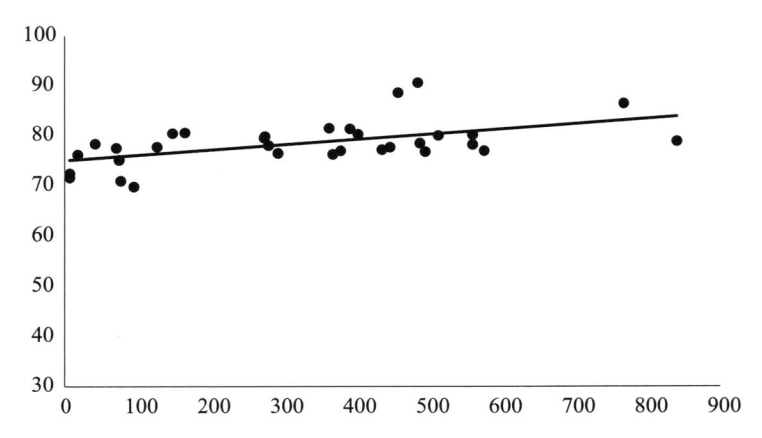

图4-3　省份PPP项目数量与省份PPP市场透明度总指数的散点图

于管理了太多的PPP项目,所以造成该地区PPP市场透明度指数较低"的猜测似乎并不成立。

人们另一个可能的疑虑在于,部分省份的PPP项目数量过少,统计学意义不大,是否还有必要参与全国排名。课题组的做法是将所有省级单位全部纳入排名榜,没有在排名时人为删除项目数过少的省级单位,以便全面客观地反映当前各省份PPP信息披露工作的现状。这是因为项目数量多少的界限不好界定,不同的读者存在不同标准,如果读者认为某些省级单位项目过少,忽略这一省份的排名信息并不影响对其他省份PPP市场透明度指数相对排名的解读。此外,一个地区项目数量为什么与PPP市场透明度指数呈现正相关,是一个非常有趣也值得讨论的话题,一个可能的原因是,PPP项目数量多的地区,主管部门安排了更多的管理人员或专门的负责人。

4.2　分阶段省级透明度结果分析

4.2.1　即时公开

接下来我们分析各个省份在即时公开和适时公开各个阶段的信息披露工作成绩。首先,表4-2给出了即时公开和适时公开PPP市场透明度指数省份排名,并且展示了2021年排名相较上一年的变化。在即时公开方面,云南、河北、山东、湖南和江苏位列排名前5位,而西藏、宁夏、北京、上海和海南位列排名最后5位。即时公开透明度指数省份排名上升最多的浙江,由2020年即时公开排名的第二十一名上升到2021年的第九名;排名下降最多的是西藏,由2020年的第一名下降了31个名次,2021年位列第三十二名。在适时公开方面,云南、河北、山东、广西和甘肃位列排名前5位,而宁夏、海南、上海、北京、新疆生产建设兵团排名最末。适时公开透明度指数省份排名上升最多的是浙江,由2020年的第二十四名跃升至2021年的第九名;排名下降最多的是河南,2021年排名相较上一年下降了6个名次,位列第十二名。

表4-2 即时公开和适时公开透明度指数省份排名

排名	2021年即时公开透明度指数	较2020年变化	2021年适时公开透明度指数	较2020年变化
1	云南	+1	云南	+1
2	河北	+4	河北	−1
3	山东	+1	山东	+2
4	湖南	−1	广西	+3
5	江苏	0	甘肃	+4
6	陕西	+1	新疆	−2
7	内蒙古	+1	吉林	−4
8	吉林	+1	四川	+9
9	甘肃	+2	浙江	+15
10	新疆	0	天津	+9
11	四川	+4	青海	−3
12	浙江	+9	河南	−6
13	安徽	−1	江苏	−3
14	辽宁	−1	湖南	−2
15	河南	−1	广东	−4
16	新疆	+4	黑龙江	−3
17	广东	−1	山西	−1
18	青海	−1	安徽	−4
19	黑龙江	+5	江西	+2

（续表）

排名	2021年即时公开透明度指数	较2020年变化	2021年适时公开透明度指数	较2020年变化
20	山西	−1	陕西	−5
21	湖北	−3	福建	−3
22	贵州	+1	辽宁	+3
23	江西	+4	湖北	−3
24	天津	+1	内蒙古	−2
25	重庆	−3	贵州	−2
26	福建	0	重庆	+1
27	广西	+3	兵团	−1
28	上海	+3	北京	0
29	北京	0	上海	0
30	海南	+2	海南	0
31	宁夏	−3	宁夏	0
32	西藏	−31		

表4−3给出了2021年度PPP项目即时公开透明度指数以及即时公开所涉及的各个阶段的透明度分指数省份排名。

表4−3 2021年即时公开透明度指数及各个阶段透明度分指数省份排名

排名	即时公开透明度指数	识别阶段	准备阶段	采购阶段	执行阶段
1	云南	云南	云南	云南	云南
2	河北	河北	河北	河北	河北
3	山东	湖南	兵团	湖南	山东
4	湖南	上海	山东	山东	内蒙古
5	江苏	山东	新疆	江苏	江苏
6	陕西	甘肃	甘肃	甘肃	湖南
7	内蒙古	新疆	山西	新疆	兵团
8	吉林	青海	广西	陕西	吉林

（续表）

排名	即时公开透明度指数	识别阶段	准备阶段	采购阶段	执行阶段
9	甘肃	陕西	吉林	广东	四川
10	新疆	江苏	湖北	内蒙古	浙江
11	四川	广西	四川	安徽	安徽
12	浙江	天津	浙江	福建	陕西
13	安徽	吉林	河南	青海	河南
14	辽宁	辽宁	内蒙古	四川	贵州
15	河南	黑龙江	江西	江西	广东
16	兵团	江西	江苏	吉林	重庆
17	广东	广东	辽宁	天津	湖北
18	青海	山西	湖南	黑龙江	黑龙江
19	黑龙江	河南	陕西	浙江	福建
20	山西	安徽	青海	河南	上海
21	湖北	兵团	黑龙江	湖北	新疆
22	贵州	湖北	贵州	重庆	山西
23	江西	内蒙古	天津	贵州	北京
24	天津	贵州	重庆	辽宁	辽宁
25	重庆	福建	广东	山西	天津
26	福建	四川	安徽	上海	广西
27	广西	浙江	北京	北京	甘肃
28	上海	重庆	海南	兵团	青海
29	北京	北京	福建	广西	海南
30	海南	海南	宁夏	海南	宁夏
31	宁夏	福建	上海	宁夏	江西
32	西藏	西藏	西藏	西藏	西藏

云南、河北和山东在各阶段均表现优异且各阶段也相对稳健，几乎没有明显短板。云南和河北在识别阶段、准备阶段、采购阶段和执行阶段均表现不错，使其在即时公开透明度指数排名中分别位列第一、第二。湖南在识别阶段、采购阶段和执行阶

段均表现不错,但其在准备阶段排名为第十八名,导致其在及时公开透明度指数排名中只能位列第六,如将来能在准备阶段更好地做好信息披露工作,排名仍有上升的空间。新疆在识别阶段、准备阶段和采购阶段表现较好,但在执行阶段表现较差,从而拉低了其在即时公开透明度指数中的排名。

西藏、宁夏、海南、北京和上海占据了即时公开透明度省级排名的最后5名。其中,上海在识别阶段的排名位列第四,但在其他阶段信息披露工作方面的糟糕表现拉低了其即时公开透明度指数排名。云南在四个阶段的排名均位列第一,这使其在即时公开透明度指数排名中位列首位。

江苏在各个阶段的排名都没有十分突出,但最终占据即时公开透明度指数第五名,而识别阶段、采购阶段和执行阶段均排名第六的甘肃几乎在各个阶段的PPP信息透明度指数都要高于江苏,但在即时公开透明度指数排名上落后于江苏,这反映了各省份PPP项目的阶段分布对课题组研究的最终结果的确存在着一定程度的影响。如果一个省份处于准备阶段的PPP项目占比较高,且这一阶段的工作做得较为出色,那么该省份很容易获得高分,因为按照第3章所述的算法,原本采购阶段和执行阶段的权重被"归并"到准备阶段和识别阶段中去了。相反,如果一个省份处于准备阶段的PPP项目并不多,那么该省份一旦在采购阶段和执行阶段中的工作略有不足,就可能对最终的透明度总指数产生不利影响。为了更清晰地反映这一问题,表4-4列出了各省份PPP项目按阶段的分布,经过对比很容易发现江苏处于准备阶段的项目占比要明显高于甘肃。当然,需要强调的是,我们这里指出项目分阶段的分布差异,只是为了解读少数省份排名结果及可能的原因,并不是说为了提高PPP市场透明度指数而应该刻意去放缓PPP项目进度。

表4-4 2021年各省份分阶段PPP项目数量

省 份	项目总数量	准备阶段	采购阶段	执行阶段
河南	841	71	239	531
山东	768	30	135	603
贵州	576	65	169	342
四川	560	10	98	452

(续表)

省　份	项目总数量	准备阶段	采购阶段	执行阶段
广东	560	21	71	468
浙江	513	13	49	451
江西	495	22	59	414
安徽	488	12	39	437
云南	485	14	91	380
河北	458	18	86	354
山西	447	53	170	224
湖北	436	30	116	290
新疆	403	12	33	358
江苏	392	10	57	325
广西	379	20	145	214
福建	368	12	31	325
湖南	363	4	33	326
辽宁	280	42	126	112
陕西	275	13	57	205
内蒙古	274	12	41	221
吉林	165	14	28	123
甘肃	148	3	32	113
黑龙江	127	6	40	81
海南	98	5	14	79
北京	77	1	5	71
重庆	75	2	28	45
天津	71	2	11	58
宁夏	47	2	6	39
青海	42	2	11	29
兵团	18	2	6	10
上海	7	0	4	3
西藏	3	1	2	0

4.2.2 适时公开

表 4-5 给出了 2021 年度 PPP 项目适时公开透明度指数以及适时公开所涉及的各个阶段的透明度分指数前十省份榜单。同样可以发现，河北和云南在各个阶段均表现抢眼，特别是河北在识别阶段和采购阶段排名均列第二。山东依靠其在识别阶段的优秀表现，在适时公开透明度指数排名中位列第三。由于采购阶段的信息披露工作重要性最高（根据专家判定矩阵的计算结果，采购阶段权重为 0.45），河北和云南凭借在采购阶段较高的指数占据了适时公开透明度指数排名的第一位和第二位。

表 4-5 2021 年适时公开透明度指数及各个阶段透明度分指数省份排名

排名	适时公开透明度指数	识别阶段	准备阶段	采购阶段
1	云南	云南	上海	云南
2	河北	河北	青海	河北
3	山东	山东	吉林	山东
4	广西	四川	云南	吉林
5	甘肃	浙江	河北	河南
6	新疆	重庆	山东	新疆
7	吉林	北京	辽宁	江苏
8	四川	广西	天津	甘肃
9	浙江	海南	广东	广西
10	天津	甘肃	黑龙江	湖南
11	青海	宁夏	广西	黑龙江
12	河南	天津	福建	广东
13	江苏	青海	安徽	内蒙古
14	湖南	新疆	湖北	天津
15	广东	江西	山西	山西
16	黑龙江	湖南	河南	陕西

(续表)

排名	适时公开透明度指数	识别阶段	准备阶段	采购阶段
17	山西	安徽	江苏	安徽
18	安徽	河南	湖南	青海
19	江西	广东	江西	福建
20	陕西	吉林	新疆	湖北
21	福建	江苏	陕西	四川
22	辽宁	山西	甘肃	浙江
23	湖北	陕西	贵州	贵州
24	内蒙古	贵州	内蒙古	江西
25	贵州	辽宁	兵团	辽宁
26	重庆	福建	四川	兵团
27	兵团	黑龙江	浙江	重庆
28	北京	湖北	重庆	上海
29	上海	内蒙古	北京	北京
30	海南	兵团	海南	海南
31	宁夏	上海	宁夏	宁夏

这份榜单的后5名则被宁夏、海南、上海、北京和新疆生产建设兵团占据。对比表4-3可以发现，其中北京、上海、宁夏和海南在即时公开信息披露方面的工作表现也不佳（参看前文分析），即时公开透明度指数也排在末尾，说明这些省份PPP项目信息公开的披露工作亟待加强。

我们使用折线图能更清楚地反映省级单位在适时公开或即时公开各个阶段的具体指数结果。图4-4展示了各个省级单位在即时公开各个阶段的指数结果，对比可以发现：识别阶段和准备阶段信息披露最充分，而采购阶段和执行阶段的指数普遍较低。这一结果基本符合预期：识别阶段和准备阶段的很多信息决定了PPP项目能否顺利通过审核，往往更受监管部门和社会参与方的重视，因而指数普遍较高。

图4-4　2021年各省份即时公开透明度指数各阶段分布

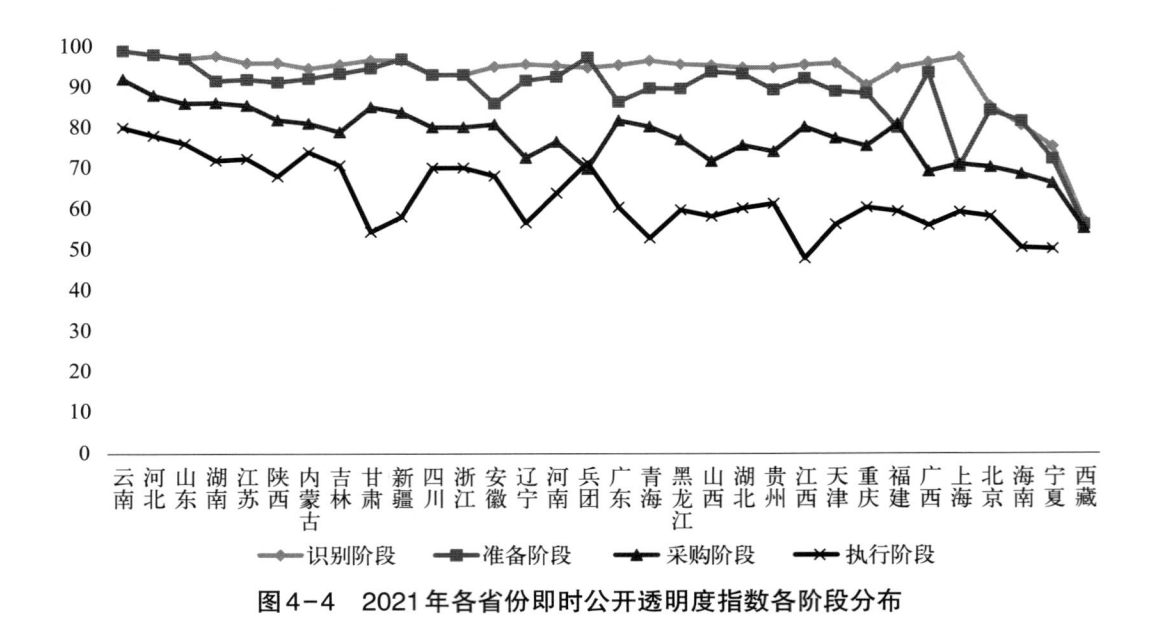

图4-5则展示了各个省级单位在适时公开各个阶段的指数结果。与即时公开的情况有所不同,适时公开在识别阶段的信息披露明显不如准备阶段与采购阶段充分。这主要是因为识别阶段涉及两个重要的PDF文件,即"两评"(物有所值评价和财政承受能力论证),课题组对这两份PDF文件进行了颇为严格的审核,很多项目没有披露或者存在"虚假"披露,导致各省份这一阶段的指数普遍相对较低。

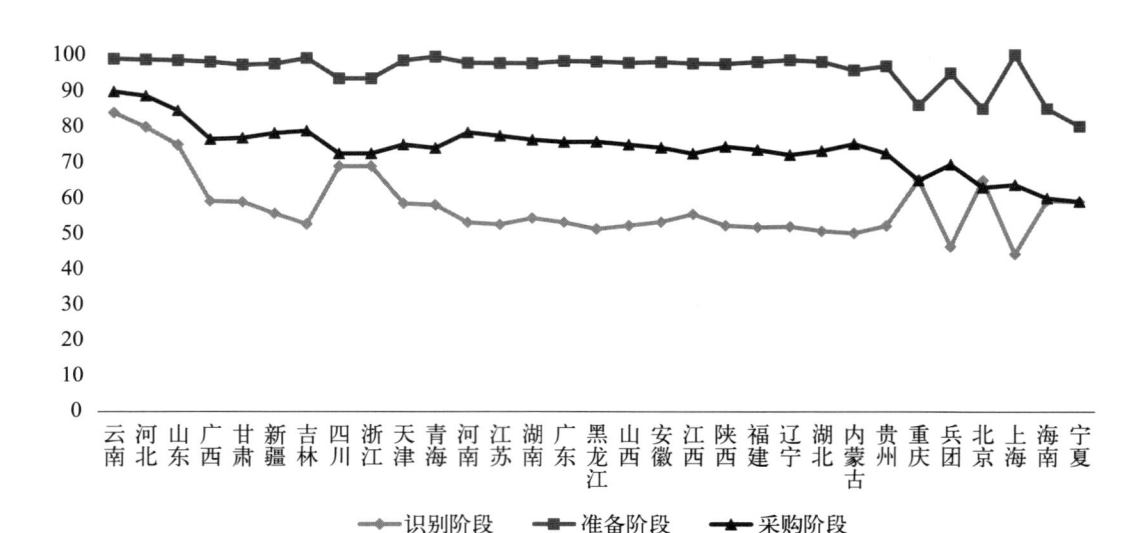

图4-5　2021年各省份适时公开透明度指数各阶段分布

4.3 "两评一案"省级结果分析

所谓"两评一案",是指"物有所值评价报告及本级行业主管部门会同财政部门的审核通过意见""财政承受能力论证报告及本级财政部门的审核通过意见"以及"实施方案附件"。"两评一案"在整个PPP项目的识别阶段和准备阶段处于非常重要的地位,也是目前我国PPP项目规范运行必不可少的重要步骤,在很大程度上将决定该PPP项目能否顺利实施。因此,我们在本小节对这几份重点报告的各省份披露情况进行简单总结。

由于"两评一案"涵盖的信息量非常丰富,往往通过长达几十页甚至上百页的PDF文件形式呈现在网站上,供社会各方进行查阅,因此,这三份PDF文件是课题组人工阅读和检查的重点对象。表4-6给出了这三个PDF文件得分的省级单位排序情况。从中可以发现,这三个PDF文件得分排名与适时公开透明度指数排名具有较高的一致性,比如云南占据了"实施方案附件"指标的第一名、"物有所值评价报告及本级行业主管部门会同财政部门的审核通过意见"指标的第二名和"财政承受能力论证报告及本级财政部门的审核通过意见"指标的第二名,正因为其得益于这三项指标的优秀表现,云南在适时公开透明度指数排名中位列第一。此外,宁夏在适时公开透明度指数排名中列在最后一位,主要就是其在这三份文件上的得分排名较差导致的,这表明宁夏在"两评一案"上的信息披露工作亟待加强。青海虽然占据了"物有所值评价报告及本级行业主管部门会同财政部门的审核通过意见"指标和"财政承受能力论证报告及本级财政部门的审核通过意见"指标的第一名,但是"实施方案附件"指标排名较差,因而其适时公开透明度指数排名只到第十一位。河北的"两评一案"指标均表现优秀,各项目排名都在前4位,因而其适时公开透明度指数位列第二。山东、广西和甘肃在"两评一案"中的工作各有优劣,因而分别在适时公开透明度指数排名中位列第三名、第四名和第五名。

表4-6 "两评一案"省级透明度排名

排名	适时公开透明度指数	物有所值评价	财政承受能力论证	实施方案
1	云南	青海	青海	云南
2	河北	云南	云南	河北

(续表)

排名	适时公开透明度指数	物有所值评价	财政承受能力论证	实施方案
3	山东	河北	吉林	山东
4	广西	吉林	河北	四川
5	甘肃	山东	天津	浙江
6	新疆	四川	福建	上海
7	吉林	浙江	广东	青海
8	四川	广东	山东	吉林
9	浙江	福建	江西	辽宁
10	天津	江西	河南	广东
11	青海	天津	四川	福建
12	河南	广西	浙江	天津
13	江苏	河南	广西	黑龙江
14	湖南	陕西	甘肃	安徽
15	广东	新疆	山西	湖北
16	黑龙江	山西	新疆	广西
17	山西	甘肃	陕西	河南
18	安徽	江苏	湖北	山西
19	江西	贵州	江苏	江苏
20	陕西	重庆	重庆	新疆
21	福建	湖北	安徽	湖南
22	辽宁	北京	贵州	江西
23	湖北	安徽	黑龙江	陕西
24	内蒙古	黑龙江	湖南	甘肃
25	贵州	湖南	北京	贵州
26	重庆	辽宁	海南	内蒙古
27	兵团	海南	内蒙古	兵团
28	北京	内蒙古	宁夏	重庆

(续表)

排名	适时公开透明度指数	物有所值评价	财政承受能力论证	实施方案
29	上海	宁夏	辽宁	北京
30	海南	兵团	兵团	海南
31	宁夏	上海	上海	宁夏

未来课题组会考虑做一些专题评估，不仅评估这些关键性指标或核心PDF文件是否披露，还将评估这些报告具体内容的质量，以进一步推动PPP项目更加规范。

5

城市指数的排名与分析

5.1 城市PPP项目分布情况概述

在前面第3章、第4章对全国层面和省级层面的PPP市场透明度指数对比分析的基础上,本章将对中国PPP项目数量相对较多的部分城市的PPP市场透明度情况展开一些分析。在中国338个地级市(自治州、地区、盟等,以下统一都视作"市")中,已经有328个城市引入了PPP模式(见表5-1),PPP模式推动范围之广,可见一斑。特别是广东、山东、河南、新疆、安徽、云南、辽宁、湖南、广西、江苏、湖北、内蒙古、河北、山西、浙江、江西、陕西、吉林、四川、福建、贵州、宁夏22个省份已经实现了PPP项目地级市的全覆盖。

表5-1 各省份引入PPP模式的城市个数

省 份	引入PPP模式的城市个数	城市总数	省 份	引入PPP模式的城市个数	城市总数
云南	16	16	江西	11	11
内蒙古	12	12	河北	11	11
吉林	9	9	河南	17	17
四川	21	21	浙江	11	11
宁夏	5	5	海南	4	4
安徽	16	16	湖北	13	13
山东	16	17	湖南	14	14
山西	11	11	甘肃	13	14
广东	21	21	福建	10	10
广西	14	14	贵州	10	10

(续表)

省 份	引入PPP模式的城市个数	城市总数	省 份	引入PPP模式的城市个数	城市总数
新疆	14	14	辽宁	15	15
陕西	13	13	青海	6	8
江苏	13	13	黑龙江	12	13
西藏	2	7			

这些开展PPP项目的城市中,有些拥有较为成熟的PPP市场,有些则刚刚起步。为了使得相关评估分析更具有稳健性、科学性,课题组在本次报告中选取了PPP项目数量较多的城市作为分析对象。为了方便画图,课题组选择了截至2021年12月31日在PPP综合信息平台中项目数量超过50个的53个地级以上城市作为城市层面PPP市场透明度指数具体分析的样本,其中项目数量超过30个的地级以上城市层面的PPP市场透明度指数的结果如附件四所示。这53个具体城市包括:广东东莞、江西赣州、贵州遵义、山东潍坊、江苏南京、河南南阳、浙江温州、贵州毕节、山东青岛、山东济宁、陕西西安、湖北武汉、河南驻马店、福建宁德、河南郑州、山东临沂、新疆乌鲁木齐、浙江杭州、江西宜春、福建泉州、河南信阳、山西临汾、山东菏泽、四川宜宾、河南洛阳、江西上饶、浙江台州、新疆巴音、河南平顶山、安徽阜阳、新疆阿克苏、浙江丽水、福建漳州、云南昆明、四川成都、河北承德、山东济南、福建福州、贵州贵阳、河北唐山、辽宁大连、山东日照、山西晋中、云南玉溪、内蒙古赤峰、贵州黔东南、广西南宁、贵州黔南、江苏徐州、河北沧、贵州黔西南、山西吕梁、河南周口。

5.2 重点城市指数的基本情况

5.2.1 总指数城市排名

这53个PPP市场发展较为成熟的城市,其2021年PPP市场透明度总指数排名如

表5-2所示。排在首位的是河北承德,指数为86.35,比全国平均水平高13.89;紧随其后的是云南昆明和云南玉溪,总指数分别达到84.82和83.23。此外,总指数在80以上的城市还有山东济宁、河北唐山、新疆阿克苏、河北沧州、山东日照、山东潍坊,这些都是PPP信息公开工作开展得相对较好的城市。

表5-2 2021年部分城市PPP市场透明度总指数

排名	城市	2021年项目数量	2021年总指数	较2020年总指数差异	2020年总指数
1	河北承德	58	86.35	+8.74	77.61
2	云南昆明	60	84.82	+14.20	70.62
3	云南玉溪	56	83.23	+10.55	72.69
4	山东济宁	77	83.08	+19.46	63.63
5	河北唐山	57	82.65	+8.29	74.36
6	新疆阿克苏	62	82.62	−1.90	84.52
7	河北沧州	52	81.96	+7.02	74.93
8	山东日照	56	80.42	+21.79	58.63
9	山东潍坊	97	80.11	+20.53	59.58
10	山东菏泽	64	79.93	+12.10	67.83
11	江苏南京	89	79.58	+1.67	77.90
12	广东东莞	135	79.14	+5.00	74.14
13	浙江丽水	61	77.88	+3.97	73.91
14	山东临沂	68	77.63	+19.47	58.16
15	浙江杭州	68	77.60	+1.62	75.98
16	山东青岛	80	77.40	+9.15	68.24
17	新疆乌鲁木齐	68	77.01	+3.55	73.46
18	安徽阜阳	62	76.49	+1.85	74.65
19	内蒙古赤峰	56	76.15	+1.06	75.10
20	山东济南	58	76.04	+18.79	57.25

(续表)

排名	城市	2021年项目数量	2021年总指数	较2020年总指数差异	2020年总指数
21	江苏徐州	53	75.95	+1.53	74.42
22	浙江台州	62	75.74	+5.39	70.35
23	浙江温州	84	75.44	+2.67	72.77
24	福建泉州	66	75.32	+1.28	74.04
25	四川宜宾	63	74.95	+5.18	69.77
26	福建宁德	70	74.29	+4.40	69.89
27	贵州贵阳	58	73.91	−2.67	76.58
28	四川成都	59	72.89	+3.61	69.27
29	江西宜春	66	72.85	+4.99	67.86
30	陕西西安	77	72.71	+2.41	70.30
31	福建漳州	61	71.81	−0.61	72.42
32	河南南阳	86	71.09	+6.42	64.67
33	新疆巴音	62	70.40	+7.65	62.75
34	河南洛阳	63	70.13	+2.14	67.99
35	江西赣州	120	69.94	+0.46	69.49
36	贵州遵义	115	69.62	+1.99	67.64
37	河南平顶山	62	69.52	+0.37	69.15
38	河南驻马店	71	69.40	+4.86	64.54
39	福建福州	58	69.08	+1.72	67.35
40	山西吕梁	51	68.84	+0.03	68.81
41	湖北武汉	74	68.35	−0.16	68.51
42	江西上饶	62	67.45	+5.69	61.76
43	广西南宁	55	66.65	−2.19	68.85
44	贵州毕节	81	65.73	−2.12	67.85
45	河南郑州	69	65.73	−0.69	66.42

(续表)

排名	城市	2021年项目数量	2021年总指数	较2020年总指数差异	2020年总指数
46	山西晋中	56	65.54	+1.47	64.08
47	山西临汾	64	64.27	+1.02	63.25
48	河南周口	51	64.25	+1.13	63.11
49	辽宁大连	56	63.91	+6.31	57.61
50	贵州黔西南	52	61.26	+2.58	58.68
51	河南信阳	65	60.94	+1.50	59.44
52	贵州黔东南	56	60.20	+1.21	58.99
53	贵州黔南	55	57.07	+2.36	54.70

通过和2020年PPP市场透明度指数进行对比可以发现，大部分地级以上城市2021年指数较2020年有所增长，尤其是山东日照，其2021年指数较2020年上升了21.79，紧随其后的是山东潍坊，较2020年上升了20.53。不过，同时也可以发现，少数地级以上城市2021年指数较2020年有所降低，降幅较大的是贵州贵阳和广西南宁，2021年总指数较2020年下降最多，分别下降了2.67和2.19。

5.2.2 与全国平均水平比较

此外，从53个城市的透明度总指数分布图来看，在大力推广PPP模式的过程中，大多数城市PPP市场透明度指数的差异并不是很明显，但也应该注意到部分城市的PPP市场透明度指数远低于其他城市。如图5-1所示，可将这53个城市的PPP市场透明度总指数的分布分成两个梯队：第一梯队城市的PPP市场透明度情况均领先于全国平均水平，即包括河北宁德到江西宜春在内的30个城市；第二梯队城市的PPP市场透明度情况则落后于全国平均水平，即包括河南南阳到贵州黔东南在内的23个城市。由于这里的分析对象都是开展PPP项目数量相对较多的城市，因而业务不熟悉不应该成为第二梯队城市PPP市场透明度指数不高的"借口"，而是说明部分城市确实需要加强PPP信息公开相关工作力度，避免出现整个PPP市场只重视规模而忽视规范化管理的问题。

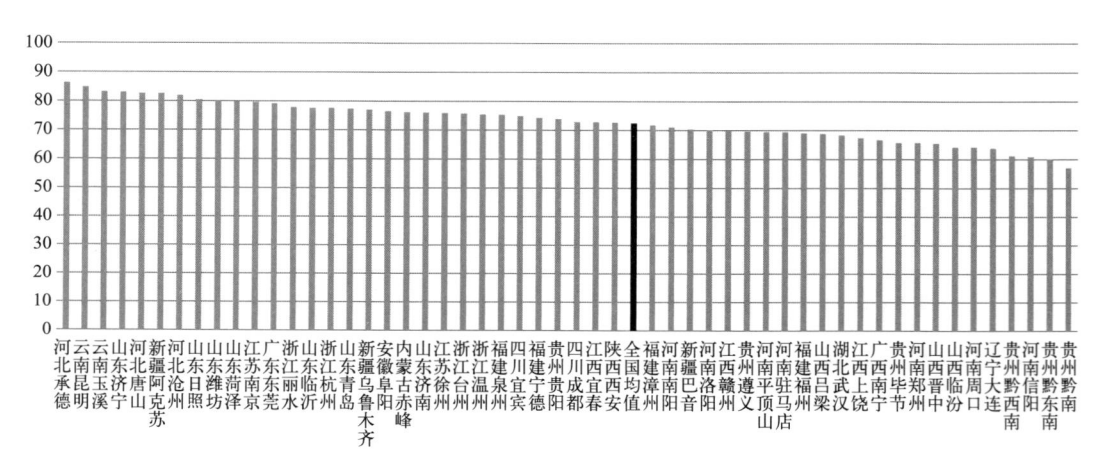

图 5-1　2021 年部分城市 PPP 市场透明度总指数分布

5.2.3　各城市即时公开和适时公开结果分析

图 5-2 和图 5-3 分别展示了这 53 个城市的即时公开透明度指数和适时公开透明度指数的结果分布。通过图 5-2 可以看出，2021 年即时公开透明度指数的平均结果高于 2020 年，但差异不大：2021 年即时公开透明度指数平均为 83.70，2020 年即时公开透明度指数平均为 82.70。同时，通过图 5-3 可以观察到，2021 年除了山东青岛、云南昆明、云南玉溪和河北承德外，其他城市的适时公开透明度指数与 2020 年差异不大。此外，还可以发现从河南承德到四川宜宾在内的大部分城市 2021 年即时公开透明度指数和适时公开透明度指数都高于 2020 年，而贵州黔南、

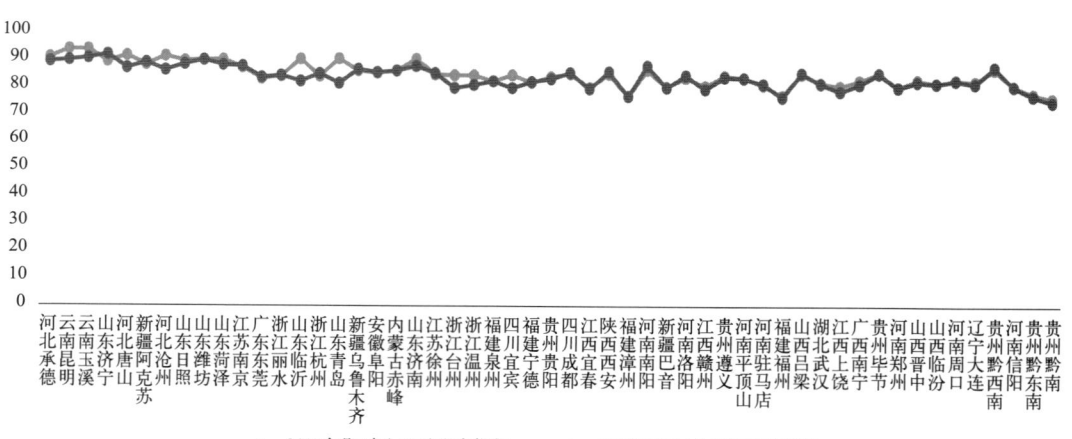

图 5-2　2020—2021 年部分城市 PPP 项目即时公开透明度指数分布

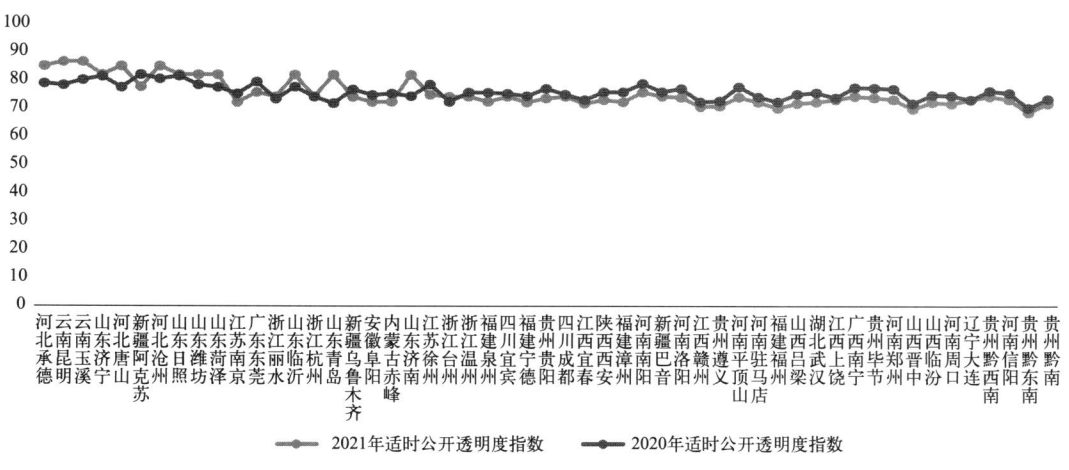

图 5-3　2020—2021 年部分城市 PPP 项目适时公开透明度指数分布

河南南阳和陕西西安等城市的即时公开透明度指数和适时公开透明度指数低于 2020 年，说明 2021 年 PPP 项目信息透明度工作做得好的城市在即时公开和适时公开方面做得都好，但是也有部分城市在即时公开和适时公开方面均在"走下坡路"。

在即时公开上，2021 年较 2020 年进步幅度位居前三的城市为山东临沂、山东青岛和浙江台州，其中，山东临沂由 2020 年的 81.23 上升到 2021 年的 89.36，山东青岛由 2020 年的 80.51 上升到 2021 年的 89.41，浙江台州由 2020 年的 78.82 上升到 2021 年的 83.47；退步最多的城市依次为山东济宁、河南南阳和浙江杭州。在适时公开上，2021 年较 2020 年进步幅度位居前三的城市为山东青岛、云南昆明和山东济南；退步最多

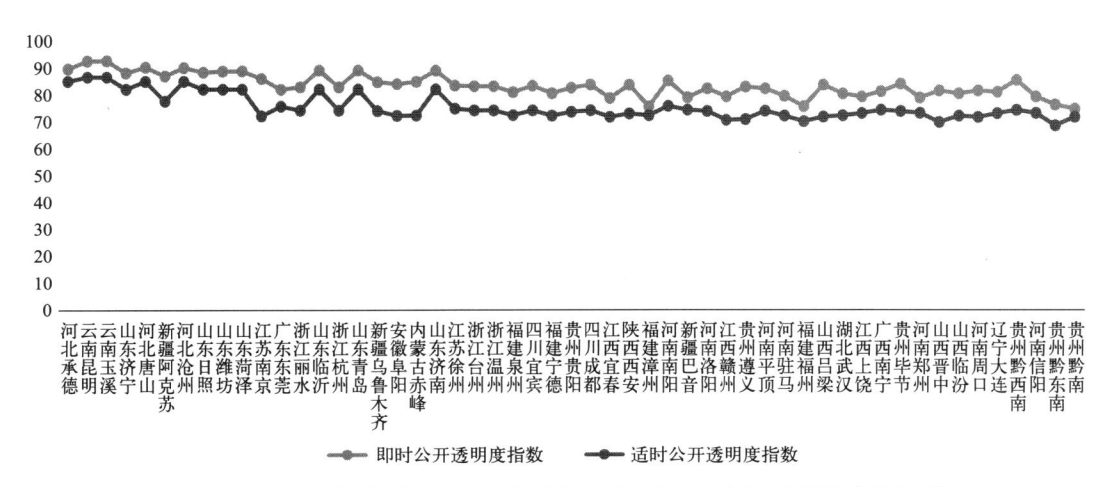

图 5-4　2021 年部分城市 PPP 项目即时公开和适时公开透明度指数分布

的城市依次为山东济宁、河南南阳和浙江杭州。而且通过图5-4也可以发现,总体而言,2021年的即时公开透明度指数高于适时公开透明度指数,说明各城市在PPP项目信息适时公开方面的工作还有待进一步加强。

5.2.4 分阶段的各城市透明度结果分析

这些城市PPP项目不同阶段的分指数结果如图5-5和图5-6所示。图5-5展示了各个城市的即时公开透明度指数在识别阶段、准备阶段、采购阶段和执行阶段的情况对比,从中可以很明显地得出如下结论:在即时公开部分,各个城市的识别阶段和准备阶段信息公开工作做得比较好,指数普遍高于其他各阶段。出现这一结果的现实原因可能在于:识别阶段、准备阶段基本信息的完善有助于吸引社会资本

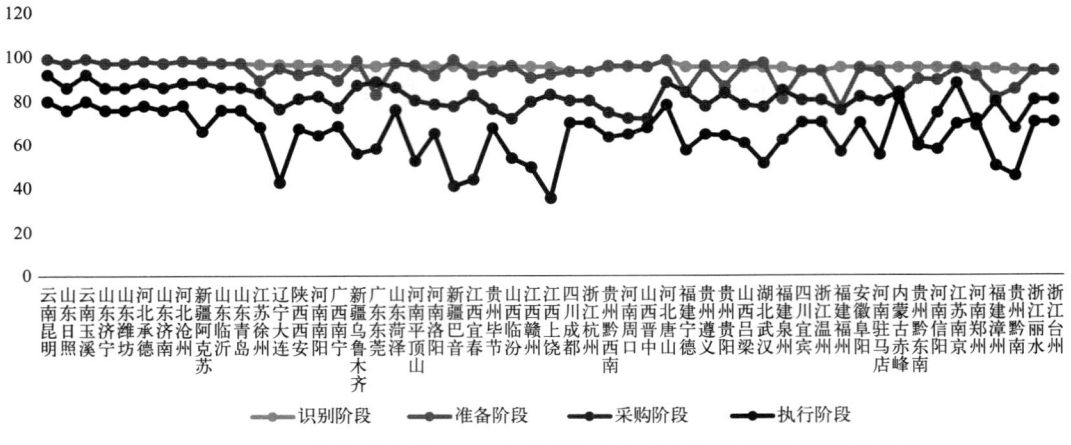

图5-5 2021年部分城市PPP项目即时公开透明度指数各阶段分布

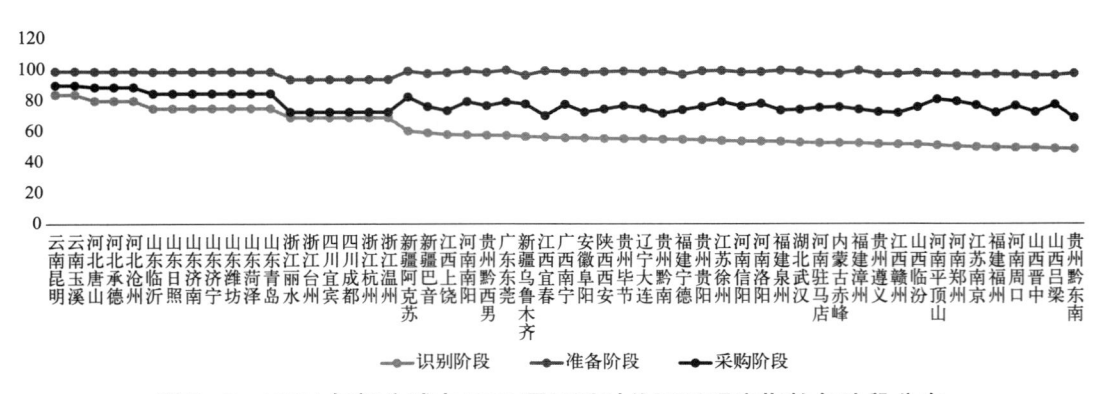

图5-6 2021年部分城市PPP项目适时公开透明度指数各阶段分布

方的参与，直接影响到PPP项目的招标结果，因而大多数项目的主管部门会较为重视识别阶段和准备阶段即时公开的信息填报，其平均指数分别达到95.50和92.80。而采购阶段和执行阶段的信息透明度指数平均分别为80.88和64.49，处在四个阶段公开情况的中下水平，且执行阶段、准备阶段的即时公开透明度指数的跳跃性很大。同时，也应该注意到，部分城市准备阶段的即时公开透明度指数是低于采购阶段和执行阶段的。

对于适时公开透明度指数的情况（见图5-6），在适时公开部分所包含的识别阶段、准备阶段和采购阶段中，明显处于最低位的是各个城市的识别阶段信息公开情况，其平均指数为60.91，而适时公开的准备阶段的信息公开工作则做得较好，平均指数达到97.71。出现这种情况可能是因为适时公开的识别阶段包括物有所值评价报告、财政承受能力论证报告、可行性研究报告等重要的报告附件，这些报告信息的披露情况经过课题组的严格考察，发现存在问题的报告数量很多，甚至会出现"虚假"披露的情况。因此，物有所值评价报告、财政承受能力论证报告、可行性研究报告的不规范导致识别阶段的适时公开透明度指数在识别、准备、采购三阶段中排名最低。同时，这53个城市之间三个阶段的适时公开透明度指数没有发生很大的跳跃。

如此鲜明的对比也可以警示各个地方相关部门应该重视"两评"的工作质量和信息公开工作，同时也提醒中央主管部门不能放松对"两评"的规范要求，由于问题普遍存在，所以有必要针对这些重点工作提出更详细、更具有可操作性的政策指引。

5.3 主要城市"两评一案"结果

本节将延续省级分析的内容，对重点城市"两评一案"的透明度结果进行分析。从表5-3可以看出，广东东莞、云南昆明、云南玉溪和福建漳州在"两评一案"报告信息披露上的工作成绩值得肯定，特别是广东东莞和福建漳州的物有所值评价报告和财政承受能力论证报告的排名分别是第一、二位，在这两项信息披露上均取得了满分的成绩,根据前文的定义,即没有信息披露不全,更没有"虚假"披露行为。云南昆明虽然在三项指标上都没有进入前5名,但综合来看其三项指标的排名都靠前,这使其在适时公开透明度指数中排名第一。

表5-3 "两评一案"城市的结果排序

排名	适时指数	物有所值评价报告	财政承受能力论证报告	实施方案
1	云南昆明	广东东莞	广东东莞	云南昆明
2	云南玉溪	福建漳州	福建漳州	云南玉溪
3	河北唐山	江苏徐州	江苏徐州	河北唐山
4	河北承德	福建泉州	贵州毕节	河北承德
5	河北沧州	新疆阿克苏	福建泉州	河北沧州
6	山东临沂	贵州毕节	新疆阿克苏	山东临沂
7	山东日照	贵州贵阳	河南南阳	山东日照
8	山东济南	云南昆明	贵州贵阳	山东济南
9	山东济宁	云南玉溪	河南洛阳	山东济宁
10	山东潍坊	贵州黔南	云南昆明	山东潍坊
11	山东菏泽	湖北武汉	云南玉溪	山东菏泽
12	山东青岛	陕西西安	安徽阜阳	山东青岛
13	新疆阿克苏	河南南阳	贵州黔南	浙江丽水
14	河南南阳	江西上饶	山西临汾	浙江台州
15	广东东莞	江西宜春	湖北武汉	四川宜宾
16	江苏徐州	河南洛阳	陕西西安	四川成都
17	贵州黔西南	河北唐山	江西宜春	浙江杭州
18	广西南宁	河北承德	内蒙古赤峰	浙江温州
19	新疆巴音	河北沧州	河北唐山	广东东莞
20	浙江丽水	安徽阜阳	河北承德	江苏徐州
21	浙江台州	内蒙古赤峰	河北沧州	福建漳州
22	四川宜宾	广西南宁	新疆巴音	福建泉州

（续表）

排名	适时指数	物有所值评价报告	财政承受能力论证报告	实施方案
23	四川成都	山东临沂	河南信阳	贵州贵阳
24	浙江杭州	山东日照	广西南宁	江西宜春
25	浙江温州	山东济南	贵州黔西南	新疆阿克苏
26	新疆乌鲁木齐	山东济宁	山东临沂	河南南阳
27	河南平顶山	山东潍坊	山东日照	贵州毕节
28	河南洛阳	山东菏泽	山东济南	湖北武汉
29	贵州毕节	山东青岛	山东济宁	贵州黔南
30	贵州贵阳	贵州黔西南	山东潍坊	广西南宁
31	河南郑州	浙江丽水	山东菏泽	陕西西安
32	河南信阳	浙江台州	山东青岛	河南洛阳
33	辽宁大连	四川宜宾	福建宁德	辽宁大连
34	江西上饶	四川成都	浙江丽水	河南信阳
35	陕西西安	浙江杭州	浙江台州	安徽阜阳
36	福建泉州	浙江温州	四川宜宾	贵州黔西南
37	福建漳州	河南平顶山	四川成都	福建宁德
38	湖北武汉	山西临汾	浙江杭州	江西上饶
39	内蒙古赤峰	河南信阳	浙江温州	山西临汾
40	山西临汾	新疆巴音	江西上饶	河南平顶山
41	河南驻马店	福建宁德	河南平顶山	新疆巴音
42	安徽阜阳	贵州遵义	福建福州	贵州黔东南
43	福建宁德	福建福州	江西赣州	河南驻马店
44	江苏南京	山西吕梁	贵州遵义	河南郑州
45	贵州黔南	河南驻马店	河南郑州	江西赣州
46	山西吕梁	河南周口	河南驻马店	贵州遵义
47	江西宜春	江西赣州	山西吕梁	内蒙古赤峰
48	河南周口	河南郑州	河南周口	福建福州
49	贵州遵义	江苏南京	山西晋中	江苏南京

(续表)

排名	适时指数	物有所值评价报告	财政承受能力论证报告	实施方案
50	江西赣州	辽宁大连	新疆乌鲁木齐	河南周口
51	福建福州	新疆乌鲁木齐	江苏南京	新疆乌鲁木齐
52	山西晋中	山西晋中	辽宁大连	山西吕梁
53	贵州黔东南	贵州黔东南	贵州黔东南	山西晋中

此外，江苏徐州在物有所值评价报告和财政承受能力论证报告方面均排在靠前的位置，但是适时公开透明度指数却排名倒数，主要归因于实施方案方面做得很差。而新疆乌鲁木齐和云南昆明在物有所值评价报告和财政承受能力论证报告方面均排在垫底的位置，在实施方案方面做得还可以。

5.4　PPP信息透明度的社会经济效益分析

本节拟分析城市层面PPP信息透明度带来的社会经济效益。事实上，如何平衡强化监管和吸引社会资本参与，以及如何提高落地率是摆在我国PPP监管部门面前的重要议题。PPP作为一种市场化、社会化的公共产品或服务的供给管理模式，引入社会资本的参与有助于发挥社会资本在技术和信息方面的优势，但同时也要防范社会资本攫取过高的私人利益。为此，建立强有力的监管体制十分必要。从2017年末以来，财政部等监管部门先后出台92号文等一系列政策文件，清退PPP项目管理库中一大批不规范的PPP项目，形成了PPP领域全方位、全过程监管的格局，拉开了PPP项目强监管的序幕。强化监管意味着政府对PPP项目质量、价格和产出绩效等进行监督，可能会压缩社会资本的利润空间，削弱社会资本的参与意愿。但与此同时，上级政府对PPP项目监管力度的增强，意味着对下级政府应承担的PPP支出责任的管控，92号文等对地方政府的监管，实际上切断了地方政府违规举债的途径，增强了社会资本对政府未来偿债能力的信心，从而可以激发社会资本的投资热情，提高项目落地率。

我们认为，PPP作为一种市场化的公共服务供给机制，需要具备与市场化相适应的管理手段和服务能力来解决社会资本私人利益和社会公众公共利益难以兼顾的问题,而增加PPP市场的透明度就是其中重要一环。PPP项目信息公开程度的提高,有助于营造各参与方诚实守信、严格履约的氛围,提高政府公信力,打消社会资本方投资PPP项目的顾虑,从而提高社会资本参与热情和项目落地率。

为了印证上述猜想,课题组匹配了手工整理的财政部政府和社会资本合作中心的PPP项目微观数据和从"企查查"网站搜索的社会资本基本信息的数据,考察了城市PPP信息透明度对社会资本参与以及PPP项目开工率的影响。

具体来说,首先,课题组对财政部政府和社会资本合作中心的PPP项目管理库进行手工整理,获得了每个管理库PPP项目在识别阶段、准备阶段、采购阶段和执行阶段的丰富信息,主要包括项目总投资、所属行业、发起时间、所属地区、社会资本出资比例等。[①]随后,课题组利用采集到的社会资本名称,在"企查查"网站上手工搜索每个PPP项目社会资本方的基本信息,主要包括社会资本注册地、实际控制人、成立时间、所属行业、企业规模等。接下来,课题组将手工整理得到的社会资本基本信息的数据和PPP项目层面的数据进行匹配,构建了一套囊括每个PPP项目基本信息以及参与的社会资本方基本信息的大样本微观数据库,在此基础上开展研究。

课题组还对初始样本进行了如下筛选:第一,考虑到PPP项目的行政级别,课题组剔除了中央级和省级的PPP项目;第二,考虑到PPP项目中参与的社会资本名称、出资比例等信息要等到PPP项目进入执行阶段才能公开,课题组的研究仅保留进入执行阶段的项目;第三,考虑到部分进入执行阶段的PPP项目的社会资本信息并没有公开,课题组也剔除了这部分样本。经过以上步骤,课题组最终获得了6 426个PPP项目、8 032个社会资本方的有效样本,样本覆盖了328个地级市。[②]

我们的分析表明:(1)平均而言,PPP信息透明度越高的城市,社会资本出资比例越高(见图5-7)。严谨的计量回归分析显示,城市PPP市场透明度指数每增加1,社会资本出资比例将提高0.705%。[③]统计数据显示,PPP市场透明度指数在80以上的城市,其PPP项目平均出资比例约为65%;PPP市场透明度指数在80以下的城市,其

[①] 部分数据由财政部政府和社会资本合作中心提供,课题组对此表示感谢。
[②] 数据不包括北京、上海、天津和重庆4个直辖市。
[③] 为了保证报告的可读性,此处隐去计量回归分析细节,感兴趣的读者可联系课题组索取。

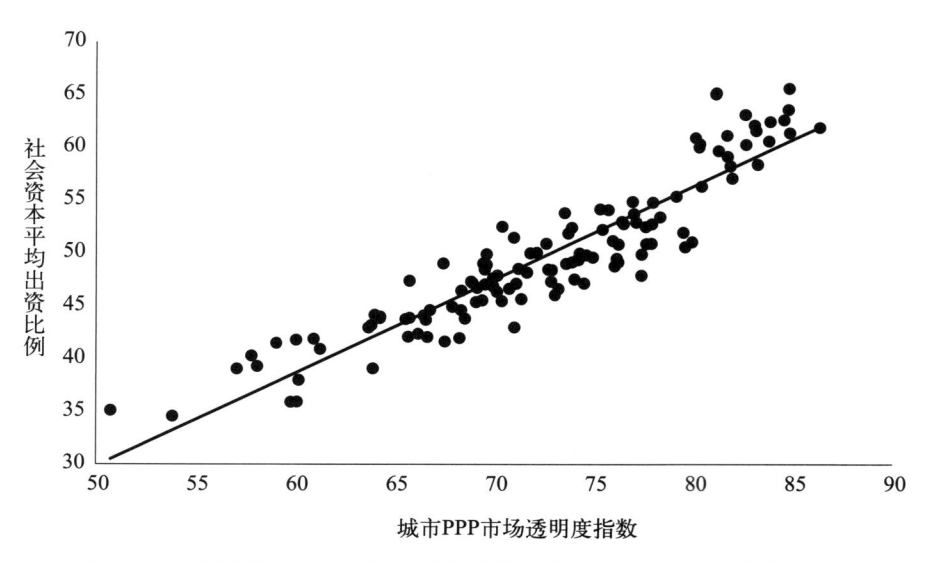

图 5-7　部分城市 PPP 市场透明度指数与社会资本平均出资比例

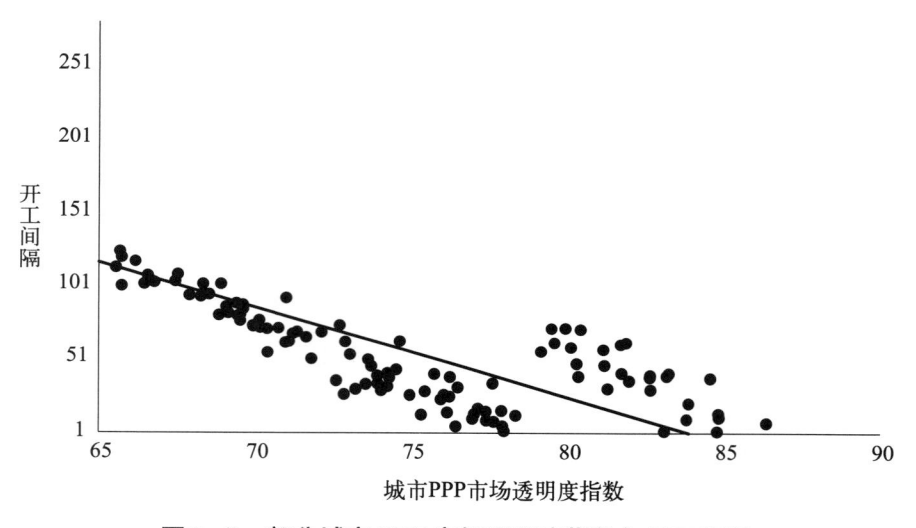

图 5-8　部分城市 PPP 市场透明度指数与开工间隔

PPP 项目平均出资比例仅为 56%。(2) 平均而言,PPP 信息透明度越高的城市,开工间隔(使用合同签订时间与项目开工时间之间的差额来度量)越短(见图 5-8);透明度越低的地区,PPP 项目越可能迟迟不开工。城市 PPP 市场透明度指数每增加 1,开工间隔将减少 8.79 天。统计数据显示,PPP 市场透明度指数在 80 以上的城市,其 PPP 项目开工间隔大概是 186 天;PPP 市场透明度指数在 80 以下的城市,其 PPP 项目开工间隔大概是 211 天。

6 总结与展望

6.1 报告总结

PPP是Public-Private Partnerships的英文首字母缩写,译为政府和社会资本合作。当前,中国的PPP模式已经不仅仅是政府的一种市场化投融资手段,更是一次全面的、系统的公共服务供给市场化社会化改革举措,因而各界对PPP的发展都寄予厚望,希望PPP能起到引领财政体制机制改革、助力公共事业全面深化改革的作用。在这一背景下,PPP项目的规范化管理就显得尤为重要,其中PPP项目及时、完善的信息公开又是PPP项目规范化管理的基础。2017年以来,财政部先后发布多份重要文件,不断强化PPP项目的信息公开管理工作:2017年初,财政部发布《政府和社会资本合作(PPP)综合信息平台信息公开管理暂行办法》,详细规定了PPP项目信息公开的各方面要求;2020年3月31日,财政部发布《政府与社会资本合作项目绩效管理操作指引》,全方位建立了完整的PPP绩效考核体系,明确了责任主体,将信息真实、公开、透明、质量纳入具体的考核细则;2021年12月16日,财政部修订发布《政府和社会资本合作(PPP)综合信息平台信息公开管理办法》,进一步拓展了责任主体,增加了信息公开内容,同时规范了信息公开的方式和时点,完善了监督机制和动态调整机制;2022年11月11日,财政部发布《关于进一步推动政府和社会资本合作(PPP)规范发展、阳光运行的通知》,从做好项目前期论证、推动项目规范运行、严防隐形债务风险以及保障项目阳光运行四个方面给出了PPP项目运行的具体指引。

在此背景下,上海财经大学PPP研究中心课题组继过去连续4年对PPP项目的信息公开工作进行评估后,又对截至2021年12月31日的中国PPP项目的最新信息公开状况进行了详细的评估。具体而言,课题组对2021年底财政部PPP管理库的10 175个项目的信息公开工作进行了详细评估,编制了一套"2021中国PPP市场透明度指数"。该指数囊括68个指标字段,并分为即时公开透明度指数、适时公开透明度指数,以及识别阶段、准备阶段、采购阶段和执行阶段等各阶段的透明度分指数。课题组采用层次分析法和专家打分法相结合的方法对指数进行合成:对于分指数下面的具体指标,按照专家对其重要程度的判定,设置不同的分值;而在分指数合成总指数时,则采用同类指数编制过程中常用的层次分析法,以保证指数编制方法的可靠性。最终,通过对指数具体结果的统计分析,课题组得到以下几个主要发现:

第一,2021年全国PPP市场透明度总指数为80.01,较2020年略有提高。这也是课题组评估中国PPP市场透明度以来,全国总指数首次达到80。进一步对PPP项目的异质性分析表明,PPP项目透明度指数没有明显的行业差异,示范项目和非示范项目的透明度指数差别也不大。

第二,省级层面的PPP市场透明度指数稳中有升,各省份PPP市场透明度指数进一步出现一定的分化趋势。前3名省份与后面省份的透明度指数表现出了不同的时间趋势:绝大多数省份2021年的透明度指数与2020年接近,有的甚至略有下降。但前3名省份的透明度指数出现了3~5不等的涨幅,逐渐拉开了与后面省份透明度指数的差距。云南(90.55)、河北(88.54)、山东(86.39)、湖南(81.43)和江苏(81.27)占据了省份榜单的前5名。

第三,多数城市PPP市场透明度指数较2020年有所提高。课题组挑选了53个PPP项目数量较多(入管理库的项目超50个)的城市,对其PPP信息公开工作进行了分析。通过和2020年PPP市场透明度指数对比可以发现,大部分地级以上城市2021年指数较2020年有所增长,尤其是山东日照,其2021年指数较2020年上升了21.79,紧随其后的是山东潍坊,较2020年上升了20.53。不过,同时也可以发现,少数地级以上城市2021年指数较2020年有所降低,降幅较大的是贵州贵阳和广西南宁,2021年指数较2020年分别下降了2.67和2.19。

第四,PPP信息透明度有助于提高地区社会资本参与热情和项目落地率。平均而言,PPP信息透明度越高的城市,社会资本出资比例越高,项目的开工间隔(使用合同签订时间与项目开工时间之间的差额来度量)也越短。

6.2 政策建议

根据本报告的分析,我们可以看到,与2020年相比,2021年中国PPP市场信息公开工作进一步稳中有进。信息公开工作的完善为PPP市场的规范发展提供了重要保障,也对财政体制机制的改革起到了牵引作用。当然,在调查研究中,我们也注意到了一些PPP市场信息公开方面存在的问题。我们提出以下几条政策建议,以期PPP信息公开工作能进一步完善,提高PPP市场的信息透明度,进而推动中国PPP项目的规范管理。

第一,完善"不适用"信息和临时性重大事项信息公开的操作规范。PPP项目涵盖了跨度很大的不同行业和领域,在合作方式、回报机制等方面也存在很大的区别,因此,有些信息可能对一些项目适用,对另外一些项目就不适用。在指数编制中,对这些不完全适用于所有项目的信息,课题组没有将其纳入指数编制的指标范围内,因为该信息如果是空白,则课题组不知道该信息是不适用于该项目,还是适用于该项目但没有公布这一信息。其实对于该类信息,如果不适用于某项目,则可以要求其特别注明"该信息不适用于本项目"或有类似表述。这样处理后,我们就可以辨别所有项目在该类信息上究竟是不适用,还是适用但未公开。此外,对于临时性重大事项信息公开的管理,也应该有类似的要求。例如,对于"重大违约及履约担保的提取情况、对公众投诉的处理情况"等临时性重大事项的信息公开,应该要求如果没有发生该类事项,应该特别注明"截至目前,本项目没有发生重大违约及履约担保的提取、公众投诉等需要披露的事项"或有其他类似表述。这一方法在上市公司、商业银行等机构的信息披露管理规范中是很常见的。

第二,加强PPP项目重点信息公开的监督检查力度。根据前文的分析,我们可以发现物有所值评价报告、财政承受能力论证报告等公布情况相对于其他信息的公开情况不够理想,因而应该加强对这些信息的监督检查力度。通过随机抽查等方式,对这些报告的披露进展进行敦促。此外,对于执行阶段等信息,要完善制度的具体抓手,敦促有关责任主体主动公开、即时公开相关信息。例如,可以通过合同约定等方式,将项目公司在执行阶段的信息披露工作与政府付费等挂钩,推动PPP项目信息公开工作。最后，为了防止虚假上传的现象，可以考虑通过关键词识别的方式进行自动化甄别。比如上传附件中不包含某些关键词的，不得上传。

第三，应将PPP项目信息透明度的建设作为PPP项目提质增效的有效制度安排予以重视。 进一步推动城市PPP项目提高信息公开质量，及时将PPP项目的信息反馈给社会公众，既不给地方政府违规举债留下空间，又不给社会资本迟迟不开工PPP项目提供可能，营造PPP项目信息公开、透明的市场氛围，打消社会资本参与PPP项目的顾虑。

6.3 未来展望

以上是我们报告的全部内容。总的来说，在2017—2020年指数编制和分析的基础上，我们通过编制指数的方式，对截至2021年底的中国PPP项目的信息公开情况进行了详细的分析。报告保持了指标体系和指数编制方法的连续性。展望来年，我们的主要工作是：

第一，构建新的指标体系，以适应新的PPP信息公开管理办法。 正如我们在第1章和第2章指出的那样，2021年12月16日，财政部发布110号文。这一新的PPP信息公开管理办法于2022年1月1日正式实施，该办法将信息公开的方式从即时公开和适时公开变成主动公开和依申请公开，并大幅增加了执行阶段信息公开的内容。因此，来年我们有必要重构指标体系，以适应这一新的管理办法。课题组将在来年的报告中使用110号文及其相应的附件作为评估依据。构想是：(1)将透明度总指数分为基础信息、准备阶段信息、采购阶段信息和执行阶段信息四个一级指标。四个一级指标下面的二级指标按照110号文要求来设定，比如采购阶段信息分为资格预审信息、项目采购信息和合同签署信息等三个二级指标。四个一级指标下面的三级指标将综合考虑110号文的要求和财政部PPP综合信息平台数据的可得性来进行设置。课题组仍将充分考虑政府主管部门、业界专家和高校学者等诸多专业人士的综合意见，使用层次分析法对指标进行赋权，最后根据三级指标得分进行加权平均，计算得到透明度总指数。(2)进一步评估信息披露的及时性，以适应新的PPP信息公开管理办法。

110号文第13条对信息公开时点作出了详细规定,因而未来课题组不光要考察信息公开与否,还将借助技术手段判断信息公开是否及时。在整个透明度评价体系中,未按110号文时点要求公开相应字段的项目会失分。

第二,进一步探索将信息质量纳入评估范围的有效手段。正如前文提及过的,本报告仅评估PPP项目的信息公开工作,不评估这些信息所代表的具体工作的质量。例如,课题组仅仅评估了PPP物有所值评价报告、财政承受能力论证报告是否得到披露,而不对物有所值评价报告、财政承受能力论证报告具体内容的优劣、科学与否等作出判断。但课题组深知这些信息都是非常重要的,因而未来可以考虑将这些重点报告的具体内容纳入专门的评估分析中,以考察各地区、各方在PPP规范化管理方面的工作业绩。

附件一　专家判定矩阵调查表

　　受亚洲开发银行的委托，上海财经大学PPP研究中心承担了《中国PPP市场透明度评估报告》的研究工作。报告将通过编制指数的方式，全面反映我国PPP市场透明度工作的成绩和不足。在指数编制过程中，不同具体指标之间包含的信息量和重要程度差异很大，因此，课题组想通过专家问卷调查的方式，确定PPP项目信息透明度各影响因素的相对权重（层次图如图3-1所示）。

　　为此，课题组根据层次分析法（AHP）的形式设计如下调查表。这种方法是在同一个层次对影响因素的重要性进行两两比较。衡量尺度划分为9个等级，其中9、7、5、3、1的数值分别对应绝对重要、十分重要、比较重要、稍微重要、同样重要，而8、6、4、2表示重要程度介于相邻的两个等级之间。

　　在下面的表格中，靠左边的等级单元格表示左列因素重要于右列因素，靠右边的等级单元格表示右列因素重要于左列因素。请根据您的看法，在相应的单元格画"√"即可。您的判断对我们科学严谨地编制PPP市场透明度指数至关重要。

　　真诚感谢您的帮助！

上海财经大学PPP研究中心课题组

									下列各组两两比较要素,对于"透明度总指数"的相对重要性如何?									
									重要性比较									
适时公开	9	8	7	6	5	4	3	2	1	2	3	4	5	6	7	8	9	即时公开

									下列各组两两比较要素,对于"适时公开"的相对重要性如何?									
									重要性比较									
识别阶段	9	8	7	6	5	4	3	2	1	2	3	4	5	6	7	8	9	准备阶段
识别阶段	9	8	7	6	5	4	3	2	1	2	3	4	5	6	7	8	9	采购阶段
准备阶段	9	8	7	6	5	4	3	2	1	2	3	4	5	6	7	8	9	采购阶段

									下列各组两两比较要素,对于"即时公开"的相对重要性如何?									
									重要性比较									
识别阶段	9	8	7	6	5	4	3	2	1	2	3	4	5	6	7	8	9	准备阶段
识别阶段	9	8	7	6	5	4	3	2	1	2	3	4	5	6	7	8	9	采购阶段
识别阶段	9	8	7	6	5	4	3	2	1	2	3	4	5	6	7	8	9	执行阶段
准备阶段	9	8	7	6	5	4	3	2	1	2	3	4	5	6	7	8	9	采购阶段
准备阶段	9	8	7	6	5	4	3	2	1	2	3	4	5	6	7	8	9	执行阶段
采购阶段	9	8	7	6	5	4	3	2	1	2	3	4	5	6	7	8	9	执行阶段

附件二 PPP综合信息平台信息公开管理暂行办法

关于印发《政府和社会资本合作（PPP）综合信息平台信息公开管理暂行办法》的通知

（财金〔2017〕1号）

各省、自治区、直辖市、计划单列市财政厅（局），新疆生产建设兵团财务局，财政部驻各省、自治区、直辖市、计划单列市财政监察专员办事处：

　　为进一步贯彻落实《国务院办公厅转发财政部　发展改革委　人民银行关于在公共服务领域推广运用政府和社会资本合作模式指导意见的通知》》（国办发〔2015〕42号）有关要求，加强和规范政府和社会资本合作（PPP）项目信息公开工作，促进PPP项目各参与方诚实守信、严格履约，保障公众知情权，推动PPP市场公平竞争、规范发展，我们研究起草了《政府和社会资本合作（PPP）综合信息平台信息公开管理暂行办法》，现印发你们，请遵照执行。

财政部

2017年1月23日

政府和社会资本合作（PPP）综合信息平台信息公开管理暂行办法

第一章　总　则

第一条　为加强和规范政府和社会资本合作（PPP）信息公开工作，促进PPP项目各参与方诚实守信、严格履约,保障公众知情权,推动PPP市场公平竞争、规范发展,依据《中华人民共和国预算法》、《中华人民共和国政府采购法》和《国务院办公厅转发财政部　发展改革委　人民银行关于在公共服务领域推广政府和社会资本合作模式指导意见的通知》(国办发〔2015〕42号)等有关规定,制定本办法。

第二条　中华人民共和国境内已纳入PPP综合信息平台的PPP项目信息公开,适用本办法。

第三条　PPP项目信息公开遵循客观、公正、及时、便利的原则。

第四条　地方各级财政部门(以下简称"财政部门")会同同级政府有关部门推进、指导、协调、监督本行政区域范围内的PPP项目信息公开工作,结合当地实际具体开展以下工作:

(一)收集、整理PPP项目信息;

(二)在PPP综合信息平台录入、维护和更新PPP项目信息;

(三)组织编制本级政府PPP项目信息公开年度工作报告;

(四)根据法律法规规定和实际需要,在其他渠道同时公开PPP项目信息;

(五)与PPP项目信息公开有关的其他工作。

政府有关部门、项目实施机构、社会资本或PPP项目公司等PPP项目参与主体应真实、完整、准确、及时地提供PPP项目信息。

第二章　信息公开的内容

第五条　项目识别阶段应当公开的PPP项目信息包括:

(一)项目实施方案概要,包含:项目基本情况(含项目合作范围、合作期限、项目产出说明和绩效标准等基本信息)、风险分配框架、运作方式、交易结构(含投融资结构、回报机制、相关配套安排)、合同体系、监管架构、采购方式选择;

(二)经财政部门和行业主管部门审核通过的物有所值评价报告,包含:定性评价的指标及权重、评分标准、评分结果;定量评价测算的主要指标、方法、过程和结果(含PSC值、PPP值)等(如有);物有所值评价通过与否的结论;

(三)经财政部门审核通过的财政承受能力论证报告,包含:本项目各年度财政支出责任数额及累计支出责任总额,本级政府本年度全部已实施和拟实施的PPP项目各年度财政支出责任数额总和及其占各年度一般公共预算支出比例情况；财政承受能力论证的测算依据、主要因素和指标等；财政承受能力论证通过与否的结论；

（四）其他基础资料，包括：新建或改扩建项目建议书及批复文件、可行性研究报告（含规划许可证、选址意见书、土地预审意见、环境影响评价报告等支撑性文件）及批复文件、设计文件及批复文件（如有）；存量公共资产建设、运营维护的历史资料以及第三方出具的资产评估报告，以及存量资产或权益转让时所可能涉及到的员工安置方案、债权债务处置方案、土地处置方案等（如有）。

第六条　项目准备阶段应当公开的PPP项目信息包括：

（一）政府方授权文件，包括对实施机构、PPP项目合同的政府方签约主体、政府方出资代表（如有）等的授权；

（二）经审核通过的项目实施方案（含同级人民政府对实施方案的批复文件），包含：项目基本情况（含项目合作范围、合作期限、项目产出说明和绩效标准等基本信息），风险分配框架，运作方式，交易结构（含投融资结构、回报机制、相关配套安排），合同体系及核心边界条件；监管架构；采购方式选择；

（三）按经审核通过的项目实施方案验证的物有所值评价报告（如有）；

（四）按经审核通过的项目实施方案验证的财政承受能力论证报告（如有）。

第七条　项目采购阶段的信息公开应遵照政府采购等相关规定执行，应当公开的PPP项目信息包括：

（一）项目资格预审公告（含资格预审申请文件）及补充公告（如有）；

（二）项目采购文件，包括竞争者须知、PPP项目合同草案、评审办法（含评审小组组成、评审专家人数及产生方式、评审细则等）；

（三）补遗文件（如有）；

（四）资格预审评审及响应文件评审结论性意见；

（五）资格预审专家、评审专家名单、确认谈判工作组成员名单；

（六）预中标、成交结果公告；

（七）中标、成交结果公告及中标通知书；

（八）项目采购阶段更新、调整的政府方授权文件（如有），包括对实施机构、PPP项目合同的政府方签约主体、政府方出资代表（如有）等的授权，

（九）同级人民政府同意签署PPP项目合同的批复文件，以及已签署的PPP项目合同，并列示主要产出说明及绩效指标、回报机制、调价机制等核心条款。

第八条　项目执行阶段应当公开的PPP项目信息包括：

（一）项目公司（如有）设立登记、股东认缴资本金及资本金实缴到位情况、增减资情况（如有）、项目公司资质情况（如有）；

（二）项目融资机构名称、项目融资金额、融资结构及融资交割情况；

（三）项目施工许可证、建设进度、质量及造价等与PPP项目合同有关约定的对照审查情况；

（四）社会资本或项目公司的运营情况（特别是出现重大经营或财务风险，可能严重影响到社会资本或项目公司正常运营的情况）及运营绩效达标情况；

（五）项目公司绩效监测报告、中期评估报告、项目重大变更或终止情况、项目定价及历次调价情况；

（六）项目公司财务报告，包括项目收费情况，项目获得的政府补贴情况，项目公司资产负债情况等内容；

（七）项目公司成本监审、PPP项目合同的变更或补充协议签订情况；

（八）重大违约及履约担保的提取情况，对公众投诉的处理情况等；

（九）本级政府或其职能部门作出的对项目可能产生重大影响的规定、决定等；

（十）项目或项目直接相关方（主要是PPP项目合同的签约各方）重大纠纷、诉讼或仲裁事项，但根据相关司法程序要求不得公开的除外；

（十一）本级PPP项目目录、本级PPP项目示范试点库及项目变化情况、本级人大批准的政府对PPP项目的财政预算、执行及决算情况等。

第九条　项目移交阶段应当公开的PPP项目信息包括：

（一）移交工作组的组成、移交程序、移交标准等移交方案；

（二）移交资产或设施或权益清单、移交资产或权益评估报告（如适用）、性能测试方案，以及移交项目资产或设施上各类担保或权益限制的解除情况；

（三）项目设施移交标准达标检测结果；

（四）项目后评价报告（含对项目产出、成本效益、监管成效、可持续性、PPP模式应用等进行绩效评价），以及项目后续运作方式。

第三章　信息公开的方式

第十条　PPP项目信息公开的方式包括即时公开和适时公开。

第十一条　即时公开是指财政部门会同有关部门和项目实施机构等依据PPP项目所处的不同阶段及对应的录入时间要求，在PPP综合信息平台录入本办法规定的相关信息时即自动公开。即时公开的内容及要求详见本办法附件。

第十二条　适时公开是指在录入本办法规定的相关信息时不自动公开，而是由财政部门会同有关部门选择在项目进入特定阶段或达成特定条件后再行公开。除本办法另有规定外，项目识别、准备、采购阶段的信息，由财政部门会同有关部门选择在项目进入执行阶段后6个月内的任一时点予以公开；项目执行阶段的信息，由财政部门会同相关部门选择在该信息对应事项确定或完成后次年的4月30日前的任一时点予以公开。前述期限届满后未选择公开的信息将转为自动公开。适时公开的内容及要求详见本办法附件。

第十三条　依照本办法公开的PPP项目信息可在财政部政府和社会资本合作中心官方网站（www.cpppc.org）上公开查询。其中PPP项目政府采购信息应当在省级以上人民政府财政部门指定的政府采购信息发布媒体上同步发布。

第四章　监督管理

第十四条　财政部对全国PPP项目信息公开情况进行评价和监督，省级财政部门负责对本省PPP项目信息公开工作进行监督管理。下级财政部门未按照本办法规定真实、完整、准确、及时录入应公开PPP项目信息的，上级财政部门应责令其限期改正；逾期拒不改正或情节严重的，予以通报批评。

第十五条　政府有关部门、项目实施机构、社会资本或PPP项目公司等PPP项目信息提供方应当对其所提供信息的真实性、完整性、准确性、及时性负责。一经发现所提供信息不真实、不完整、不准确、不及时的，PPP项目信息提供方应主动及时予以修正、补充或采取其他有效补救措施。如经财政部门或利益相关方提供相关材料证实PPP项目信息提供方未按照规定提供信息或存在其他不当情形的，财政部门可以责令其限期改正；无正当理由拒不改正的，财政部门可将该项目从项目库中清退。被清退的项目自清退之日起一年内不得重新纳入PPP综合信息平台。

第十六条　财政部门应会同政府有关部门在每年2月28日前完成上一年度本级政府实施的PPP项目信息公开年度工作报告，报送省级财政部门，并由省级财政部门在每年3月31日前汇总上报至财政部。报告内容应包括：

（一）即时和适时公开PPP项目信息的情况；

（二）PPP项目信息公开工作存在的主要问题及改进情况；

（三）其他需要报告的事项。

第十七条　财政部门工作人员在PPP项目信息公开监督管理工作中存在滥用职权、玩忽职守、徇私舞弊等违法违纪行为的，按照《公务员法》《行政监察法》《财政违法行为处罚处分条例》等国家有关规定追究相应责任；涉嫌犯罪的，移送司法机关处理。

第十八条　公民、法人或者其他组织可以通过PPP综合信息平台对PPP项目信息公开情况提供反馈意见，相关信息提供方应及时予以核实处理。

第五章　附　则

第十九条　PPP综合信息平台是指依据《关于规范政府和社会资本合作（PPP）综合信息平台运行的通知》（财金〔2015〕166号）由财政部建立的全国PPP综合信息管理和发布平台，包含项目库、机构库、资料库三部分。

第二十条　PPP项目信息公开涉及国家秘密、商业秘密、个人隐私、知识产权，可能会危及国家安全、公共安全、经济安全和社会稳定或损害公民、法人或其他组织的合法权益的，依照相关法律法规处理。

第二十一条　本办法自2017年3月1日起施行。

PPP项目信息公开要求

项目所处阶段	公开内容	公开方式	公开的时点	信息提供方
项目识别	项目概况、项目合作范围、合作期限、项目运作方式、采购社会资本方式的选择	即时公开	实施方案编制完成之日起10个工作日内	项目发起方

（续表）

项目所处阶段	公开内容	公开方式	公开的时点	信息提供方
项目识别	交易结构（含投融资结构、回报机制、相关配套安排）、项目产出说明和绩效标准、风险分配框架、合同体系、监管体系	适时公开	进入项目执行阶段后6个月内	项目发起方
	物有所值定性评价指标及权重、评分标准、评分结果	即时公开	报告定稿之日起10个工作日内	
	物有所值评价通过与否的评价结论（含财政部门会同行业部门对报告的审核意见）	即时公开	实施方案批复文件下发后10个工作日内	
	审核通过的物有所值评价报告（含财政部门对报告的批复文件）	适时公开	进入项目执行阶段后6个月内	
	本项目以及年度全部已实施和拟实施的PPP项目财政支出责任数额及年度预算安排情况，以及每一年度全部PPP项目从预算中安排的支出责任占一般公共预算支出比例情况	即时公开	实施方案批复文件下发后10个工作日内	
	财政承受能力论证的测算依据、主要因素和指标	即时公开	报告定稿之日起10个工作日内	
	通过财政承受能力论证与否的结论	即时公开	实施方案批复文件下发后10个工作日内	
	审核通过的财政承受能力论证报告（含财政部门对报告的批复文件）	适时公开	进入项目执行阶段后6个月内	
	新建或改扩建项目建议书及批复文件	适时公开	进入项目执行阶段后6个月内	实施机构
	可行性研究报告（含全套支撑性文件）及批复文件，设计文件及批复文件（如适用）	适时公开	进入项目执行阶段后6个月内	实施机构
	存量公共资产或权益的资产评估报告，以及存量资产或权益转让时所可能涉及到的各类方案等（如适用）	适时公开	进入项目执行阶段后6个月内	实施机构

（续表）

项目所处阶段	公开内容	公开方式	公开的时点	信息提供方
项目准备	政府方授权文件,包括对实施机构、PPP项目合同的政府方签约主体、政府方出资代表(如适用)等的授权	即时公开	授权后10个工作日内	项目所在地本级政府
项目准备	项目概况、项目合作范围、合作期限、项目运作方式、采购社会资本方式的选择	即时公开	进入采购程序后10个工作日内	实施机构
项目准备	交易结构(含投融资结构、回报机制、相关配套安排)、项目产出说明和绩效标准、风险分配框架、核心边界条件、合同体系、监管体系	适时公开	进入项目执行阶段后6个月内	实施机构
项目准备	政府对实施方案的审核批复文件	即时公开	批复文件下发后10个工作日内	实施机构
项目准备	审核通过的项目实施方案及修正案	适时公开	进入项目执行阶段后6个月内	实施机构
项目采购	项目资格预审公告(含资格预审申请文件)	即时公开	资格预审公告发布后10个工作日内	实施机构
项目采购	项目采购文件、补遗文件(如有)	适时公开	进入项目执行阶段后6个月内	实施机构
项目采购	资格预审评审报告及响应文件评审报告中专家组评审结论性意见,附资格预审专家和评审专家名单	适时公开	进入项目执行阶段后6个月内	采购监管机构
项目采购	确认谈判工作组成员名单	适时公开	进入项目执行阶段后6个月内	实施机构
项目采购	预中标及成交结果公告;中标、成交结果公告及中标通知书;	即时公开	依法律规定及采购文件约定	实施机构、采购监管机构
项目采购	已签署的PPP项目合同	适时公开	进入项目执行阶段后6个月内	实施机构
项目采购	PPP项目合同核心条款,应包括主要产出说明、绩效指标回报机制、调价机制	即时公开	项目合同经人民政府审核通过后10个工作日内	实施机构、项目公司

（续表）

项目所处阶段	公开内容	公开方式	公开的时点	信息提供方
项目采购	本项目政府支出责任确认文件或更新调整文件（如适用），以及同级人大（或人大常委会）将本项目财政支出责任纳入跨年度预算的批复文件（如适用）	适时公开	进入项目执行阶段后6个月内	实施机构
	项目采购阶段调整、更新的政府方授权文件（如有）	即时公开	项目合同经人民政府审核通过后10个工作日内的附件依据相关法律规定公开	实施机构
项目执行	项目公司设立登记、股东认缴及实缴资本金情况、增减资（如适用）	即时公开	设立时及资本金到位后10个工作日内	项目公司
	融资额度、融资主要条件及融资交割情况	适时公开	对应事项确定或完成后次年的4月30日前	项目公司
	项目施工许可证、建设进度、质量及造价等与PPP项目合同的符合性审查情况	即时公开	依据PPP项目合同约定；如PPP项目合同未约定时，则在对应活动结束后次年的4月30日前予以公开	实施机构、项目公司
	社会资本或项目公司的年度运营情况及运营绩效达标情况	即时公开	依据PPP项目合同约定；如PPP项目合同未约定时，则在对应活动结束后次年的4月30日前予以公开	项目公司
	项目公司绩效监测报告、中期评估报告、项目重大变更或终止情况、项目定价及历次调价情况	即时公开	依据PPP项目合同约定；如PPP项目合同未约定时，则在对应活动结束后次年的4月30日前予以公开	实施机构
	项目公司成本监审、所有的PPP合同修订协议或补充协议	适时公开	对应活动结束后次年的4月30日前	实施机构、项目公司
	项目公司财务报告相关内容，包括项目收费情况，项目获得的政府补贴情况，项目公司资产负债情况等	适时公开	对应活动结束后次年的4月30日前	项目公司
	重大违约及履约担保的提取情况，对公众投诉的处理情况等	即时公开	发生之日起10个工作日内	实施机构
	本级政府或其职能部门作出的对项目可能产生重大影响的规定、决定等	即时公开	规定及决定下发后10个工作日	实施机构

（续表）

项目所处阶段	公开内容	公开方式	公开的时点	信息提供方
项目执行	项目或项目直接相关方重大纠纷、涉诉或涉仲情况	即时公开	除本办法另有规定外，发生后10个工作日内	项目公司
	本级PPP项目目录、本级PPP项目示范试点库及项目变化情况、本级人大批准的政府对PPP项目的财政预算、执行及决算情况等	即时公开	依法律规定（如有）公开或每季度公开	
项目移交	移交工作组的组成、移交程序、移交标准等移交方案	即时公开	移交方案确定后10个工作日内	实施机构
	移交资产或设施或权益清单、移交资产或权益评估报告（如适用）、性能测试方案	即时公开	清单或报告定稿或测试完成后10个工作日内	实施机构
	移交项目资产或设施上各类担保或权益限制的解除情况（如适用）	即时公开	对应解除完成后10个工作日内	实施机构、项目公司
	项目设施移交标准达标检测结果	即时公开	达标检测结果出具后10个工作日内	实施机构
	项目后评价报告，以及项目后续运作方式	即时公开	后评估报告定稿或项目后续运作方式确定后10个工作日内	实施机构

附件三　政府和社会资本合作（PPP）综合信息平台信息公开管理办法

关于修订发布《政府和社会资本合作（PPP）综合信息平台信息公开管理办法》的通知

（财金〔2021〕110号）

各省、自治区、直辖市、计划单列市财政厅（局），新疆生产建设兵团财政局：

《政府和社会资本合作（PPP）综合信息平台信息公开管理暂行办法》（财金〔2017〕1号）施行以来，对促进PPP项目各方诚实守信、严格履约，保障公众知情权和监督权，推动PPP市场公平竞争和规范发展发挥了积极作用。为加强和规范政府和社会资本合作（PPP）信息公开工作，我们组织修订了《政府和社会资本合作（PPP）综合信息平台信息公开管理办法》，现印发给你们，请遵照执行。

财政部

2021年12月16日

政府和社会资本合作（PPP）综合信息平台信息公开管理办法

第一章　总　则

第一条　为加强和规范政府和社会资本合作（PPP）信息公开工作，促进PPP项目参与方诚实守信、严格履约，保障公众知情权，推动PPP市场公平竞争、规范发展，依据《中华人民共和国政府信息公开条例》《国务院关于进一步深化预算管理制度改革的意见》(国发〔2021〕5号)、《中共中央办公厅国务院办公厅〈关于全面推进政务公开工作的意见〉》等有关规定,制定本办法。

第二条　中华人民共和国境内已纳入PPP综合信息平台的PPP项目及其参与方信息公开,适用本办法。

第三条　本办法所称PPP综合信息平台是指由财政部建立的全国PPP综合信息管理和发布平台。本办法所称PPP项目参与方包括财政部门、行业主管部门、项目实施机构、社会资本、金融机构、项目公司、咨询机构、专家等。

第四条　PPP项目信息和PPP项目参与方信息公开坚持以公开为常态、不公开为例外,遵循公正、公平、合法、便民的原则。

第五条　财政部负责指导、监督PPP综合信息平台信息公开工作。县级以上地方财政部门负责组织、指导、协调、监督本行政区域内的PPP项目信息和PPP项目参与方信息公开工作。

第六条　PPP项目参与方应落实责任,在PPP综合信息平台真实、完整、准确、及时录入、更新PPP项目信息及PPP项目参与方信息。

第二章　信息公开的内容

第七条　PPP综合信息平台项目库储备清单中拟采用PPP模式实施的项目(以下简称储备清单项目)应当公开项目概况、行业主管部门、项目实施机构、发起情况、项目联系人及联系方式等基础信息。纳入PPP综合信息平台项目管理库的PPP项目(以下简称管理库项目)应当公开基础信息以及准备阶段、采购阶段、执行阶段相关信息。社会资本、金融机构、咨询机构和专家等PPP项目参与方应当公开其基本信息、参与PPP项目情况等信息。

第八条　管理库项目准备阶段应当公开的信息主要包括:(一)立项信息,包括计划开发年度,新建或改扩建项目的项目建议书批复、可行性研究报告批复、供地方案批复、环境影响评价批复、初步设计批复等;(二)绩效管理信息,包括绩效目标、绩效指标体系、付费机制等;(三)物有所值信息,包括物有所值评价报告及审核意见等;(四)财政承受能力论证信息,包括财政承受能力论证报告及审核意见等;(五)实施方案信息,包括经审核通过的实施方案及审核意见等;(六)其他应当公开的信息。

第九条　管理库项目采购阶段应当公开的信息主要包括：(一)资格预审信息，包括项目资格预审公告及文件、资格预审文件评审结论性意见等；(二)项目采购信息，包括项目采购方式、(预)中标或成交结果公告、中标或成交通知书等；(三)合同签署信息，包括PPP项目合同审核批准情况、政府方授权文件调整更新情况、已签署的PPP项目合同等；(四)采购阶段方案调整情况，包括采购前调整的实施方案及审核意见、物有所值评价报告及审核意见、财政承受能力论证报告及审核意见，采购后财政支出责任信息等；(五)其他应当公开的信息。

第十条　管理库项目执行阶段应当公开的信息主要包括：(一)社会资本方或项目公司信息，包括中标社会资本方或项目公司基本信息、项目公司股权结构、增减资情况说明、履约保证措施等；(二)项目融资信息，包括融资机构、金额等；(三)履约信息，包括项目建设信息、绩效管理信息、项目公司运营信息、合作期间重大事件、合同变更信息、项目移交信息等；(四)财政实际支出信息，包括项目投资竣工决算数、财政实际支出等；(五)其他应当公开的信息。

第三章　信息录入与公开方式

第十一条　储备清单项目信息由行业主管部门(或政府指定的机关、事业单位)录入、更新。管理库项目准备阶段、采购阶段的信息主要由项目实施机构、本级财政部门录入、更新；执行阶段的信息主要由项目实施机构、项目公司(未设立项目公司的为社会资本)、金融机构、本级财政部门录入、更新。社会资本、金融机构、咨询机构和专家等PPP项目参与方信息主要由各参与方在PPP综合信息平台相关模块录入、更新。

第十二条　PPP项目信息公开的方式包括主动公开和依申请公开。PPP项目参与方应当落实责任，按要求在PPP综合信息平台录入PPP项目信息。县级以上地方财政部门应对PPP项目参与方所录入的项目信息进行确认，并对本级所公开PPP项目信息的真实性、完整性、准确性、及时性负责。

第十三条　主动公开的项目基础信息在项目经省级财政部门审核纳入储备清单后公开；主动公开的项目准备阶段信息在项目经省级财政部门审核并纳入管理库后或进入执行阶段后公开；主动公开的项目采购阶段信息在参与方录入后公开，或在项目经省级财政部门审核进入执行阶段后公开；主动公开的项目执行阶段信息在参与方录入后公开，或在相关事项完成后次年4月30日前公开。退出管理库的项目将保留项目相关信息并显示处于已退库状态。

第十四条　除主动公开的项目信息及按本办法第十七条规定不予公开的信息外，其他PPP项目信息适用依申请公开。公民、法人或者其他组织可以向地方各级人民政府、以及对外以自己名义履行行政管理职能的县级以上人民政府部门（含派出机构、内设机构）的政府信息公开工作机构申请获取相关项目信息。依申请公开项目信息的申请要求、申请程序、答复时间等按照《中华人民共和国政府信息公开条例》规定执行。

第十五条　PPP项目参与方信息公开的方式为主动公开。PPP项目参与方信息录入主体对所公开信息的真实性、完整性、准确性、及时性负责。主动公开的PPP项目参与方信息在录入PPP综合信息平台后公开。

第十六条　主动公开的PPP项目信息和PPP项目参与方信息实行动态调整机制，财政部政府和社会资本合作中心（以下简称财政部PPP中心）可根据政策法规、行业发展、监管要求、市场需求等变化情况，就主动公开信息条目、录入主体、公开时点等提出动态调整建议，经财政部同意后，及时在财政部PPP中心官方网站（www.cpppc.org）上公布。

第十七条　PPP项目信息和PPP项目参与方信息中涉及《中华人民共和国政府信息公开条例》第十四条、第十五条、第十六条、第三十二条及其他不予公开情形的信息，可按规定不予公开。

第四章　监督管理

第十八条　县级以上地方财政部门应加强对本级PPP项目信息公开情况的跟踪管理，组织、协调PPP项目参与方及时录入、更新和公开项目信息。省级财政部门应定期对管理库本地区全部PPP项目信息录入、更新和公开情况进行检查和监督管理。

第十九条　处于准备、采购阶段的管理库项目，项目信息更新周期不得超过6个月；处于执行阶段的管理库项目，项目信息更新周期不得超过12个月。逾期未按要求更新项目信息的，PPP综合信息平台将自动显示项目处于停滞状态，由县级以上地方财政部门督促项目相关参与方在3个月内完成整改。对于未纳入管理库自行以PPP名义实施的项目,以及违反本办法信息公开管理要求且未在限期内完成整改的项目,不得安排PPP项目相关财政资金。

第二十条　经查实PPP项目参与方未按照规定录入、更新信息或存在其他不当情形的,县级以上财政部门可以责令其限期改正;无正当理由拒不改正的,县级以上财政部门可按相关规定将项目从项目库中清退,并对PPP项目参与方进行通报。

第二十一条　县级以上财政及相关部门工作人员在PPP项目信息公开监督管理工作中存在滥用职权、玩忽职守、徇私舞弊等违法违规行为的,依法追究相应责任;涉嫌犯罪的,依法移送有关机关处理。

第二十二条　省级财政部门应建立与财政部当地监管局的PPP项目信息共享机制,主动接受财政监督、审计监督。公民、法人或者其他组织可以就PPP项目信息公开情况向PPP项目参与方提供反馈意见,PPP项目参与方应及时予以核实处理。

第五章　附　则

第二十三条　国际多双边贷(赠)款机构参与的PPP项目,涉及该机构的相关信息公开适用该机构信息公开管理相关规定。按规定可以公开的信息由本级财政部门会同项目实施机构指定相关国内参与方代为录入、更新。

第二十四条　本办法自2022年1月1日起施行。《政府和社会资本合作(PPP)综合信息平台信息公开管理暂行办法》(财金〔2017〕1号)同时废止。

第二十五条　本办法由财政部负责解释。

附件四 PPP信息公开和规范管理制度目录

序号	发布时间	文件号	文件	发布者
1	2013.12.19	财政部74号令	《政府采购非招标采购方式管理办法》	财政部
2	2014.09.23	财金〔2014〕76号	《关于推广运用政府和社会资本合作模式有关问题的通知》	财政部
3	2014.11.29	财金〔2014〕113号	《关于印发政府和社会资本合作模式操作指南(试行)的通知》	财政部
4	2014.11.30	财金〔2014〕112号	《关于政府和社会资本合作示范项目实施有关问题的通知》	财政部
5	2014.12.30	财金〔2014〕156号	《关于规范政府和社会资本合作合同管理工作的通知》	财政部
6	2014.12.31	财金〔2014〕215号	《关于印发〈政府和社会合作项目政府采购管理办法〉的通知》	财政部
7	2014.12.31	财金〔2014〕214号	《关于印发〈政府采购竞争性磋商采购方式管理暂行办法〉的通知》	财政部
8	2015.02.13	财建〔2015〕29号	《关于推进市政公共领域开展政府和社会资本合作项目推介工作的通知》	财政部 住建部
9	2015.03.10	发改投资〔2015〕445号	《关于推进开发性金融支持政府和社会资本合作有关工作的通知》	国家发改委
10	2015.04.07	财金〔2015〕21号	《关于印发〈政府和社会合作项目财政承受能力论证指引〉的通知》	财政部
11	2015.05.19	国办发〔2015〕42号	《国务院办公厅转发财政部发展改革委人民银行关于在公共服务领域推广政府和社会资本合作模式指导意见的通知》	国务院办公厅

（续表）

序号	发布时间	文件号	文件	发布者
12	2015.06.25	财金〔2015〕57号	《关于进一步做好政府和社会资本合作项目示范工作的通知》	财政部
13	2015.12.18	财金〔2015〕166号	《关于规范政府和社会资本合作（PPP）综合信息平台运行的通知》	财政部
14	2015.12.18	财金〔2015〕167号	《关于印发〈PPP物有所值评价指引（试行）〉的通知》	财政部
15	2016.01		《中华人民共和国政府和社会资本合作法（征求意见稿）》	财政部
16	2016.05.28	财金〔2016〕32号	《关于进一步共同做好政府和社会资本合作（PPP）有关工作的通知》	国家发改委、财政部
17	2016.10.20	财金〔2016〕92号	《关于印发〈政府和社会资本合作项目财政管理暂行办法〉的通知》	财政部
18	2016.12.21	发改投资〔2016〕2698号	《关于推进传统基础设施领域政府和社会资本合作（PPP）项目资产证券化相关工作的通知》	国家发改委
19	2016.12.30	财金〔2016〕144号	《财政部政府和社会资本合作（PPP）专家库管理办法》	财政部
20	2017.01.23	财金〔2017〕1号	《关于印发〈政府和社会资本合作（PPP）综合信息平台信息公开管理暂行办法〉的通知》	财政部
21	2017.03.22	财金〔2017〕8号	《关于印发〈政府和社会资本合作（PPP）咨询机构库管理暂行办法〉的通知》	财政部
22	2017.10.19		《政府和社会资本合作（PPP）项目资产支持证券挂牌条件确认指南和信息披露指南》	上海证券交易所
23	2017.11.10	财办金〔2017〕92号	《关于规范政府和社会资本合作（PPP）综合信息平台项目库管理的通知》	财政部
24	2019.03.07	财金〔2019〕10号	《财政部关于推进政府和社会资本合作规范发展的实施意见》	财政部
25	2020.03.16	财金〔2020〕13号	《政府和社会资本合作（PPP）项目绩效管理操作指引》	财政部
26	2021.12.16	财金〔2021〕110号	《关于修订发布〈政府和社会资本合作（PPP）综合信息平台信息公开管理办法〉的通知》	财政部
27	2022.11.11	财金〔2022〕119号	《关于进一步推动政府和社会资本合作（PPP）规范发展、阳光运行的通知》	财政部

附件五　项目数大于30的城市PPP市场透明度排名

排名	城市	2021年项目数量	即时公开透明度指数	适时公开透明度指数	透明度总指数
1	河北承德	58	89.87	80.85	86.35
2	河北衡水	39	90.17	76.51	84.84
3	云南昆明	60	92.81	72.33	84.82
4	云南大理	41	92.96	71.98	84.78
5	云南红河	46	92.79	71.70	84.56
6	云南楚雄	36	92.78	69.92	83.86
7	新疆博尔塔拉	48	87.06	78.69	83.80
8	云南玉溪	56	92.85	68.20	83.23
9	山东东营	34	88.38	75.01	83.16
10	山东济宁	77	88.39	74.79	83.08
11	河北唐山	57	90.54	70.30	82.65
12	云南曲靖	42	93.18	66.13	82.63
13	新疆阿克苏	62	87.25	75.38	82.62
14	河北沧州	52	90.33	68.86	81.96
15	河北邢台	41	90.34	68.62	81.87
16	河北石家	40	90.36	68.20	81.72
17	云南文山	34	93.12	63.82	81.70

(续表)

排名	城市	2021年项目数量	即时公开透明度指数	适时公开透明度指数	透明度总指数
18	山东德州	39	88.75	69.61	81.28
19	安徽宣城	37	88.72	69.37	81.17
20	河北邯郸	49	90.75	66.12	81.14
21	山东日照	56	88.62	67.57	80.42
22	湖南常德	33	86.19	71.19	80.34
23	湖南湘西	39	86.66	70.32	80.29
24	山东潍坊	97	89.03	66.15	80.11
25	山东菏泽	64	89.12	65.55	79.93
26	江苏南京	89	86.27	69.11	79.58
27	湖南长沙	44	86.16	69.02	79.48
28	广东东莞	135	82.24	74.28	79.14
29	浙江衢州	40	83.19	70.74	78.33
30	浙江宁波	50	83.06	70.00	77.96
31	浙江湖州	46	83.22	69.61	77.91
32	浙江丽水	61	83.19	69.58	77.88
33	山东临沂	68	89.36	59.28	77.63
34	浙江杭州	68	83.11	68.99	77.60
35	山东青岛	80	89.41	58.61	77.40
36	吉林长春	46	84.03	66.98	77.38
37	四川巴中	44	83.17	67.70	77.13
38	新疆乌鲁木齐	68	85.05	64.44	77.01
39	江苏宿迁	40	84.89	64.54	76.95
40	安徽阜阳	62	84.29	64.30	76.49
41	四川广元	34	83.26	65.70	76.42
42	安徽亳州	36	82.50	66.46	76.24
43	四川乐山	32	83.29	65.16	76.22
44	内蒙古赤峰	56	85.09	62.17	76.15

（续表）

排名	城　　市	2021年项目数量	即时公开透明度指数	适时公开透明度指数	透明度总指数
45	山东济南	58	89.29	55.32	76.04
46	江苏徐州	53	83.75	63.75	75.95
47	浙江台州	62	83.47	63.66	75.74
48	浙江温州	84	83.43	62.94	75.44
49	福建泉州	66	81.26	66.04	75.32
50	四川宜宾	63	83.57	61.46	74.95
51	安徽滁州	37	81.23	64.31	74.63
52	江西九江	34	81.14	64.14	74.51
53	福建宁德	70	80.77	64.16	74.29
54	安徽蚌埠	31	79.08	66.64	74.23
55	内蒙古呼伦贝尔	34	82.40	61.44	74.23
56	江西萍乡	41	82.65	60.54	74.03
57	四川凉山	42	83.77	58.51	73.92
58	贵州贵阳	58	82.91	59.85	73.91
59	广东惠州	45	79.41	64.83	73.72
60	广东江门	45	84.21	57.07	73.62
61	安徽安庆	50	79.83	63.71	73.54
62	四川南充	38	83.69	56.83	73.22
63	山东烟台	48	90.15	46.27	73.04
64	四川成都	59	83.98	55.53	72.89
65	江西宜春	66	78.97	63.27	72.85
66	陕西西安	77	83.92	55.18	72.71
67	湖北宜昌	40	81.98	57.91	72.60
68	安徽六安	41	80.98	58.29	72.13
69	福建漳州	61	75.89	65.42	71.81
70	贵州六盘水	45	82.62	54.45	71.64
71	江苏淮安	40	84.60	50.63	71.35

（续表）

排名	城 市	2021年项目数量	即时公开透明度指数	适时公开透明度指数	透明度总指数
72	浙江金华	43	84.63	50.22	71.21
73	河南南阳	86	85.47	48.61	71.09
74	河南新乡	50	84.36	50.09	71.00
75	安徽宿州	41	80.74	55.71	70.98
76	湖北荆门	31	84.30	49.55	70.75
77	新疆巴音	62	79.26	56.55	70.40
78	山西太原	38	82.19	51.91	70.38
79	湖北孝感	34	80.09	54.62	70.16
80	河南洛阳	63	82.59	50.65	70.13
81	江西赣州	120	79.55	54.91	69.94
82	河南安阳	44	80.18	53.90	69.93
83	贵州遵义	115	83.28	48.26	69.62
84	江西抚州	48	79.18	54.63	69.61
85	河北保定	50	92.18	34.10	69.53
86	河南平顶山	62	82.57	49.11	69.52
87	湖北黄冈	32	82.48	49.07	69.45
88	河南驻马店	71	79.83	53.10	69.40
89	江西吉安	35	78.45	54.57	69.14
90	福建福州	58	75.99	58.26	69.08
91	湖北咸宁	33	80.78	50.35	68.91
92	山西吕梁	51	83.95	45.20	68.84
93	内蒙古鄂尔多斯	32	81.48	48.27	68.53
94	湖北武汉	74	80.70	49.03	68.35
95	山西长治	43	82.26	46.56	68.34
96	广西玉林	34	86.29	40.07	68.26
97	河南焦作	33	84.87	41.35	67.90
98	辽宁沈阳	36	83.02	43.31	67.53

（续表）

排名	城　　市	2021年项目数量	即时公开透明度指数	适时公开透明度指数	透明度总指数
99	江西上饶	62	79.53	48.55	67.45
100	贵州铜仁	37	81.16	44.28	66.78
101	广西南宁	55	81.52	43.40	66.65
102	河南濮阳	48	80.89	44.16	66.57
103	海南海口	46	69.56	61.62	66.46
104	河南商丘	38	83.79	38.62	66.17
105	贵州毕节	81	84.33	36.63	65.73
106	河南郑州	69	79.15	44.73	65.73
107	广西柳州	41	78.44	45.70	65.67
108	山西晋中	56	81.83	40.07	65.54
109	山西临汾	64	80.74	38.52	64.27
110	河南周口	51	81.86	36.70	64.25
111	河南开封	41	78.49	41.31	63.99
112	辽宁大连	56	81.30	36.72	63.91
113	辽宁朝阳	34	86.83	27.86	63.83
114	湖北恩施	31	80.72	37.04	63.68
115	贵州黔西南	52	85.75	22.96	61.26
116	河南信阳	65	79.67	31.65	60.94
117	贵州黔东南	56	76.67	34.45	60.20
118	山西忻州	37	80.35	28.44	60.11
119	海南省直	46	71.59	42.01	60.06
120	湖北襄阳	46	77.01	32.90	59.80
121	山西运城	38	79.79	26.62	59.06
122	贵州安顺	34	76.17	29.83	58.09
123	山西大同	35	81.15	21.30	57.81
124	贵州黔南	55	75.13	28.83	57.07
125	广西百色	31	71.60	26.09	53.85
126	广西桂林	32	68.20	23.44	50.74

后 记

这份《2021中国PPP市场透明度报告》是由上海财经大学PPP研究中心课题组通力合作、共同撰写的。课题组核心成员包括上海财经大学公共经济与管理学院投资系方芳教授、宗庆庆副教授和石成博士生。课题组在2017—2020年连续四年PPP市场透明度指数编制的基础上,对截至2021年底的中国PPP市场的信息公开状况进行调查、分析和评估。评估过程中,课题组尽可能延续保持了指标体系和指数编制的稳定性,从而保证了2021年PPP市场透明度与前四年的评估结果可比,同时也对比分析了2021年PPP项目信息公开与前一年的情况变化。课题组希望能够通过准确、客观地反映中国PPP市场的信息公开状况,为中国PPP事业的健康持续发展尽绵薄之力。

本研究项目的顺利完成,得益于各方的大力支持与帮助。首先,上海财经大学公共经济与管理学院克服种种困难,为本课题的顺利开展提供了宝贵的经费资助。此外,财政部政府和社会资本合作中心为本课题的顺利开展给予了宝贵的数据支持,在此一并谢过。但需要再次说明的是,本报告是由课题组独立完成的,仅代表课题组的学术观点,并不代表上述机构的官方观点。

最后,上海财经大学公共经济与管理学院的许多研究生和本科生参与了本项目数据收集和整理等助研工作,课题组在此一并致谢。

课题组再次对各方给予的支持和帮助表示最诚挚的谢意,同时也欢迎各界专家和从业者对课题组的工作提出宝贵意见和建议,以期未来编制的PPP市场透明度指数更加科学严谨。具体可与课题组成员联系:

宗庆庆老师(邮箱:zong.qingqing@mail.sufe.edu.cn)

PPP

such institutions above.

Finally, gratitude should also be extended to a number of postgraduates and undergraduates from the School of Public Economics and Administration at SUFE, for their contributions to data collection, consolidation and other research assistance work in the project.

At the end, the Research Group would like to express its sincerest thanks to all parties for their support and assistance. We also welcome valuable opinions and suggestions with regard to our work from all experts and professionals, with a view to formulating PPP market transparency index in a more scientific and rigorous manner in the future. Please contact our members for more details:

Zong Qingqing (email: zong.qingqing@mail.sufe.edu.cn)

Postscript

The *2021 China PPP Market Transparency Report* was prepared by the Research Group of PPP Research Center at Shanghai University of Finance and Economics (SUFE). The Research Group is comprised of the following leading members: professor Fang Fang, associate professor Zong Qingqing and PhD candidate Shi Cheng, all from the Investment Department of the School of Public Economics and Administration, SUFE. Based on the PPP Market Transparency Index prepared in 2017–2020, the Research Group has carried out investigation, analysis and evaluation concerning the information disclosure landscape of the Chinese PPP market by the end of 2021. During the evaluation, the Research Group has tried all the best to maintain the stability of the index system and index compilation methods, thus ensuring the comparability of PPP market transparency results in 2021 with those in the previous years. Meanwhile, the information disclosure of PPP projects in 2021 has also been put in comparison with that in the preceding years. The Group hopes that its work could accurately and objectively reflect the information disclosure status of the Chinese PPP market, thereby contributing to the healthy and sustainable development of the PPP in China.

The successful completion of the research project relies on the strong support and assistance of other organizations. First of all, School of Public Economics and Administration at SUFE has provided valuable financial support for the smooth implementation of the project. Second, the Group would like to thank the China Public Private Partnerships Center (CPPPC) for its data support. However, it needs to be stated again that this Report, prepared independently by the Research Group, represents the academic opinions of the Research Group and doesn't represent the official opinions of

Appendix V Ranking of Cities with Over 30 Projects in PPP Market Transparency Index

Ranking	City	Number of projects in 2021	Transparency index of immediate disclosure	Transparency index of disclosure in due time	Transparency Index
109	Linfen, Shanxi	64	80.74	38.52	64.27
110	Zhoukou, Henan	51	81.86	36.70	64.25
111	Kaifeng, Henan	41	78.49	41.31	63.99
112	Dalian, Liaoning	56	81.30	36.72	63.91
113	Chaoyang, Liaoning	34	86.83	27.86	63.83
114	Enshi Prefecture, Hubei	31	80.72	37.04	63.68
115	Qianxinan, Guizhou	52	85.75	22.96	61.26
116	Xinyang, Henan	65	79.67	31.65	60.94
117	Qiandongnan, Guizhou	56	76.67	34.45	60.20
118	Xinzhou, Shanxi	37	80.35	28.44	60.11
119	Hainan	46	71.59	42.01	60.06
120	Xiangyang, Hubei	46	77.01	32.90	59.80
121	Yuncheng, Shanxi	38	79.79	26.62	59.06
122	Anshun, Guizhou	34	76.17	29.83	58.09
123	Datong, Shanxi	35	81.15	21.30	57.81
124	Qiannan, Guizhou	55	75.13	28.83	57.07
125	Baise, Guangxi	31	71.60	26.09	53.85
126	Guilin, Guangxi	32	68.20	23.44	50.74

Ranking	City	Number of projects in 2021	Transparency index of immediate disclosure	Transparency index of disclosure in due time	Transparency Index
85	Baoding, Hebei	50	92.18	34.10	69.53
86	Pingdingshan, Henan	62	82.57	49.11	69.52
87	Huanggang, Hubei	32	82.48	49.07	69.45
88	Zhumadian, Henan	71	79.83	53.10	69.40
89	Ji'an, Jiangxi	35	78.45	54.57	69.14
90	Fuzhou, Fujian	58	75.99	58.26	69.08
91	Xianning, Hubei	33	80.78	50.35	68.91
92	Lvliang, Shanxi	51	83.95	45.20	68.84
93	Erdos, Inner Mongolia	32	81.48	48.27	68.53
94	Wuhan, Hubei	74	80.70	49.03	68.35
95	Changzhi, Shanxi	43	82.26	46.56	68.34
96	Yulin, Guangxi	34	86.29	40.07	68.26
97	Jiaozuo, Henan	33	84.87	41.35	67.90
98	Shenyang, Liaoning	36	83.02	43.31	67.53
99	Shangrao, Jiangxi	62	79.53	48.55	67.45
100	Tongren, Guizhou	37	81.16	44.28	66.78
101	Nanning, Guangxi	55	81.52	43.40	66.65
102	Puyang, Henan	48	80.89	44.16	66.57
103	Haikou, Hainan	46	69.56	61.62	66.46
104	Shangqiu, Henan	38	83.79	38.62	66.17
105	Bijie, Guizhou	81	84.33	36.63	65.73
106	Zhengzhou, Henan	69	79.15	44.73	65.73
107	Liuzhou, Guangxi	41	78.44	45.70	65.67
108	Jinzhong, Shanxi	56	81.83	40.07	65.54

(continued)

Appendix V Ranking of Cities with Over 30 Projects in PPP Market Transparency Index

Ranking	City	Number of projects in 2021	Transparency index of immediate disclosure	Transparency index of disclosure in due time	Transparency Index
61	Anqing, Anhui	50	79.83	63.71	73.54
62	Nanchong, Sichuan	38	83.69	56.83	73.22
63	Yantai, Shandong	48	90.15	46.27	73.04
64	Chengdu, Sichuan	59	83.98	55.53	72.89
65	Yichun, Jiangxi	66	78.97	63.27	72.85
66	Xi'an, Shaanxi	77	83.92	55.18	72.71
67	Yichang, Hubei	40	81.98	57.91	72.60
68	Lu'an, Anhui	41	80.98	58.29	72.13
69	Zhangzhou, Fujian	61	75.89	65.42	71.81
70	Liupanshui, Guizhou	45	82.62	54.45	71.64
71	Huai'an, Jiangsu	40	84.60	50.63	71.35
72	Jinhua, Zhejiang	43	84.63	50.22	71.21
73	Nanyang, Henan	86	85.47	48.61	71.09
74	Xinxiang, Henan	50	84.36	50.09	71.00
75	Suzhou, Anhui	41	80.74	55.71	70.98
76	Jingmen, Hubei	31	84.30	49.55	70.75
77	Bayingolin, Xinjiang	62	79.26	56.55	70.40
78	Taiyuan, Shanxi	38	82.19	51.91	70.38
79	Xiaogan, Hubei	34	80.09	54.62	70.16
80	Luoyang, Henan	63	82.59	50.65	70.13
81	Ganzhou, Jiangxi	120	79.55	54.91	69.94
82	Anyang, Henan	44	80.18	53.90	69.93
83	Zunyi, Guizhou	115	83.28	48.26	69.62
84	Fuzhou, Jiangxi	48	79.18	54.63	69.61

(continued)

Ranking	City	Number of projects in 2021	Transparency index of immediate disclosure	Transparency index of disclosure in due time	Transparency Index
39	Suqian, Jiangsu	40	84.89	64.54	76.95
40	Fuyang, Anhui	62	84.29	64.30	76.49
41	Guangyuan, Sichuan	34	83.26	65.70	76.42
42	Haozhou, Anhui	36	82.50	66.46	76.24
43	Leshan, Sichuan	32	83.29	65.16	76.22
44	Chifeng, Inner Mongolia	56	85.09	62.17	76.15
45	Jinan, Shandong	58	89.29	55.32	76.04
46	Xuzhou, Jiangsu	53	83.75	63.75	75.95
47	Taizhou, Zhejiang	62	83.47	63.66	75.74
48	Wenzhou, Zhejiang	84	83.43	62.94	75.44
49	Quanzhou, Fujian	66	81.26	66.04	75.32
50	Yibin, Sichuan	63	83.57	61.46	74.95
51	Chuzhou, Anhui	37	81.23	64.31	74.63
52	Jiujiang, Jiangxi	34	81.14	64.14	74.51
53	Ningde, Fujian	70	80.77	64.16	74.29
54	Bengbu, Anhui	31	79.08	66.64	74.23
55	Hulunbeier, Inner Mongolia	34	82.40	61.44	74.23
56	Pingxiang, Jiangxi	41	82.65	60.54	74.03
57	Liangshan, Sichuan	42	83.77	58.51	73.92
58	Guiyang, Guizhou	58	82.91	59.85	73.91
59	Huizhou, Guangdong	45	79.41	64.83	73.72
60	Jiangmen, Guangdong	45	84.21	57.07	73.62

(continued)

Appendix V Ranking of Cities with Over 30 Projects in PPP Market Transparency Index

Ranking	City	Number of projects in 2021	Transparency index of immediate disclosure	Transparency index of disclosure in due time	Transparency Index
15	Xingtai, Hebei	41	90.34	68.62	81.87
16	Shijiazhuang, Hebei	40	90.36	68.20	81.72
17	Wenshan, Yunnan	34	93.12	63.82	81.70
18	Dezhou, Shandong	39	88.75	69.61	81.28
19	Xuancheng, Anhui	37	88.72	69.37	81.17
20	Handan, Hebei	49	90.75	66.12	81.14
21	Rizhao, Shandong	56	88.62	67.57	80.42
22	Changde, Hunan	33	86.19	71.19	80.34
23	Xiangxi, Hunan	39	86.66	70.32	80.29
24	Weifang, Shandong	97	89.03	66.15	80.11
25	Heze, Shandong	64	89.12	65.55	79.93
26	Nanjing, Jiangsu	89	86.27	69.11	79.58
27	Changsha, Hunan	44	86.16	69.02	79.48
28	Dongguan, Guangdong	135	82.24	74.28	79.14
29	Quzhou, Zhejiang	40	83.19	70.74	78.33
30	Ningbo, Zhejiang	50	83.06	70.00	77.96
31	Huzhou, Zhejiang	46	83.22	69.61	77.91
32	Lishui, Zhejiang	61	83.19	69.58	77.88
33	Linyi, Shandong	68	89.36	59.28	77.63
34	Hangzhou, Zhejiang	68	83.11	68.99	77.60
35	Qingdao, Shandong	80	89.41	58.61	77.40
36	Changchun, Jilin	46	84.03	66.98	77.38
37	Bazhong, Sichuan	44	83.17	67.70	77.13
38	Urumqi, Xinjiang	68	85.05	64.44	77.01

(continued)

Appendix V Ranking of Cities with Over 30 Projects in PPP Market Transparency Index

Ranking	City	Number of projects in 2021	Transparency index of immediate disclosure	Transparency index of disclosure in due time	Transparency Index
1	Chengde, Hebei	58	89.87	80.85	86.35
2	Hengshui, Hebei	39	90.17	76.51	84.84
3	Kunming, Yunnan	60	92.81	72.33	84.82
4	Dali, Yunnan	41	92.96	71.98	84.78
5	Honghe, Yunnan	46	92.79	71.70	84.56
6	Chuxiong, Yunnan	36	92.78	69.92	83.86
7	Bortala Prefecture, Xinjiang	48	87.06	78.69	83.80
8	Yuxi, Yunnan	56	92.85	68.20	83.23
9	Dongying, Shandong	34	88.38	75.01	83.16
10	Jining, Shandong	77	88.39	74.79	83.08
11	Tangshan, Hebei	57	90.54	70.30	82.65
12	Qujing, Yunnan	42	93.18	66.13	82.63
13	Aksu, Xinjiang	62	87.25	75.38	82.62
14	Cangzhou, Hebei	52	90.33	68.86	81.96

(continued)

Appendix IV List of PPP Information Disclosure and Regulatory Management Systems

No.	Issued on	Document No.	Document	Issued by
17	October 20, 2016	Cai Jin [2016] No.92	*Circular on Issuing the Interim Measures for the Administration of Finance for Public-private Partnership Projects*	Ministry of Finance
18	December 21, 2016	Fa Gai Tou Zi [2016] No.2698	*Circular on Relevant Work Concerning the Promotion of Asset Securitization of PPP Projects in Infrastructure Sector*	National Development and Reform Commission
19	December 30, 2016	Cai Jin [2016] No.144	*Administrative Measures of the Ministry of Finance for the Public-Private Partnership (PPP) Expert Database*	Ministry of Finance
20	January 23, 2017	Cai Jin [2017] No.1	*Circular on Issuing the Interim Measures for Administration of Information Disclosure for Public-Private Partnership Integrated Information Platform*	Ministry of Finance
21	March 22, 2017	Cai Jin [2017] No.8	*Circular on Issuing the Interim Measures for the Administration of PPP Consulting Agency Database*	Ministry of Finance
22	October 19, 2017		*Guidelines for Qualification for Asset-backed Securities' Listing and Information Disclosure in PPP Projects*	Shanghai Stock Exchange
23	November 10, 2017	Cai Ban Jin [2017] No.92	*Circular on Regulating Project Database of the National PPP Integrated Information Platform*	Ministry of Finance
24	March 7, 2019	Cai Jin [2019] No.10	*Guide of the Ministry of Finance on Promoting the Regulated Development of Public-Private Partnership*	Ministry of Finance
25	March 16, 2020	Cai Jin [2020] No.13	*Guideline for Public-Private Partnership (PPP) Project Performance Management*	Ministry of Finance
26	December 16, 2021	Cai Jin [2021] No.110	*Circular on Amending and Issuing the Measures for the Administration of Information Disclosure for Public-Private Partnership Integrated Information Platform*	Ministry of Finance
27	November 11, 2022	Cai Jin [2022] No.119	*Circular on Further Promoting the Standardized Development and Transparent Operation of Public-Private Partnership*	Ministry of Finance

No.	Issued on	Document No.	Document	Issued by
8	February 13, 2015	Cai Jian [2015] No.29	*Circular on Promoting Public-Private Partnership Projects in Municipal Public Utilities*	Ministry of Finance Ministry of Housing and Urban-Rural Development
9	March 10, 2015	Fa Gai Tou Zi [2015] No.445	*Circular on Relevant Work Concerning the Promotion of the Development Financial Support for Public-Private Partnership*	National Development and Reform Commission
10	April 7, 2015	Cai Jin [2015] No.21	*Circular on Issuing the Guidelines for the Financial Affordability Assessment of the Public-Private Partnership Projects*	Ministry of Finance
11	May 19, 2015	Guo Ban Fa [2015] No.42	*Notice of the General Office of the State Council on Forwarding the Guideline of the Ministry of Finance, the National Development and Reform Commission, and the People's Bank of China on the Promotion of Public-Private Partnership (PPP) Model in Public Service Sector*	The General Office of the State Council
12	June 25, 2015	Cai Jin [2015] No.57	*Circular on Further Effectively Implementing the Demonstration of Public-Private Partnership Projects*	Ministry of Finance
13	December 18, 2015	Cai Jin [2015] No.166	*Circular on Regulating the Operation of the Public-Private Partnership (PPP) Integrated Information Platform*	Ministry of Finance
14	December 18, 2015	Cai Jin [2015] No.167	*Circular on Issuing Guidelines for Value-for-money Evaluation of PPP (Trial)*	Ministry of Finance
15	January 2016		*The Public-Private Partnership Law of the People's Republic of China (Exposure Draft)*	Ministry of Finance
16	May 28, 2016	Cai Jin [2016] No.32	*Circular on Further Effectively and Jointly Implementing Public-Private Partnerships*	National Development and Reform Commission, Ministry of Finance

(continued)

Appendix IV List of PPP Information Disclosure and Regulatory Management Systems

No.	Issued on	Document No.	Document	Issued by
1	December 19, 2013	No.74 Decree of Ministry of Finance	*Measures for the Administration of Government Procurement in No-bid Procurement Model*	Ministry of Finance
2	September 23, 2014	Cai Jin [2014] No.76	*Circular on Issues Concerning the Promotion and Application of the Public-Private Partnership Model*	Ministry of Finance
3	November 29, 2014	Cai Jin [2014] No.113	*Circular on Issuing the Operational Guidelines for Public-Private Partnership Model (Trial)*	Ministry of Finance
4	November 30, 2014	Cai Jin [2014] No.112	*Circular on Issues Concerning the Implementation of the Demonstration Projects of Public-Private Partnership*	Ministry of Finance
5	December 30, 2014	Cai Jin [2014] No.156	*Circular on Regulating the Contract Management of Public-Private Partnership*	Ministry of Finance
6	December 31, 2014	Cai Jin [2014] No.215	*Circular on Issuing the Administrative Measures for Government Procurement under Public-Private Partnership Projects*	Ministry of Finance
7	December 31, 2014	Cai Jin [2014] No.214	*Circular on Issuing the Interim Measures for the Administration of Competitive Consultation of Government Procurement*	Ministry of Finance

(continued)

information sharing mechanism with local regulatory authorities of the Ministry of Finance, and accept financial supervision and audit supervision. Citizens, legal persons or other organizations may provide feedback on PPP project information disclosure to PPP project participants, who shall verify the same and handle it in a timely manner.

Chapter V Supplementary Provisions

Article 23 For a PPP project involving an international multilateral or bilateral lending (sponsoring) institution, the disclosure of information on the institution shall be governed by its information disclosure management regulations. The information that may be disclosed according to such regulations shall be entered and updated by the financial department at the same level in conjunction with a domestic party designated by the project implementing organization.

Article 24 The Measures will come into force on January 1, 2022. The *Interim Measures for the Administration of Information Disclosure for Public-Private Partnership Integrated Information Platform* (Cai Jin [2017] No.1) shall be abolished simultaneously.

Article 25 The Measures shall be construed by the Ministry of Finance.

bounded by Articles 14, 15, 16, 32 of the Regulations on Open Government Information of the People's Republic of China and other non-disclosure provisions may not be disclosed.

Chapter IV Supervision and Administration

Article 18 Local financial departments at or above the county level shall strengthen the tracking and management of information disclosure of PPP projects at the same level, and organize and coordinate PPP project participants to enter, update and disclose project information in a timely manner. Provincial financial departments shall regularly check, supervise and manage the information entry, update and disclosure of all PPP projects included in the management database within their jurisdictions.

Article 19 For management database projects in the preparation and procurement stages, the project information update cycle shall be less than 6 months; for management database projects in the implementation stage, the project information update cycle shall be less than 12 months. Where project information is not updated as required within the cycle, the PPP integrated information platform will automatically display the project as "suspended", and the local finance department at or above the county level will urge the project participants to complete corrections within 3 months. Projects that are not included in the management database but operate in the name of PPP, and projects that fail to complete corrections before the specified time — which violates the information disclosure management requirements herein — are not entitled to PPP funds.

Article 20 Where it is verified that any PPP project participant fails to enter or update information as required or falls under other improper circumstances, the financial department above the county level may urge it to make corrections before the specified time; if it refuses to correct without justifiable reasons, the financial department above the county level may remove the project from the database according to applicable regulations and make public the PPP project participants involved.

Article 21 The personnel of finance and relevant departments above the county level will be subject to corresponding liabilities if they abuse their power, neglect duty, practice favoritism, or have any other violations during the supervision and management of the PPP project information disclosure; if suspected of committing a crime, they will be transferred to judicial organs.

Article 22 Provincial financial departments should establish a PPP project in the reserve list; preparation stage information that is voluntarily disclosed shall be made public after the project is reviewed by the provincial financial department and included in the management database or after the project comes to the implementation stage; procurement stage information that is voluntarily disclosed shall be made public after such information is entered by participants, or after the project is approved by the provincial financial department and comes to the implementation stage; implementation stage information that is voluntarily disclosed shall be made public after such information is entered by participants, or after relevant matters are completed and before April 30 of the following year. Projects that have been removed from the management database must keep their information and are marked as "removed" in the database.

Article 14   PPP project information — other than the project information that is voluntarily disclosed and the information that should not be disclosed as stipulated by Article 17 hereof — shall be disclosed upon application. Citizens, legal persons or other organizations may apply for project information to the local people's governments at all levels, as well as the government information disclosure divisions of government departments above the county level (including external and internal agencies) that perform administrative functions in their own names. The requirements, procedures, and response cycle for project information disclosure upon application are subject to the *Regulations on Open Government Information of the People's Republic of China.*

Article 15   Information on PPP project participants shall be disclosed on a voluntary basis. Those who enter the information on PPP project participants shall be responsible for its truthfulness, completeness, accuracy, and timeliness. The information on PPP project participants that is voluntarily disclosed is made public after being entered into the PPP integrated information platform.

Article 16   The information on PPP projects and PPP project participants that is voluntarily disclosed is subject to a dynamic adjustment mechanism. The China Public Private Partnerships Center (hereinafter referred to as the CPPPC) may, according to changes in policies and regulations, industry developments, regulatory requirements, and market demands, provide dynamic adjustment suggestions on the information to be disclosed voluntarily, the parties who are required to enter the information, the disclosure time, and so on, and announce such suggestions via the CPPPC's official website (www.cpppc.org) in a timely manner upon approval by the Ministry of Finance.

Article 17   The information on PPP projects and PPP project participants that is

Article 10　Regarding management database projects, the information to be disclosed during the implementation phase includes: 1. Information on corporate partners or project companies, including the basic information of bid-winning corporate partners or project companies, the equity structure of project companies, the description of capital changes, and performance bonds; 2. Project financing information, including financing institutions, and financing amount; 3. Contract performance information, including project construction information, performance management information, project company operation information, major events during the cooperation period, contract change information, and project handover information. 4. Information on actual financial expenditures, including final accounts and actual financial expenditure; 5. Other information that should be disclosed.

Chapter III　Information Entry and Manner of Disclosure

Article 11　Information on reserve list projects shall be entered and updated by competent industry departments (or public organizations designated by the government). Information on management database projects in the preparation and procurement stages is primarily entered and updated by project implementing organizations and financial departments at the same level; information on projects in the implementation stage is primarily entered and updated by project implementing organizations, project companies (or corporate partners, if no project company has not been established), financial institutions, and financial departments at the same level. Information on PPP project participants such as corporate partners, financial institutions, consulting agencies, and experts is primarily entered and updated by themselves via corresponding modules on the PPP integrated information platform.

Article 12　PPP project information may be disclosed voluntarily or upon application. PPP project participants shall perform their responsibilities for entering information on PPP projects on the PPP integrated information platform as required. Local financial departments at or above the county level shall verify the project information provided by PPP project participants, and be responsible for the truthfulness, completeness, accuracy, and timeliness of the PPP project information disclosed at the same level.

Article 13　Basic project information that is voluntarily disclosed shall be made public after the project is reviewed by the provincial financial department and included platform (hereinafter referred to as the reserve list projects) that plan to employ the PPP model shall disclose basic information such as project overview, competent industry department, project implementing organization, initiation status, and project contacts. The PPP projects included in the Project Management Database of the PPP integrated information platform (hereinafter referred to as management database projects) shall disclose basic information, alongside information related to the preparation, procurement and implementation stages. PPP project participants such as corporate partners, financial institutions, consulting agencies, and experts shall disclose their basic information, participation in PPP projects, and other information.

Article 8　Regarding management database projects, the information to be disclosed during the preparatory phase includes: 1. Project approval information, including the planned project cycle, approvals of the construction or expansion proposal, approvals of the feasibility study report, approvals of the land supply plan, approvals of environmental impact assessment, and approvals of preliminary design; 2. Performance management information, including performance goals, performance indicator systems and payment mechanisms; 3. Value-for-money information, including value-for-money assessment reports and review opinions; 4. Financial affordability assessment information, including the financial affordability assessment report and review opinions; 5. Implementation program information, including the reviewed and approved implementation program and review opinions; 6. Other information that should be disclosed.

Article 9　Regarding management database projects, the information to be disclosed during the procurement phase includes: 1. Prequalification information, including project prequalification announcements and documents, and concluding observations with respect to prequalification documents; 2. Project procurement information, including project procurement methods, announcements of the (pre-)bid winning and transaction results, and notices of bid winning or transaction; 3. Contract signing information, including the review and approval of PPP project contracts, the adjustment and update of government authorization documents, and signed PPP project contracts; 4. Program adjustment in the procurement stage, including the adjusted implementation program and review opinions before procurement, the value-for-money assessment report and review opinions, the financial affordability assessment report and review opinions, and the information on financial expenditure liability after procurement; 5. Other information that should be disclosed.

Measures for the Administration of Information Disclosure for Public-Private Partnership Integrated Information Platform

Chapter I General Provisions

Article 1 The Measures are hereby formulated in order to strengthen and regulate the information disclosure of Public-Private Partnership ("PPP") projects, encourage various parties to PPP projects to act in good faith and strictly honor their agreements, protect the public's right to know and promote fair competition and regulated development of the PPP market, in accordance with the *Regulations on Open Government Information of the People's Republic of China*, the *Opinions of the State Council on Further Deepening the Reform of the Budget Management System* (Guo Fa [2021] No.5), the *Opinions of the General Office of the CPC Central Committee on Comprehensively Promoting the Disclosure of Government Affairs* and other applicable regulations.

Article 2 The Measures apply to the disclosure of information about the PPP projects within the territory of the People's Republic of China that have been included in the PPP integrated information platform, alongside their participants.

Article 3 The PPP integrated information platform refers to the PPP integrated information management and release platform for the whole country established by the Ministry of Finance. PPP project participants include financial departments, competent industry authorities, project implementing organizations, corporate partners, financial institutions, project companies, consulting agencies, experts, and so on.

Article 4 The information on PPP projects and PPP project participants should be disclosed in principle, with impartiality, fairness, legality, and public convenience in mind.

Article 5 Information disclosure on the PPP integrated information platform is guided and supervised by the Ministry of Finance. Local financial departments at or above the county level are responsible for organizing, directing, coordinating, and supervising the disclosure of PPP project information and PPP project participant information within respective administrative regions.

Article 6 PPP project participants shall perform their responsibilities for entering and updating information on PPP projects and PPP project participants on the PPP integrated information platform in a truthful, complete, accurate, and timely manner.

Chapter II Contents Subject to Disclosure

Article 7 Projects in the Project Reserve List of the PPP integrated information

Appendix III Measures for the Administration of Information Disclosure for Public-Private Partnership Integrated Information Platform

Circular on Amending and Issuing the Measures for the Administration of Information Disclosure for Public-Private Partnership Integrated Information Platform
(Cai Jin [2021] No.110)

To the financial offices (bureaus) of all provinces, autonomous regions, municipalities directly under the Central Government and cities specifically designated in the state plan, and the Financial Bureau of Xinjiang Production and Construction Corps,

Since its enforcement, the *Interim Measures for Administration of Information Disclosure for Public-Private Partnership Integrated Information Platform* (Cai Jin [2017] No.1) has played a significant role in encouraging all parties to PPP projects to act in good faith and strictly honor their agreements, protecting the public's right to know and supervise, and promoting fair competition and standardized development of the PPP market. The *Measures for Administration of Information Disclosure for Public-Private Partnership Integrated Information Platform* are thus revised in order to strengthen and regulate the information disclosure of public-private partnership (PPP) projects. The document is now distributed for your execution.

Ministry of Finance
December 16, 2021

Appendix II Interim Measures for the Administration of Information Disclosure for Public-Private Partnership Integrated Information Platform

Stage	Contents to be disclosed	Manner of disclosure	Time limit	Information provider
Transfer	Release of various security or interests on the assets or facilities to be transferred (if applicable)	Immediate disclosure	Within ten working days after the corresponding release	Executive agency and project company
	Detection results on the satisfaction of the transfer standards for project facilities	Immediate disclosure	Within ten working days after the issue of detection results	Implementing organization
	Post assessment report and the subsequent operation mode of the project	Immediate disclosure	Within ten working days after the post evaluation report is finalized or the subsequent operation manner of the project is determined	Implementing organization

Stage	Contents to be disclosed	Manner of disclosure	Time limit	Information provider
Implementation	Related contents of the financial report of the project company, including payment for the project, the government subsidy granted to the project, and the assets and liabilities of the project company and others	Disclosure in due time	Before April 30 of the year following the end of corresponding activities	Project company
	Major breach of contract and withdrawal of performance bond, handling of public complaints, etc.	Immediate disclosure	Within ten working days upon occurrence	Implementing organization
	Provisions or decisions made by the government at the corresponding level or its functional departments that may have a significant impact on the project	Immediate disclosure	Within ten working days after the issue of provisions and decisions	Implementing organization
	Major disputes, litigations or arbitrations with respect to the project or the parties directly related to the project	Immediate disclosure	Except as otherwise provided in the Measures, within ten working days upon occurrence	Project company
	Directory of the PPP projects at the same level, pilot library thereof and changes to the projects as well as the budget, implementation and settlement situations of governments for the PPP projects as approved by the people's congresses at the same level	Immediate disclosure	Disclosed or quarterly disclosed as required by the law (if any)	
Transfer	Composition of the transfer working group, transfer procedures, transfer standards, and other transfer programs	Immediate disclosure	Within ten working days after the transfer program is determined	Implementing organization
	List of the assets or facilities or interests to be transferred, assessment report on the assets or equity to be transferred (if applicable), scheme on performance test	Immediate disclosure	Within ten working days after the list or report is finalized or after the end of the test	Implementing organization

(continued)

Appendix II Interim Measures for the Administration of Information Disclosure for Public-Private Partnership Integrated Information Platform

Stage	Contents to be disclosed	Manner of disclosure	Time limit	Information provider
Implementation	Registration of the project company, capital subscribed by the shareholders and availability of the capital, increase or decrease of the capital (if applicable)	Immediate disclosure	Upon incorporation and within ten working days after the capital fund is obtained	Project company
	Financing limit, key terms and closing conditions	Disclosure in due time	Before April 30 of the year following the determining or completion of matters corresponding to the information	Project company
	Review of the project construction permits, construction progress, quality and cost and others made based on the PPP project contracts	Immediate disclosure	According to the PPP project contracts; if the PPP project contracts do not make any provisions, prior to April 30 in the next year after the end of corresponding activities	Executive agency and project company
	Annual operation of private capital partners or the project company and satisfaction of the operational performance	Immediate disclosure	According to the PPP project contracts; if the PPP project contracts do not make any provisions, prior to April 30 in the next year after the end of corresponding activities	Project company
	Project company's performance monitoring report, interim assessment report, major changes or termination of the project, project pricing and previous adjustments	Immediate disclosure	According to the PPP project contracts; if the PPP project contracts do not make any provisions, prior to April 30 in the next year after the end of corresponding activities	Implementing organization
	Cost monitoring and review of the project company, alteration agreements on the PPP project contracts or supplementary agreements	Disclosure in due time	Before April 30 of the year following the end of corresponding activities	Implementing organization Project company

(continued)

Stage	Contents to be disclosed	Manner of disclosure	Time limit	Information provider
Procurement	Project procurement documents, addenda (if any)	Disclosure in due time	Within six months after entering into the implementation phase	Implementing organization
	Concluding observations with respect to the review report of prequalification and response documents, including the list of prequalification experts and review experts	Disclosure in due time	Within six months after entering into the implementation phase	Procurement authority
	List of the working group of negotiation about confirmation	Disclosure in due time	Within six months after entering into the implementation phase	Implementing organization
	Announcement of pre-bid winners and transaction results, the announcement of the bid-winning and transaction results and the letter of acceptance;	Immediate disclosure	As agreed according to the law and the procurement documents	Executive agency, procurement authority
	Signed PPP project contracts	Disclosure in due time	Within six months after entering into the implementation phase	Implementing organization
	Key terms of PPP project contract, listing main output specifications, return mechanism for performance indicators, and the price adjustment mechanism	Immediate disclosure	Within ten working days after the project contract is approved by the people's government	Executive agency and project company
	Government's responsibility confirmation documents for the expenditure of the project or the update or adjustment documents (if applicable) of the people's congress at the same level (or the NPC Standing Committee) including the financial expenditure liability of the project into budgets which span two years	Disclosure in due time	Within six months after entering into the implementation phase	Implementing organization
	Government's authorization documents (if any) for the adjustment and updates during the project procurement process	Immediate disclosure	Appendices to the project contract approved by the people's government within ten working days will be made	Implementing organization

(continued)

Appendix II Interim Measures for the Administration of Information Disclosure for Public-Private Partnership Integrated Information Platform

Stage	Contents to be disclosed	Manner of disclosure	Time limit	Information provider
Identification	Asset evaluation report with respect to the stocked public assets or equity, and various programs and others (if applicable) that may be involved in the transfer of stocked assets or equity	Disclosure in due time	Within six months after entering into the implementation phase	Implementing organization
Preparation	Authorized documents of the government, including the authorization of the parties to the implementing agency, the contracting parties of the PPP project contract, the government's investment representatives (if applicable), etc.	Immediate disclosure	Within ten working days after authorization	Local government at the same level
	Introduction to the project, the cooperation scope, the cooperation term, the operation mode, selection of the mode of purchasing social capital	Immediate disclosure	Within ten working days after entering into the procurement procedures	Implementing organization
	Transaction structure (including financing structure, return mechanism and relevant supporting arrangements), project output specification and performance standards, risk allocation framework, core boundary conditions, contracts and regulatory system	Disclosure in due time	Within six months after entering into the implementation phase	Implementing organization
	Government's approval documents with respect to the implementation programs	Immediate disclosure	Within ten working days after the issue of approval documents	Implementing organization
	Project implementation program as examined and approved and amendments thereto	Disclosure in due time	Within six months after entering into the implementation phase	Implementing organization
Procurement	Prequalification announcements (including prequalification application documents)	Immediate disclosure	Within ten working days after the issue of the prequalification announcement	Implementing organization

(continued)

Stage	Contents to be disclosed	Manner of disclosure	Time limit	Information provider
Identification	Value-for-money evaluation report that has been examined and approved (including the approval documents issued by the finance departments)	Disclosure in due time	Within six months after entering into the implementation phase	
	Financial expenditure liabilities of the project and those of the PPP projects implemented and to be implemented in the year and annual budget arrangements, and the ratio of expenditure for all the PPP projects out of the budget in each year in the expenditure of the general public budget	Immediate disclosure	Within ten working days after the issue of approval documents with respect to the implementation programs	
	Measurement basis, key factors and indicators of the financial affordability assessment	Immediate disclosure	Within ten working days after the report is finalized	
	Conclusions on whether the financial affordability assessment passes or not	Immediate disclosure	Within ten working days after the issue of approval documents with respect to the implementation programs	
	Financial affordability assessment report that has been examined and approved (including the approval documents issued by the finance departments)	Disclosure in due time	Within six months after entering into the implementation phase	
	Proposals for new or renovated or expanded projects and approval documents	Disclosure in due time	Within six months after entering into the implementation phase	Implementing organization
	Feasibility study report (including a full set of supporting documents) and approval documents, design documents and approval documents (if applicable)	Disclosure in due time	Within six months after entering into the implementation phase	Implementing organization

(continued)

Chapter V Supplementary Provisions

Article 19 The PPP integrated information platform consisting of three parts, i.e., project library, institution library and document library, refers to the PPP integrated information management and release platform for the whole country established by the Ministry of Finance according to the *Circular on Regulating the Operation of the Public-Private Partnership (PPP) Integrated Information Platform* (Cai Jin [2015] No.166).

Article 20 In the event that the PPP project information disclosure involves state secrets, trade secrets, personal privacy, intellectual property rights, which may endanger national security, public safety, economic security and social stability or harm legitimate rights and interests of the citizens, legal persons or other organizations, it will be handled in accordance with relevant laws and regulations.

Article 21 The Measures will come into force as of March 1, 2017.

Requirements for Information Disclosure of PPP Projects

Stage	Contents to be disclosed	Manner of disclosure	Time limit	Information provider
Identification	Introduction to the project, the cooperation scope, the cooperation term, the operation mode, selection of the mode of purchasing social capital	Immediate disclosure	Within ten working days from the date of completion of the implementation programs	Project initiator
	Transaction structure (including financing structure, return mechanism and relevant supporting arrangements), project output specification and performance standards, risk allocation framework, contracts and regulatory system	Disclosure in due time	Within six months after entering into the implementation phase	Project initiator
	Value-for-money qualitative assessment indicators and weights, scoring standards, scoring results	Immediate disclosure	Within ten working days after the report is finalized	
	Conclusions on whether value-for-money evaluation is passed or not (including opinions of the finance departments in concert with industry departments)	Immediate disclosure	Within ten working days after the issue of approval documents with respect to the implementation programs	

(continued)

shall be responsible for the authenticity, completeness, accuracy and timeliness of the information provided. Once the information provided is untrue, incomplete, inaccurate and not provided timely, the PPP project information provider shall take the initiative to amend, supplement or take other effective remedial measures in a timely manner. If the provider of the PPP project information is confirmed with related materials produced by the finance departments or stakeholders not providing information in accordance with the provisions or falls under other improper circumstances, the finance departments may order it to correct within a time limit; if it refuses to correct without justifiable reasons, the finance departments can weed out the project from the project library. The project being weeded out may not be included into the PPP integrated information platform within one year since the date on which it is weeded out.

Article 16   The finance department shall, in conjunction with the relevant government departments, complete the annual report on the disclosure of information about the PPP projects implemented by the government at the same level for the previous year before February 28 each year, submit it to the finance department at the provincial level, which will report the information to the Ministry of Finance before March 31 each year after making summarization. The report shall include:

1. circumstances on disclosure of the PPP project information on an instant basis and made in due time;

2. major issues occurred during the disclosure of the PPP project information and improvements thereof; and

3. other matters that need to be reported.

Article 17   The personnel of the finance departments will be subject to corresponding liabilities according to the *Civil Servant Law*, the *Law on Administrative Supervision*, the *Regulations on the Penalties and Sanctions against Illegal Financial Conducts* and other related provisions of the State if they abuse their power, neglect of duty, play favoritism and commit irregularities and have any other violations during the supervision and management of the PPP project information disclosure; if they are suspected of constituting a crime, they will be transferred to judicial organs.

Article 18   Citizens, legal persons or other organizations may provide feedbacks to the PPP project information disclosure situation through the PPP integrated information platform, and the relevant information provider shall verify the same and handle it in a timely manner.

disclosure are detailed in the appendix to the Measures.

Article 12　To make disclosure in due time refers to the disclosure of the relevant information as stipulated in the Measures by the finance departments, in concert with the related departments when the project enters into a specific stage or reaches a specific condition rather than automatic disclosure upon the entry of the relevant information. Except as otherwise provided in the Measures, the information during the project identification, preparation and procurement processes will be disclosed by the finance departments in conjunction with the relevant departments at any time within six months after the entry into the implementation phase of the project; The information during the implementation phase will be made available to the public by the finance departments in conjunction with the relevant departments at any time before April 30 of the year following the determining or completion of matters corresponding to the information. The information not made available to the public after the expiration of the foregoing period of time will be opened to the public automatically. The contents and requirements of making disclosure in due time are detailed in the appendix to the Measures.

Article 13　The PPP project information made available to the public according to the Measures may be inquired on the official website of China Public Private Partnerships Center (www.cpppc.org). Information on government procurement of PPP projects shall be published at the media designated by the finance department of a people's government above provincial level.

Chapter IV　Supervision and Administration

Article 14　The Ministry of Finance will evaluate and supervise the disclosure of the PPP project information all over the country, and the provincial finance department is responsible for the supervision and management of the PPP project information to be disclosed in the said province. Where the finance departments at lower level do not enter into the PPP project information that shall be made available to the public on a truly, complete, accurate and timely basis, the finance departments at higher level shall order them to make corrections within a time limit; if they refuse to make corrections or the circumstances are serious, they will be criticized.

Article 15　The relevant government departments, project implementation agencies, corporate partners or PPP project company and other PPP project information providers company and others;

7. cost monitoring and review of the project company, alteration of PPP project contracts or signing of supplementary agreements;

8. major breach of contract and withdrawal of performance bond, handling of public complaints, etc.;

9. provisions or decisions made by the government at the corresponding level or its functional departments that may have a significant impact on the project;

10. major disputes, litigations or arbitrations with respect to the project or of the parties directly related to the project (mainly the contracting parties to the PPP project contracts), except those forbidden according to the relevant judicial proceedings; and

11. the directory of the PPP projects at the same level, pilot library thereof and changes to the projects as well as the budget, implementation and settlement situations of governments for the PPP projects as approved by the people's congresses at the same level.

Article 9 The PPP project information to be disclosed during the project transfer phase includes:

1. composition of the transfer working group, transfer procedure, transfer standards and other transfer programs;

2. list of the assets or equity or interests to be transferred, assessment report on the assets or equity to be transferred (if applicable), scheme on performance test, and the release of various security or interests on the assets or facilities to be transferred;

3. detection results on satisfaction of the transfer standards for project facilities; and

4. post evaluation reports (including evaluation for the project output, cost effectiveness, regulatory effectiveness, sustainability, PPP model applications, etc.), as well as the subsequent operation manner.

Chapter III Manner of Information Disclosure

Article 10 PPP project information can be disclosed immediately or in due time.

Article 11 To make disclosure immediately refers to the automatic disclosure of the related information as stipulated by the Measures via the PPP integrated information platform made by the finance departments, in concert with the related departments, the project implementing organizations and others according to the different stages of the PPP projects and the corresponding entry time. The contents and requirements of the instant

3. addenda (if any);

4. concluding observations with respect to the review of prequalification and response documents;

5. the list of prequalification experts, review experts and the working group of negotiation about confirmation;

6. announcement of pre-bid winners and transaction results;

7. the announcement of the bid-winning and transaction results and the letter of acceptance;

8. the authorization documents of the government updated and adjusted during the procurement process (if any), including the authorization granted to the executive agency, the governments signing the PPP project contract, the government's investment representatives (if any) and others; and

9. the document of the people's government at the same level on consent to sign the PPP project contracts, and the signed PPP project contract, listing main output specifications and performance indicators, the return mechanism, the price adjustment mechanism and other core provisions.

Article 8 The PPP project information to be disclosed during the project implementation phase includes:

1. registration of the project company (if any), capital subscribed by the shareholders and availability of the capital, increase or decrease of the capital (if any), qualifications of the project company (if any);

2. name of the financing institution, amount of funds raised for the project, the financing structure and particulars on the financing delivery;

3. review of the project construction permits, construction progress, quality and cost and others made based on the related agreements under the PPP project contracts;

4. the operation of corporate partners or the project company (especially major business or financial risks that may seriously affect the normal operation of the corporate partners or the project company) and satisfaction of the operational performance;

5. the project company's performance monitoring report, interim evaluation report, major changes or termination of the project, project pricing and previous price adjustments;

6. the financial report of the project company, including payment for the project, the government subsidy granted to the project, and the assets and liabilities of the project

4. Other basic information, including: proposals for new or renovated or expanded projects and approval documents, feasibility study report (including planning permits, siting opinions, land pre-review opinion, environmental impact assessment report and other supporting documents) and approval documents, design documents and approval documents (if any); historical materials of construction and operation maintenance of stocked public assets as well as the asset evaluation report issued by a third party and the employees placement scheme, claim and debt disposal programs, land disposal programs and others (if any) that may be involved in the transfer of stocked assets or equity.

Article 6　The PPP project information to be disclosed during the project preparatory phase includes:

1. the authorization documents of the government, including the authorization granted to the executive agency, the governments signing the PPP project contract, the government's investment representatives (if any) and others;

2. the examined and approved project implementation program (including the approval documents of the people's government at the same level with respect to the implementation programs), including: basic information of the project (including the project cooperation scope, cooperation period, project output specification, performance standards and other basic information), risk allocation framework, operation mode, transaction structure (including financing structure, return mechanism and relevant supporting arrangements), contracts and core boundary conditions; regulatory framework; selection of the purchase mode;

3. the value-for-money evaluation report that has been verified based on the examined and approved project implementation program, if any; and

4. the financial affordability assessment report that has been verified based on the examined and approved project implementation program, if any.

Article 7　The disclosure of information in the procurement process shall comply with the provisions on government procurement and other provisions, and the PPP project information to be disclosed shall include:

1. prequalification announcements (including prequalification application documents) and supplementary announcement (if any);

2. project procurement documents, including notes to competitors, PPP project contract (draft), review methods (including composition of the review group, the number of review experts and the producing way thereof, the review rules, etc.);

information platform;

3. organize to prepare the annual work report of their government-level PPP project information disclosure;

4. make available the PPP project information in other channels at the same time in accordance with laws and regulations and actual needs; and

5. other efforts related to the PPP project information disclosure.

Relevant government departments, project implementing organizations, corporate partners or PPP project company and other PPP project participants shall provide the PPP project information in a truly, complete, accurate and timely manner.

Chapter II Contents Subject to Disclosure

Article 5 The PPP project information to be disclosed during the project identification phase includes:

1. summary of the implementation program, including: basic information of the project (including the project cooperation scope, cooperation period, project output specification, performance standards and other basic information), risk allocation framework, operation mode, transaction structure (including financing structure, return mechanism and relevant supporting arrangements), contracts, regulatory framework, selection of the purchase mode;

2. the value-for-money evaluation report that has been examined and approved by the finance departments and the competent industry authority, including: qualitative evaluation indicators and weights, scoring standards, scoring results; main indicators, methods, processes and results (including PSC value, PPP value), etc. (if any) for the purpose of quantitative evaluation; conclusions on whether value-for-money evaluation is passed or not;

3. the financial affordability assessment report that has been examined and approved by the finance departments, including: liabilities of fiscal expenditure of each year and total expenditure liabilities, total liabilities of fiscal expenditure of the PPP projects implemented by the government at the same level in current year and that of the PPP projects to be implemented for various years, and ratios of them in the general public budget expenditures of various years; measurement basis, key factors and indicators of the financial affordability assessment as well as others; and conclusions on whether the financial affordability assessment is passed or not;

Public-Private Partnership Integrated Information Platform, which are distributed for your execution.

Ministry of Finance
January 23, 2017

Interim Measures for the Administration of Information Disclosure for Public-Private Partnership Integrated Information Platform

Chapter I General Provisions

Article 1 In order to strengthen and standardize the information disclosure of Public-Private Partnership ("PPP") projects, cause various parties to the PPP projects to act in good faith and strictly honor their agreements, protect the public's right to know and promote fair competition and regulated development of the PPP market, the *Interim Measures for the Administration of Information Disclosure for Public-Private Partnership Integrated Information Platform* (the "Measures") are hereby formulated in accordance with the *Budget Law of the People's Republic of China*, the *Government Procurement Law of the People's Republic of China*, the *Circular of the General Office of State Council on Forwarding the Guidelines of the Ministry of Finance, the National Development and Reform Commission and the People's Bank of China on Promoting the Public-Private Partnership Model in the Public Service Sectors* (Guo Ban Fa [2015] No.42) and other related provisions.

Article 2 The Measures apply to the disclosure of information about the PPP projects within the territory of the People's Republic of China that have been included in the PPP integrated information platform.

Article 3 PPP project information disclosure shall be conducted in the principles of objectiveness, fairness, timeliness and convenience.

Article 4 Local finance departments at all levels (hereinafter referred to as the "finance departments") will, in conjunction with the related departments of the government at the same level, promote, guide, coordinate and supervise the PPP project information disclosure work within their respective administrative region and carry out the following work in combination with local realities:

1. collect and sort out the PPP project information;

2. enter into, maintain and update the PPP project information via the PPP integrated

Appendix II Interim Measures for the Administration of Information Disclosure for Public-Private Partnership Integrated Information Platform

Circular on Issuing the Interim Measures for Administration of Information Disclosure for Public-Private Partnership Integrated Information Platform
(Cai Jin [2017] No.1)

To the financial offices (bureaus) of all provinces, autonomous regions, municipalities directly under the Central Government and cities specifically designated in the state plan, the Financial Bureau of Xinjiang Production and Construction Corps, and the Financial Supervision Commissioner Offices of the Ministry of Finance at all provinces, autonomous regions, municipalities directly under the Central Government and cities specifically designated in the state plan,

In order to further carry out the related requirements of the Circular of the General Office of the State Council on Forwarding the Guiding Opinions of the Ministry of Finance, the National Development and Reform Commission and the People's Bank of China on Promoting the Public-Private Partnership Model in the Public Service Sectors (Guo Ban Fa [2015] No.42), strengthen and standardize the information disclosure of Public-Private Partnership ("PPP") projects, cause various parties to the PPP projects to act in good faith and strictly honor their agreements, protect the public's right to know and promote fair competition and regulated development of the PPP market, we hereby formulate the *Interim Measures for the Administration of Information Disclosure for*

In paired comparison, what is the relative importance of the two factors to the "total transparency index"?

	Comparison of importance	
Disclosure in due time	9 8 7 6 5 4 3 2 1 2 3 4 5 6 7 8 9	Immediate disclosure

In paired comparison, what is the relative importance of the two factors to the "disclosure in due time"?

	Comparison of importance	
Identification stage	9 8 7 6 5 4 3 2 1 2 3 4 5 6 7 8 9	Preparation stage
Identification stage	9 8 7 6 5 4 3 2 1 2 3 4 5 6 7 8 9	Procurement stage
Preparation stage	9 8 7 6 5 4 3 2 1 2 3 4 5 6 7 8 9	Procurement stage

In paired comparison, what is the relative importance of the two factors to the "immediate disclosure"?

	Comparison of importance	
Identification stage	9 8 7 6 5 4 3 2 1 2 3 4 5 6 7 8 9	Preparation stage
Identification stage	9 8 7 6 5 4 3 2 1 2 3 4 5 6 7 8 9	Procurement stage
Identification stage	9 8 7 6 5 4 3 2 1 2 3 4 5 6 7 8 9	Implementation stage
Preparation stage	9 8 7 6 5 4 3 2 1 2 3 4 5 6 7 8 9	Procurement stage
Preparation stage	9 8 7 6 5 4 3 2 1 2 3 4 5 6 7 8 9	Implementation stage
Procurement stage	9 8 7 6 5 4 3 2 1 2 3 4 5 6 7 8 9	Implementation stage

Appendix I Determination Matrix Survey for Experts

Entrusted by the Asian Development Bank, the PPP Research Center of Shanghai University of Finance and Economics undertakes the China PPP Market Transparency Assessment Report, which involves preparing an index to holistically reflect the achievements and deficiencies in the information disclosure efforts within China's PPP market. In the process of index preparation, the amount of information contained in each specific indicator and its degree of importance vary greatly. Therefore, the Research Group intends to determine the relative weight among the influencing factors of information transparency of PPP projects through an expert survey (the hierarchy chart is shown in Figure 3-1).

To this end, the Research Group has designed the survey below based on the Analytic Hierarchy Process (AHP), which makes paired comparison on the importance of influencing factors at the same hierarchy. The measurement scale is divided into 9 levels, of which the values of 9, 7, 5, 3 and 1 correspond to absolutely more important, more important, relatively more important, slightly more important, and equally important, while 8, 6, 4 and 2 indicate that the importance is between two adjacent levels.

In the tables below, the left cells indicate that the factors on the left are more important than those on the right, and the right cells indicate that factors on the right are more important than those on the left. Please tick "√" in the corresponding cell based on your own understanding. Your judgment is critical to our scientific and rigorous preparation of the PPP market transparency index.

Thanks for your help!

Research Group of PPP Research Center at
Shanghai University of Finance and Economics

will be deducted if a project fails to provide information within the timeframe specified in No.110 Document.

Second, effective approaches to including information quality into the scope of assessment will be further explored. As mentioned in the preceding paragraphs, this Report only assesses the information disclosure work of PPP projects, but not the quality of the information disclosed. For example, the Research Group has assessed whether the value-for-money report and financial affordability report were disclosed but without assessment of their quality. Therefore, the content of these key project reports should direct special assessment and analysis in the future, with an aim of examining the standardized management of PPP projects in all regions and of all stakeholders.

6.3 Outlook

That's all for the 2022 China PPP Market Transparency Report. Based on the index compilation and analysis in 2017–2020, and by means of index preparation, substantial data and analysis on the information disclosure of PPP projects in China as of the end of 2021 are provided. The Report has maintained the continuity of the index system and index compilation methods. Looking ahead, the Research Group has identified the following priorities:

First, a new index system will be established in line with the new PPP information disclosure management policy. As described in Chapter 1 and Chapter 2, on December 16, 2021, the Ministry of Finance released the No.110 Document, which will come into force on January 1, 2022. The document has changed information disclosure methods from immediate disclosure and disclosure in due time to voluntary disclosure and disclosure upon application, and increased a large amount of information to be disclosed in the implementation stage. Therefore, the Report's index system must be adapted to the new management regulation in the coming years. The No.110 Document and its annexes will be used as the assessment basis for years to come. The initial idea is: (1) The general transparency index is divided into four primary indexes — basic information, preparation stage information, procurement stage information and implementation stage information. The secondary indexes are set as required by the No.110 Document: For example, procurement stage information is divided into three secondary indexes: prequalification information, project procurement information and contract signing information. The tertiary indexes are set with reference to the No.110 Document, as well as data availability on the MOF's PPP Integrated Information Platform. Still, the Research Group will take into full account the opinions of professionals such as government authorities, industry experts, and university researchers, weight indexes using the AHP, and finally calculate the general transparency index according to the weighted average of the three-level indexes. (2) The timeliness of information disclosure is further assessed in compliance with the new policy. Given that Article 13 of the No.110 Document stipulates in detail the time points of information disclosure, the Research Group will not only examine whether the information is disclosed, but also employ technological means to judge whether the information is disclosed in a timely manner. In the transparency evaluation system, corresponding points analyzing PPP information disclosure performance. A possible remedy may be to require the project to insert a notation to the effect of "the information item does not apply to this project". From this, it is possible to discern whether the information item is inapplicable, or if the project has failed to disclose the information. In addition, there should be similar requirements for the management of disclosure on major temporary events. For instance, for the disclosure of information on temporary major events such as "material breach and withdrawal of performance bond, handling of public complaints, etc.", projects should be requested to state that "as of now, the project has no material breach and withdrawal of performance bond, handling of public complaints and other issues to be disclosed" or similar expressions, if there are no corresponding events. This practice is common in the information disclosure management standards of listed companies, commercial banks and other institutions.

Second, to strengthen the supervision and inspection of the disclosure of key information in PPP projects. Based on the above analysis, the Research Group found that the disclosure of value-for-money report and financial affordability report was less desirable compared with the rest. Accordingly, it is advised that the supervision and inspection over disclosure outcomes should be strengthened. Random inspection may be utilized to supervise the disclosure of these project reports. In addition, concerning the information to be disclosed at implementation stage, it may be necessary to improve the system and regulations, urging responsible parties to disclose relevant information in a proactive and timely manner. For example, it is feasible to link information disclosure by project companies at the implementation stage with payment by the government by means of contractual covenants, etc. Finally, automatically screening the documents by keyword identification may be helpful in the prevention of false uploads. The screening could require attachments without certain keywords were not approved for upload, thereby improving the quality of information disclosure.

Third, to place a high value on information transparency as an effective institutional arrangement for improving the quality and efficiency of PPP projects. Cities should be further urged to improve the quality of information disclosure and make such information public in a timely manner in order to prevent local governments from borrowing unlawfully and social capital from delaying PPP projects. It is vital to create a market environment in which PPP project information is accessible and transparent, and to relieve the concerns of social capital players.

Third, most cities delivered PPP market transparency indexes higher than those in 2020. The Research Group selected 53 cities that managed a relatively large number of PPP projects (>50 projects in the Management Database) for more detailed analysis. Comparison with the indexes in 2020 shows that most cities above the prefecture level scored higher in 2021 than in 2020. Among them, the largest increase was delivered by Rizhao of Shandong, the 2021 overall score of which increased by 21.79 points compared to 2020, followed by Weifang of Shandong, with increase of 20.53 points from 2020. However, there were also several cities recording lower scores in 2021 than in 2020, represented by Guiyang of Guizhou and Xining of Guangxi — the two saw the greatest drop in overall score, which was 2.67 and 2.19, respectively.

Fourth, information transparency helps increase the engagement of social capital and the implementation rate of projects. On average, cities with higher PPP information transparency showed a larger share of private capital contributions, as well as a shorter project launch cycle (measured by the interval between the time of contract signing and the time of project launch).

6.2 Policy Suggestions

To conclude the above analysis, in 2021 China has made steady progress regarding the information disclosure in PPP market compared with the previous year. The results observed in this Report suggest the progress in PPP information disclosure is leading reform in infrastructure and services. Notwithstanding these achievements, the Research Group also identified issues related to the disclosure of PPP market information. Therefore, the following are offered as policy improvement opportunities and enhancements, with a view to further improving the PPP information disclosure work, further raising the information disclosure transparency in the PPP market, and promoting the standardized management of PPP projects in China.

First, to improve the operational norms for the disclosure of "inapplicable" information and temporary major events. PPP projects cover a wide range of sectors and fields, which have varied cooperation methods, return mechanisms, etc. It is difficult to ascertain in analyzing results if information is required to be disclosed but not lodged, or if it is not applicable. Accordingly, this limits the extent of research scope when aspects: performing proper preliminary project demonstration, promoting standardized project operation, prohibiting hidden debt risks, and ensuring transparent project operation.

Against this backdrop, the Research Group of PPP Research Center at the Shanghai University of Finance and Economics (SUFE), following the evaluation of the information disclosure of PPP projects in the past four years, carried out a detailed assessment on the latest status as of December 31, 2021. The Research Group assessed in detail the information disclosure work of 10 175 projects included into MOF's PPP Project Management Database as of the end of 2021, and compiled a set of "2021 China PPP Market Transparency Index", which incorporates 68 index fields and is divided into transparency index of immediate disclosure, transparency index of disclosure in due time, and transparency sub-indexes at each stage, i.e., identification, preparation, procurement, and implementation. Regarding the synthesis of indexes, the Research Group adopted an approach combining analytic hierarchy process (AHP) and expert scoring: for specific indexes, different scores were set according to the importance determined by selected experts; and for the synthesis of sub-indexes, the Research Group adopted AHP, a method commonly used in the compilation of similar indexes, thus guaranteeing the reliability of the index preparation method. In the end, through the statistical analysis of final results, the Research Group obtained the following findings:

First, the overall national PPP market transparency index 2021 was 80.01, a slight improvement from 2020. This is also the first time that the national average score has reached 80 since the Research Group started this project. Further analysis on heterogeneity shows no obvious difference in the transparency indexes between industries or between demonstration and non-demonstration projects.

Second, the overall PPP market information transparency index at the provincial level rose steadily, yet with a larger gap between different provinces. The transparency indexes of the top three provinces and the following provinces clearly demonstrated divergent trends: in 2021, most provinces scored similarly — if not slightly lower — compared with 2020. However, the top three provinces' scores increased by about 3~5 points, gradually expanding the gap with the rest. The top five provinces are Yunnan Province (90.55), Hebei Province (88.54), Shandong Province (86.39), Hunan Province (81.43) and Jiangsu Province (81.27).

6.1 Report Summary

PPPs is the acronym for Public-Private Partnerships. At present, China's PPP model is not only a means of market-oriented investment and financing by government, but also has become a comprehensive and systematic market and social reform on the provision of public infrastructure and services. Therefore, all stakeholders (both internal and external) have high expectations for the further development and implementation of PPP, hoping it could play a key role in leading the reform of public finance system and assisting the public sector in deepening reforms. In this context, standardized arrangements for the management of PPP projects is particularly important, in which the timely and complete information disclosure of PPP projects serves as the basis. Since 2017, the Ministry of Finance (MOF) has introduced a number of key documents to continuously reinforce management over the information disclosure of PPP projects: in early 2017, the Ministry released the *Interim Measures for the Administration of Information Disclosure for Public-Private Partnership Integrated Information Platform*, which details all the requirements for PPP project information disclosure; on March 31, 2020, the Ministry released the *Guideline for PPP Project Performance Management* to establish a complete PPP performance management system, identify responsible parties, and include the authenticity, openness, transparency, and quality of information into specific assessment rules; on December 16, 2021, the Ministry amended and released the *Measures for the Administration of Information Disclosure for Public-Private Partnership Integrated Information Platform*, which expands the scope of responsible parties, increases the information to be disclosed, specifies how and when information disclosure should be completed, and establishes a sound supervision mechanism and a sound dynamic adjustment mechanism; on November 11, 2022, the Ministry released the *Circular on Further Promoting the Standardized Development and Transparent Operation of Public-Private Partnership*, providing a specific operation guideline for PPP projects from four

Report Summary and Outlook

Every increase of 1 point in a city's information transparency index leads to a decrease of 8.79 days in the launch cycle. Statistics show that cities with an information transparency index of 80 or more recorded a PPP project launch cycle of about 186 days; while the figure for cities with a score of less than 80 was approximately 211 days.

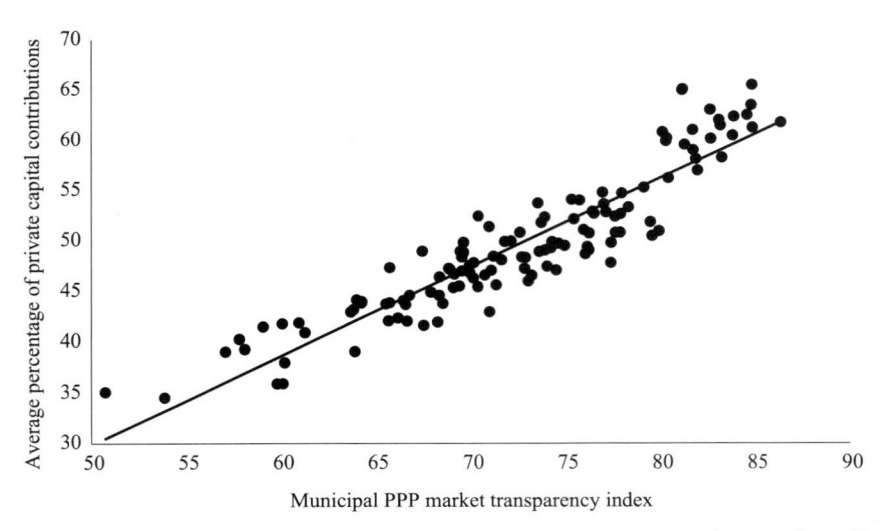

Figure 5-7 Transparency Index and Average Percentage of Private Capital Contributions of Selected Cities

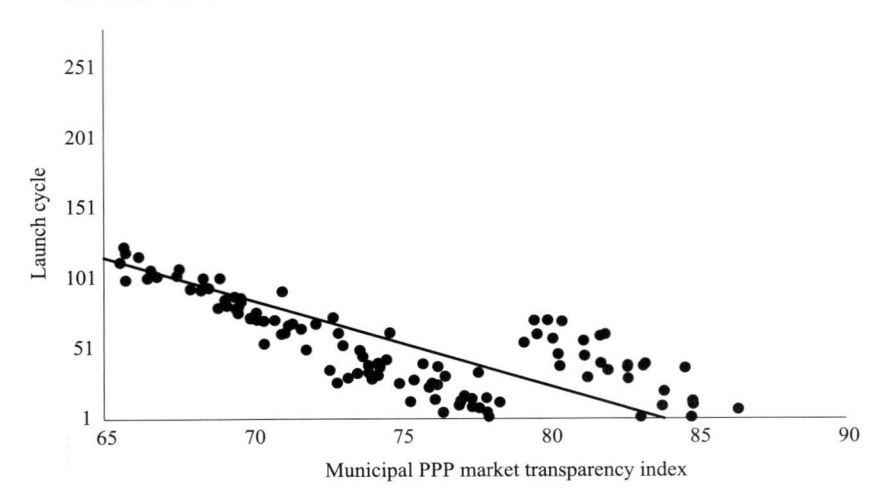

Figure 5-8 Transparency Index and Average Project Launch Cycle of Selected Cities

capital investment.[①] According to statistics, cities with an information transparency index of above 80 recorded a private capital contribution rate of around 65% on average; while the figure for cities with a score of below 80 was only 56%. (2) On average, cities with higher PPP information transparency showed a shorter project launch cycle (measured by the interval between the time of contract signing and the time of project launch) (see Figure 5-8); in cities with poorer transparency, PPP projects were more likely to delay.

[①] For the readability of the Report, details of the econometric regression analysis are omitted, which you may request from the Research Group if you are interested.

of PPP project information will contribute to an atmosphere of honesty, trustworthiness, and compliance among all parties. It raises public trust and dispels social capital's concerns, resulting in increased social capital engagement and project implementation.

To verify the above conjecture, the Research Group matched the micro-data on PPP projects manually retrieved from of the CPPPC with the profiles of social capital available on Qcc.com, and investigated the impact of PPP information transparency on private capital engagement and PPP project implementation rate.

To begin, the Research Team obtained a wealth of information on PPP projects in the identification, preparation, procurement, and implementation phases in the CPPPC's Management Database through manual reorganization. It primarily includes a project's total investment, industry, time of initiation, location, percentage of social capital contribution, and so on.[①] The Research Group then manually searched Qcc.com for the basic information on the social capital involved, including its place of registration, actual controller, time of establishment, industry, size, and more. Following that, the basic information on the social capital was matched with the data on corresponding PPP projects to constitute a large-sample, micro-database that incorporates the basic information of each PPP project and its social capital parties. Research was performed on this basis.

Primary samples were also screened as follows: first, given the administrative level of PPP projects, central and provincial PPP projects were eliminated; second, only projects at the implementation stage were included in the research, since the information on private capital, such as its name and contribution rate, are not made public until the implementation phase; third, some PPP projects that failed to disclose its private capital information at the implementation stage was removed as well. After the above steps, a total of 6 426 PPP projects and 8 032 social capital organizations were acquired as valid samples, covering 328 prefecture-level cities.[②]

The findings of the analysis are: (1) On average, cities with higher PPP information transparency showed a larger share of private capital contributions (see Figure 5–7). Rigorous econometric regression analysis shows that every 1 point increase in a city's information transparency index leads to a 0.705% increase in the percentage of social

---

[①] CPPPC has also provided some data directly to the Research Group, for which the Research Group would like to show gratitude.

[②] Four municipalities directly under the central government — Beijing, Shanghai, Tianjin and Chongqing — were excluded.

Xuzhou, Jiangsu, despite its desirable performance in disclosing value-for-money and financial affordability reports, didn't rank high in the index of disclosure in due time, mainly attributable to its poor work regarding implementation program. Urumqi, Xinjiang and Kunming, Yunnan ranked among the last in disclosing information on value-for-money and financial affordability, with average performance in terms of implementation program.

5.4 Analysis of Social and Economic Benefits of PPP Information Transparency

This section includes an analysis of the social and economic benefits brought about by PPP information transparency at the city level. How to balance stronger supervision and better social capital participation, and how to increase the implementation rate are priorities of China's PPP regulatory authorities. For PPP, a market-oriented, society-based supply management model for public products or services, social capital offers advantages in technology and information, but in the meantime it should be prevented from capturing excessive private benefits. To this end, it is necessary to establish a strong regulatory system. Since the end of 2017, the Ministry of Finance and other regulators have introduced an array of policies such as the No.92 Document, and removed a great deal of non-standard PPP projects from the Management Database. A pattern of all-round and whole-process supervision therefore takes place in the PPP sector, marking the start of reinforced supervision over PPP projects. Reinforced supervision means that the government supervises the quality, price and output performance of PPP projects, which may compress the profit margin of social capital and discourage its engagement. While on the other hand, enhanced supervision of PPP projects by the higher-level government implies that the control of the PPP expenditure liability that the lower-level government should bear, as well as the supervision of local governments by such policies as the No.92 Document, deprives local governments of the tools for borrowing illegally. This boosts social capital's trust in the government's ability to repay its debts, encouraging investment and project implementation.

PPP is a market-oriented public infrastructure and services mechanism that requires market-compatible management means and service capabilities to address the balance between the private interests of social capital and the public interests. Increased transparency in the PPP market is a critical part of the solution. The improved disclosure

Ranking	Transparency index of disclosure in due time	Value-for-money assessment	Financial affordability assessment	Implementation program
30	Guiyang, Guizhou	Qianxinan, Guizhou	Weifang, Shandong	Nanning, Guangxi
31	Zhengzhou, Henan	Lishui, Zhejiang	Heze, Shandong	Xi'an, Shaanxi
32	Xinyang, Henan	Taizhou, Zhejiang	Qingdao, Shandong	Luoyang, Henan
33	Dalian, Liaoning	Yibin, Sichuan	Ningde, Fujian	Dalian, Liaoning
34	Shangrao, Jiangxi	Chengdu, Sichuan	Lishui, Zhejiang	Xinyang, Henan
35	Xi'an, Shaanxi	Hangzhou, Zhejiang	Taizhou, Zhejiang	Fuyang, Anhui
36	Quanzhou, Fujian	Wenzhou, Zhejiang	Yibin, Sichuan	Qianxinan, Guizhou
37	Zhangzhou, Fujian	Pingdingshan, Henan	Chengdu, Sichuan	Ningde, Fujian
38	Wuhan, Hubei	Linfen, Shanxi	Hangzhou, Zhejiang	Shangrao, Jiangxi
39	Chifeng, Inner Mongolia	Xinyang, Henan	Wenzhou, Zhejiang	Linfen, Shanxi
40	Linfen, Shanxi	Bayingolin, Xinjiang	Shangrao, Jiangxi	Pingdingshan, Henan
41	Zhumadian, Henan	Ningde, Fujian	Pingdingshan, Henan	Bayingolin, Xinjiang
42	Fuyang, Anhui	Zunyi, Guizhou	Fuzhou, Fujian	Qiandongnan, Guizhou
43	Ningde, Fujian	Fuzhou, Fujian	Ganzhou, Jiangxi	Zhumadian, Henan
44	Nanjing, Jiangsu	Lvliang, Shanxi	Zunyi, Guizhou	Zhengzhou, Henan
45	Qiannan, Guizhou	Zhumadian, Henan	Zhengzhou, Henan	Ganzhou, Jiangxi
46	Lvliang, Shanxi	Zhoukou, Henan	Zhumadian, Henan	Zunyi, Guizhou
47	Yichun, Jiangxi	Ganzhou, Jiangxi	Lvliang, Shanxi	Chifeng, Inner Mongolia
48	Zhoukou, Henan	Zhengzhou, Henan	Zhoukou, Henan	Fuzhou, Fujian
49	Zunyi, Guizhou	Nanjing, Jiangsu	Jinzhong, Shanxi	Nanjing, Jiangsu
50	Ganzhou, Jiangxi	Dalian, Liaoning	Urumqi, Xinjiang	Zhoukou, Henan
51	Fuzhou, Fujian	Urumqi, Xinjiang	Nanjing, Jiangsu	Urumqi, Xinjiang
52	Jinzhong, Shanxi	Jinzhong, Shanxi	Dalian, Liaoning	Lvliang, Shanxi
53	Qiandongnan, Guizhou	Qiandongnan, Guizhou	Qiandongnan, Guizhou	Jinzhong, Shanxi

Ranking	Transparency index of disclosure in due time	Value-for-money assessment	Financial affordability assessment	Implementation program
4	Chengde, Hebei	Quanzhou, Fujian	Bijie, Guizhou	Chengde, Hebei
5	Cangzhou, Hebei	Aksu, Xinjiang	Quanzhou, Fujian	Cangzhou, Hebei
6	Linyi, Shandong	Bijie, Guizhou	Aksu, Xinjiang	Linyi, Shandong
7	Rizhao, Shandong	Guiyang, Guizhou	Nanyang, Henan	Rizhao, Shandong
8	Jinan, Shandong	Kunming, Yunnan	Guiyang, Guizhou	Jinan, Shandong
9	Jining, Shandong	Yuxi, Yunnan	Luoyang, Henan	Jining, Shandong
10	Weifang, Shandong	Qiannan, Guizhou	Kunming, Yunnan	Weifang, Shandong
11	Heze, Shandong	Wuhan, Hubei	Yuxi, Yunnan	Heze, Shandong
12	Qingdao, Shandong	Xi'an, Shaanxi	Fuyang, Anhui	Qingdao, Shandong
13	Aksu, Xinjiang	Nanyang, Henan	Qiannan, Guizhou	Lishui, Zhejiang
14	Nanyang, Henan	Shangrao, Jiangxi	Linfen, Shanxi	Taizhou, Zhejiang
15	Dongguan, Guangdong	Yichun, Jiangxi	Wuhan, Hubei	Yibin, Sichuan
16	Xuzhou, Jiangsu	Luoyang, Henan	Xi'an, Shaanxi	Chengdu, Sichuan
17	Qianxinan, Guizhou	Tangshan, Hebei	Yichun, Jiangxi	Hangzhou, Zhejiang
18	Nanning, Guangxi	Chengde, Hebei	Chifeng, Inner Mongolia	Wenzhou, Zhejiang
19	Bayingolin, Xinjiang	Cangzhou, Hebei	Tangshan, Hebei	Dongguan, Guangdong
20	Lishui, Zhejiang	Fuyang, Anhui	Chengde, Hebei	Xuzhou, Jiangsu
21	Taizhou, Zhejiang	Chifeng, Inner Mongolia	Cangzhou, Hebei	Zhangzhou, Fujian
22	Yibin, Sichuan	Nanning, Guangxi	Bayingolin, Xinjiang	Quanzhou, Fujian
23	Chengdu, Sichuan	Linyi, Shandong	Xinyang, Henan	Guiyang, Guizhou
24	Hangzhou, Zhejiang	Rizhao, Shandong	Nanning, Guangxi	Yichun, Jiangxi
25	Wenzhou, Zhejiang	Jinan, Shandong	Qianxinan, Guizhou	Aksu, Xinjiang
26	Urumqi, Xinjiang	Jining, Shandong	Linyi, Shandong	Nanyang, Henan
27	Pingdingshan, Henan	Weifang, Shandong	Rizhao, Shandong	Bijie, Guizhou
28	Luoyang, Henan	Heze, Shandong	Jinan, Shandong	Wuhan, Hubei
29	Bijie, Guizhou	Qingdao, Shandong	Jining, Shandong	Qiannan, Guizhou

(continued)

for-money and financial affordability led to the poorest performance of disclosure in due time at identification stage among all stages. No outstanding fluctuation is found in the disclosure in due time index of the three stages among 53 cities.

The results are a signal to local authorities that due attention should be made to the information disclosure effort for the "Two Assessments", as well as a reminder to the national competent authorities to keep tightening the regulatory requirements for "Two Assessments". Due to the pervasiveness of the problem, it is necessary to propose a more detailed and operable policy guide for these key tasks.

5.3 Analysis on Municipal Transparency Indexes of "Two Assessments and One Program"

This section is a continuation of the provincial analysis, examining the transparency of the "Two Assessments and One Program" in key cities. Table 5–3 shows the performance of Dongguan of Guangdong, Kunming of Yunnan, Yuxi of Yunnan and Zhangzhou of Fujian in disclosing the "Two Assessments and One Program" is worthy of recognition. Dongguan and Zhangzhou ranked first and second in the disclosure of information relating to value-for-money and financial affordability, with a perfect score. According to the definition above, the two cities were recorded with neither incomplete disclosure nor "false" disclosure. Although Kunming, Yunnan did not rank among the top five in any of the three indicators, its relatively high ranking in all of them resulted in its first place in the disclosure in due time index as a whole.

Table 5–3 Municipal Transparency Rankings of "Two Assessments and One Program"

Ranking	Transparency index of disclosure in due time	Value-for-money assessment	Financial affordability assessment	Implementation program
1	Kunming, Yunnan	Dongguan, Guangdong	Dongguan, Guangdong	Kunming, Yunnan
2	Yuxi, Yunnan	Zhangzhou, Fujian	Zhangzhou, Fujian	Yuxi, Yunnan
3	Tangshan, Hebei	Xuzhou, Jiangsu	Xuzhou, Jiangsu	Tangshan, Hebei

(continued)

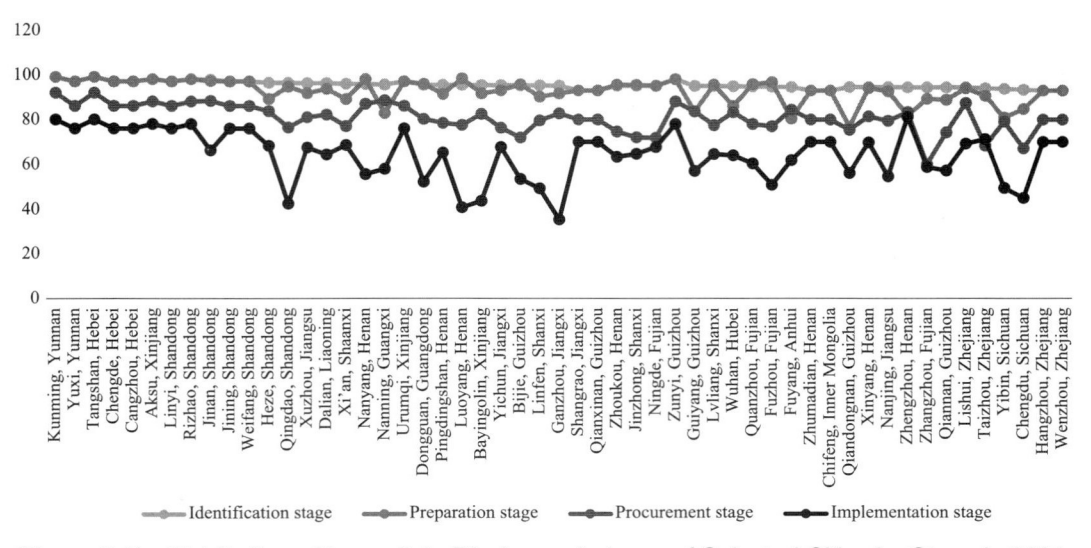

Figure 5–5　Distribution of Immediate Disclosure Indexes of Selected Cities by Stage in 2021

Conversely, for disclosure in due time (see Figure 5–6), the index at identification stage was significantly lower than those at preparation and procurement phases. The identification stage average index was 60.91, while the index at the preparation stage averaged up to 97.71. The possible reason for such difference relates to the requirement raised by disclosure in due time at the identification stage as to disclose value-for-money assessment report, financial affordability assessment report and other essential attachments. All of these were rigorously reviewed by the Research Group. Many reports were found problematic and/or "forged". Therefore, the non-standard reporting of value-

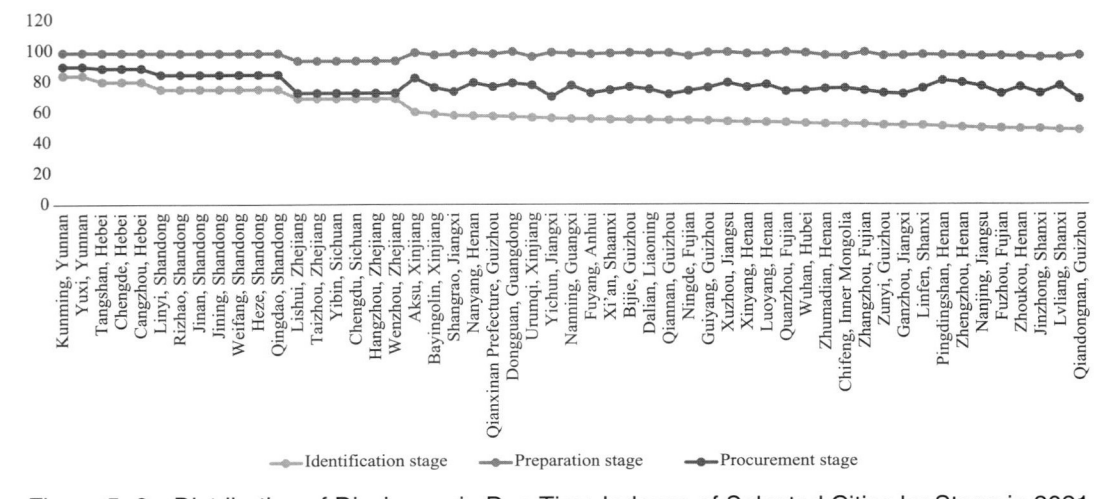

Figure 5–6　Distribution of Disclosure in Due Time Indexes of Selected Cities by Stage in 2021

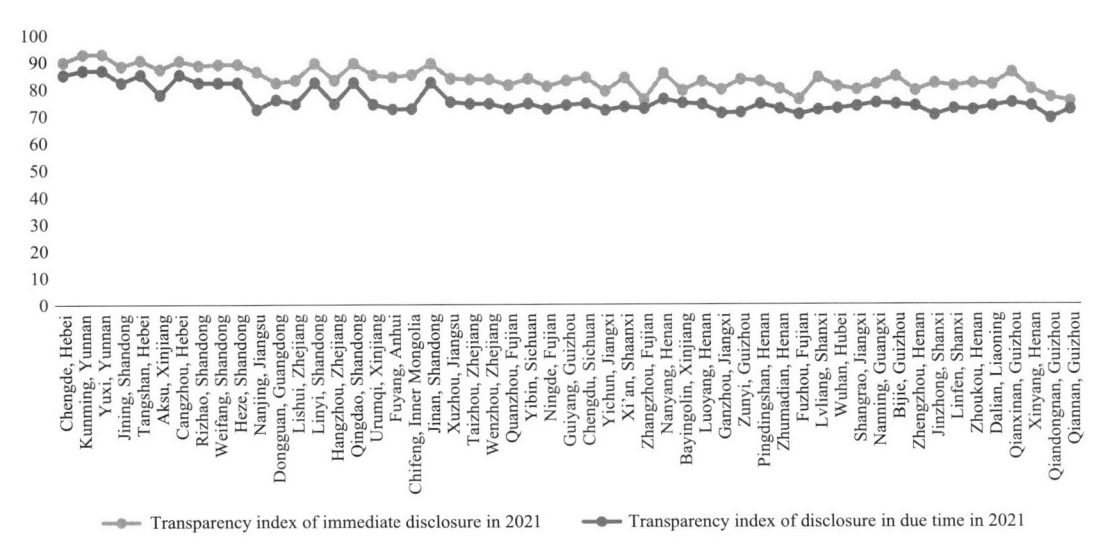

Figure 5-4   Distribution of Immediate Disclosure Indexes and Disclosure in Due Time Indexes of Selected Cities in 2021

Nanyang of Henan, and Hangzhou of Zhejiang declined the most. Figure 5-4 indicates that the overall immediate disclosure index is higher than the index of disclosure in due time in 2021, calling for more efforts in the information disclosure in due time by cities.

5.2.4　Analysis on Municipal Index by Stage

The municipal sub-indexes at different stages are shown in Figure 5-5 and Figure 5-6. Figure 5-5 shows the immediate disclosure index of each city at the stages of identification, preparation, procurement and implementation. The results indicate that in relation to immediate information disclosure requirements, cities have performed better during the identification and preparation phases, with scores generally higher than those at the rest stages. The reason may be that the completeness of basic information in identification and preparation stages helps attract social capital and directly improves the tendering results of PPP projects. As a result, it is likely most project management departments will pay more attention to the information to be immediately disclosed at the two stages, resulting in average indexes of 95.50 and 92.80 respectively. The average information transparency indexes at procurement and implementation stages were 80.88 and 64.49 respectively, lower than the other two, along with great fluctuation. Meanwhile, it should also be noted that the immediate disclosure indexes of some cities in the preparation stage were lower than those in procurement and implementation stages.

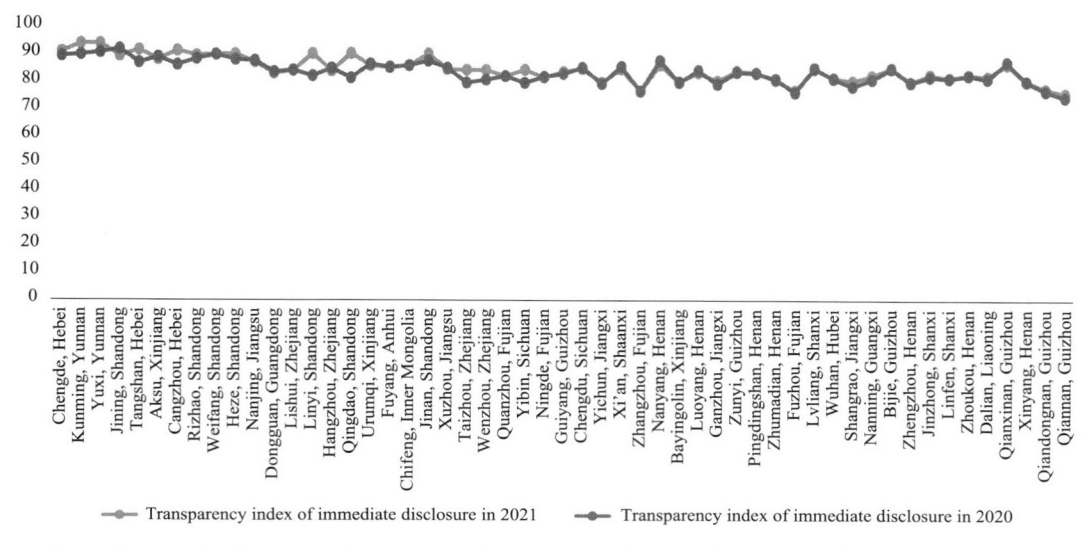

Figure 5–2   Distribution of Immediate Disclosure Indexes of Selected Cities in 2020–2021

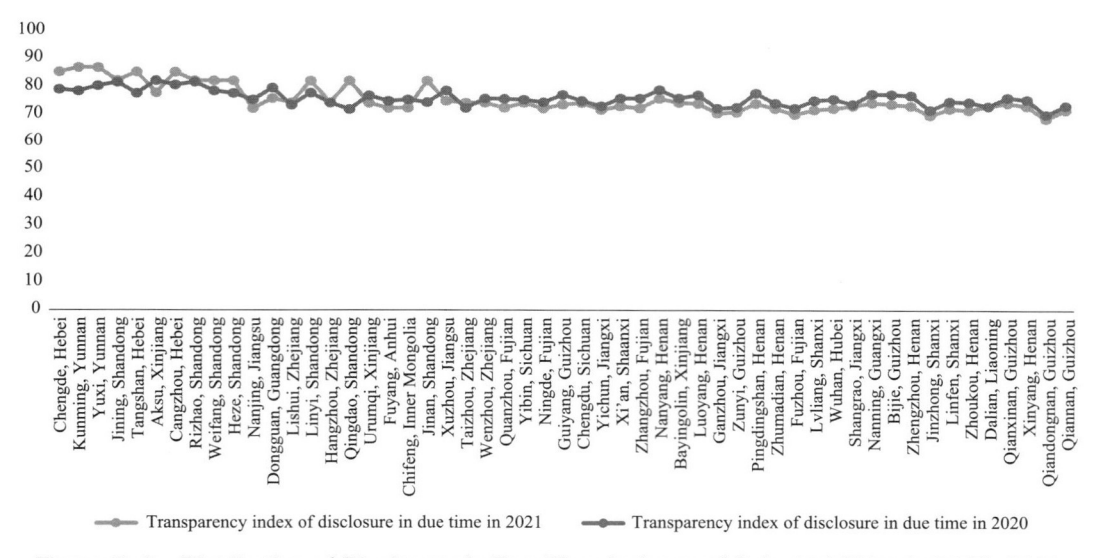

Figure 5–3   Distribution of Disclosure in Due Time Indexes of Selected Cities in 2020–2021

As far as immediate disclosure is concerned, the top three cities that made the largest improvement in 2021 compared with 2020 are: Linyi of Shandong (from 81.23 to 89.36 points), Qingdao of Shandong (from 80.51 to 89.41 points) and Taizhou of Zhejiang (from 78.82 to 83.47 points); while the cities with the most prominent drop are Jining in Shandong, Nanyang in Henan and Hangzhou in Zhejiang. Regarding disclosure in due time, the top three cities that improved most in 2021 compared with 2020 are Qingdao in Shandong, Kunming in Yunnan, and Jinan in Shandong; while Jining of Shandong,

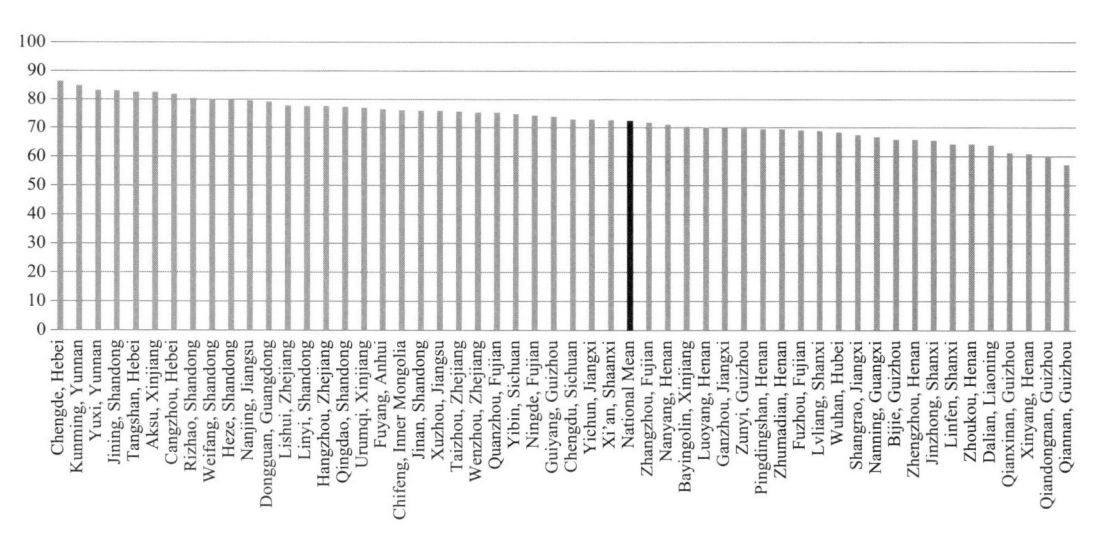

Figure 5–1   Distribution of Overall Transparency Indexes of Selected Cities in 2021

between Nanyang, Henan and Qiandongnan, Guizhou. As most of the cities analyzed manage large numbers of PPP projects, inexperience should not be a factor for poor PPP market transparency indexes delivered by the cities in the second group. Instead, it means that some cities do need to strengthen their efforts related to PPP information disclosure to avoid the negligence in standardized management.

5.2.3 Analysis on Municipal Index by Immediate Disclosure/ Disclosure in Due Time

Figure 5–2 and Figure 5–3 show the distribution of the immediate disclosure indexes and the disclosure in due time indexes of 53 cities. As shown in Figure 5–2, the average immediate disclosure index 83.7 in 2021 was higher than the 82.70 in 2020, representing a minor variance. At the same time, it can be observed from Figure 5–3 that all the cities other than Qingdao of Shandong, Kunming of Yunnan, Yuxi of Yunnan and Chengde of Hebei scored similarly in terms of disclosure in due time in 2021 and 2020. Also, the majority of cities from Chengde of Hebei to Yibin of Sichuan scored higher in both immediate disclosure and disclosure in due time indexes in 2021 than 2020; while Qiannan of Guizhou, Nanyang of Henan and Xi'an of Shaanxi did the opposite. It indicates that the good performance of cities in PPP project information transparency was attributable to their high scores in both immediate disclosure and disclosure in due time. On the other hand, there were several cites delivering worse performance in both dimensions.

Ranking	City	Number of projects in 2021	Overall index in 2021	Variance from general index in 2020	Overall index in 2020
43	Nanning, Guangxi	55	66.65	−2.19	68.85
44	Bijie, Guizhou	81	65.73	−2.12	67.85
45	Zhengzhou, Henan	69	65.73	−0.69	66.42
46	Jinzhong, Shanxi	56	65.54	+1.47	64.08
47	Linfen, Shanxi	64	64.27	+1.02	63.25
48	Zhoukou, Henan	51	64.25	+1.13	63.11
49	Dalian, Liaoning	56	63.91	+6.31	57.61
50	Qianxinan, Guizhou	52	61.26	+2.58	58.68
51	Xinyang, Henan	65	60.94	+1.50	59.44
52	Qiandongnan, Guizhou	56	60.20	+1.21	58.99
53	Qiannan, Guizhou	55	57.07	+2.36	54.70

Comparison with the indexes in 2020 shows that most cities above the prefecture level scored higher in 2021 than in 2020. Among them, the largest increase was delivered by Rizhao of Shandong, the 2021 overall score of which increased by 21.79 points compared to 2020, followed by Weifang of Shandong, with an increase of 20.53 points from 2020. However, there were also several cities recording a lower score, represented by Guiyang of Guizhou and Xining of Guangxi - the two saw the greatest drop in overall score, which was 2.67 and 2.19, respectively.

5.2.2 Comparison with National Average

The distribution of the general transparency indexes of 53 cities shows that as the PPP model gains popularity, no significant differences were seen in PPP market information transparency between most cities, despite several exceptions. By the index, these cities can be classified into two main groups, as shown in Figure 5–1. The first group includes 30 cities with leading PPP market transparency performance across the nation, i.e., those ranking between Ningde, Hebei and Yichun, Jiangxi; and the second group consists of 23 cities that lagged behind the national average, i.e., those ranking

Ranking	City	Number of projects in 2021	Overall index in 2021	Variance from general index in 2020	Overall index in 2020
19	Chifeng, Inner Mongolia	56	76.15	+1.06	75.10
20	Jinan, Shandong	58	76.04	+18.79	57.25
21	Xuzhou, Jiangsu	53	75.95	+1.53	74.42
22	Taizhou, Zhejiang	62	75.74	+5.39	70.35
23	Wenzhou, Zhejiang	84	75.44	+2.67	72.77
24	Quanzhou, Fujian	66	75.32	+1.28	74.04
25	Yibin, Sichuan	63	74.95	+5.18	69.77
26	Ningde, Fujian	70	74.29	+4.40	69.89
27	Guiyang, Guizhou	58	73.91	−2.67	76.58
28	Chengdu, Sichuan	59	72.89	+3.61	69.27
29	Yichun, Jiangxi	66	72.85	+4.99	67.86
30	Xi'an, Shaanxi	77	72.71	+2.41	70.30
31	Zhangzhou, Fujian	61	71.81	−0.61	72.42
32	Nanyang, Henan	86	71.09	+6.42	64.67
33	Bayingolin, Xinjiang	62	70.40	+7.65	62.75
34	Luoyang, Henan	63	70.13	+2.14	67.99
35	Ganzhou, Jiangxi	120	69.94	+0.46	69.49
36	Zunyi, Guizhou	115	69.62	+1.99	67.64
37	Pingdingshan, Henan	62	69.52	+0.37	69.15
38	Zhumadian, Henan	71	69.40	+4.86	64.54
39	Fuzhou, Fujian	58	69.08	+1.72	67.35
40	Lvliang, Shanxi	51	68.84	+0.03	68.81
41	Wuhan, Hubei	74	68.35	−0.16	68.51
42	Shangrao, Jiangxi	62	67.45	+5.69	61.76

(continued)

markets, the overall ranking of PPP market transparency index in 2021 is shown in Table 5–2. Chengde, Hebei Province, ranked first, with an index of 86.35 points, 13.89 points higher than the national average; followed by Kunming of Yunnan and Yuxi of Yunnan, scoring 84.82 and 83.23 points, respectively. In addition, cities with a total score of 80 points or above include Jining of Shandong, Tangshan of Hebei, Aksu of Xinjiang, Cangzhou of Hebei, Rizhao of Shandong and Weifang of Shandong. The index outcomes suggest that these cities have performed well in terms of PPP information disclosure.

Table 5–2 Overall Transparency Indexes of Selected Cities in 2021

Ranking	City	Number of projects in 2021	Overall index in 2021	Variance from general index in 2020	Overall index in 2020
1	Chengde, Hebei	58	86.35	+8.74	77.61
2	Kunming, Yunnan	60	84.82	+14.20	70.62
3	Yuxi, Yunnan	56	83.23	+10.55	72.69
4	Jining, Shandong	77	83.08	+19.46	63.63
5	Tangshan, Hebei	57	82.65	+8.29	74.36
6	Aksu, Xinjiang	62	82.62	−1.90	84.52
7	Cangzhou, Hebei	52	81.96	+7.02	74.93
8	Rizhao, Shandong	56	80.42	+21.79	58.63
9	Weifang, Shandong	97	80.11	+20.53	59.58
10	Heze, Shandong	64	79.93	+12.10	67.83
11	Nanjing, Jiangsu	89	79.58	+1.67	77.90
12	Dongguan, Guangdong	135	79.14	+5.00	74.14
13	Lishui, Zhejiang	61	77.88	+3.97	73.91
14	Linyi, Shandong	68	77.63	+19.47	58.16
15	Hangzhou, Zhejiang	68	77.60	+1.62	75.98
16	Qingdao, Shandong	80	77.40	+9.15	68.24
17	Urumqi, Xinjiang	68	77.01	+3.55	73.46
18	Fuyang, Anhui	62	76.49	+1.85	74.65

(continued)

Province	Number of cities with PPP model	Total number of cities	Province	Number of cities with PPP model	Total number of cities
Xinjiang	14	14	Liaoning	15	15
Shaanxi	13	13	Qinghai	6	8
Jiangsu	13	13	Heilongjiang	12	13
Xizang	2	7			

Some cities have mature PPP markets, while others are relatively new to PPP projects. For the purposes of this Report, the Research Group selected the cities that have introduced a large number of PPP projects for analysis. Specifically, 53 cities were selected as samples for analysis of municipal PPP market transparency. They were cities above the prefecture level with more than 50 projects registered in the PPP Integrated Information Platform as of December 31, 2021. For the results of the PPP Market Transparency Index in cities above the prefecture level with more than 30 projects, please see Appendix IV. The 53 cities are: Dongguan of Guangdong, Ganzhou of Jiangxi, Zunyi of Guizhou, Weifang of Shandong, Nanjing of Jiangsu, Nanyang of Henan, Wenzhou of Zhejiang, Bijie of Guizhou, Qingdao of Shandong, Jining of Shandong, Xi'an of Shaanxi, Wuhan of Hubei, Zhumadian of Henan, Ningde of Fujian, Zhengzhou of Henan, Linyi of Shandong, Urumchi of Xinjiang, Hangzhou of Zhejiang, Yichun of Jiangxi, Quanzhou of Fujian, Xinyang of Henan, Linfen of Shanxi, Heze of Shandong, Yibin of Sichuan, Luoyang of Henan, Shangrao of Jiangxi, Taizhou of Zhejiang, Bayingol of Xinjiang, Pingdingshan of Henan, Fuyang of Anhui, Aksu of Xinjiang, Lishui of Zhejiang, Zhangzhou of Fujian, Kunming of Yunnan, Chengdu of Sichuan, Chengde of Hebei, Jinan of Shandong, Fuzhou of Fujian, Guiyang of Guizhou, Tangshan of Hebei, Dalian of Liaoning, Rizhao of Shandong, Jinzhong of Shanxi, Yuxi of Yunnan, Chifeng of Inner Mongolia, Qiandongnan of Guizhou, Nanning of Guangxi, Qiannan of Guizhou, Xuzhou of Jiangsu, Cangzhou of Hebei, Qianxinan of Guizhou, Lvliang of Shanxi and Zhoukou of Henan.

5.2 Municipal PPP Market Transparency Index

5.2.1 Municipal Ranking

Of the 53 cities selected, all of which could be described as relatively mature PPP

5.1 Municipal Distribution of PPP Projects

Drawing on the same methodology for comparative analysis of the PPP market transparency indexes at national level and at provincial level in Chapter 3 and Chapter 4, this Chapter presents some analysis on the transparency of the PPP market in some cities with a large number of PPP projects. In the 338 prefecture-level cities (autonomous prefecture, prefecture, league, etc., are all defined as "city" hereinafter), 328 cities have introduced the PPP model (see Table 5–1). The PPP model is far-reaching, especially in 22 provinces, that is, Guangdong, Shandong, Henan, Xinjiang, Anhui, Yunnan, Liaoning, Hunan, Guangxi, Jiangsu, Hubei, Inner Mongolia, Hebei, Shanxi, Zhejiang, Jiangxi, Shaanxi, Jilin, Sichuan, Fujian, Guizhou and Ningxia, where PPP projects have covered all prefecture-level cities.

Table 5–1 Number of Cities with PPP Model in Each Province

Province	Number of cities with PPP model	Total number of cities	Province	Number of cities with PPP model	Total number of cities
Yunnan	16	16	Jiangxi	11	11
Inner Mongolia	12	12	Hebei	11	11
Jilin	9	9	Henan	17	17
Sichuan	21	21	Zhejiang	11	11
Ningxia	5	5	Hainan	4	4
Anhui	16	16	Hubei	13	13
Shandong	16	17	Hunan	14	14
Shanxi	11	11	Gansu	13	14
Guangdong	21	21	Fujian	10	10
Guangxi	14	14	Guizhou	10	10

(continued)

5

Municipal Rankings and Analysis

Ranking	Transparency index of disclosure in due time	Value-for-money assessment	Financial affordability assessment	Implementation program
26	Chongqing	Liaoning	Hainan	Inner Mongolia
27	XPCC	Hainan	Inner Mongolia	XPCC
28	Beijing	Inner Mongolia	Ningxia	Chongqing
29	Shanghai	Ningxia	Liaoning	Beijing
30	Hainan	XPCC	XPCC	Hainan
31	Ningxia	Shanghai	Shanghai	Ningxia

In the future, the Research Group will consider carrying out a number of special assessments to check not only whether these key fields or core PDF files are disclosed, but also the quality of these reports, with an aim to further promote the standardization and transparency of PPP projects.

Table 4-6 Provincial Transparency Rankings of "Two Assessments and One Program"

Ranking	Transparency index of disclosure in due time	Value-for-money assessment	Financial affordability assessment	Implementation program
1	Yunnan	Qinghai	Qinghai	Yunnan
2	Hebei	Yunnan	Yunnan	Hebei
3	Shandong	Hebei	Jilin	Shandong
4	Guangxi	Jilin	Hebei	Sichuan
5	Gansu	Shandong	Tianjin	Zhejiang
6	Xinjiang	Sichuan	Fujian	Shanghai
7	Jilin	Zhejiang	Guangdong	Qinghai
8	Sichuan	Guangdong	Shandong	Jilin
9	Zhejiang	Fujian	Jiangxi	Liaoning
10	Tianjin	Jiangxi	Henan	Guangdong
11	Qinghai	Tianjin	Sichuan	Fujian
12	Henan	Guangxi	Zhejiang	Tianjin
13	Jiangsu	Henan	Guangxi	Heilongjiang
14	Hunan	Shaanxi	Gansu	Anhui
15	Guangdong	Xinjiang	Shanxi	Hubei
16	Heilongjiang	Shanxi	Xinjiang	Guangxi
17	Shanxi	Gansu	Shaanxi	Henan
18	Anhui	Jiangsu	Hubei	Shanxi
19	Jiangxi	Guizhou	Jiangsu	Jiangsu
20	Shaanxi	Chongqing	Chongqing	Xinjiang
21	Fujian	Hubei	Anhui	Hunan
22	Liaoning	Beijing	Guizhou	Jiangxi
23	Hubei	Anhui	Heilongjiang	Shaanxi
24	Inner Mongolia	Heilongjiang	Hunan	Gansu
25	Guizhou	Hunan	Beijing	Guizhou

(continued)

and the finance industry at the same level", the "financial affordability report and approval documents by the finance department at the same level" and "attachments to implementation program". The "Two Assessments and One Program" takes a very important position at the identification and preparation stages of a PPP project, and is also an indispensable step in the normal operation of PPP projects in China, enough to determine whether a PPP project can be implemented smoothly or not. Accordingly, this section briefly summarizes the disclosure of these key reports in all provinces.

The "Two Assessments and One Program" documents contain extensive and complex information, prepared in PDF files and published on the website. It is not unusual for the PDF files to extend to tens or even hundreds of pages for the public to review. Three PDF files were subject to the Research Group's manual reading and checking — "value for money", "financial affordability", "implementation program". Table 4-6 shows the provincial rankings of the scores of the three PDF files. It shows that the rankings are highly consistent with that of disclosure in due time index. For example, Yunnan took the first place in "attachments to implementation program", the second place in "value-for-money assessment report and approval documents by the competent industry authority and the finance industry at the same level", and the second place in the "financial affordability report and approval documents by the finance department at the same level". The province's excellent performance in the three indicators earned it the first place in the disclosure in due time index. Ningxia ranked the last in the same ranking, mainly attributable to its low score in the disclosure of the three documents. Therefore, the city should dedicate more efforts to this aspect. Qinghai took the first place in the ranking of "value-for-money assessment report and approval documents by the competent industry authority and the finance industry at the same level" and "financial affordability report and approval documents by the finance department at the same level", but due to its low scores in "attachments to implementation program", its general index of disclosure in due time ranked No.11 only. Hebei performed well in "Two Assessments and One Program", ranking among top four in all three documents, so it retained its second place in the overall ranking of disclosure in due time index. Shandong, Guangxi and Gansu delivered a mixed performance in "Two Assessments and One Program", making them rank from No.3 to No.5 in the general list.

with expectations as the more detailed information at the identification and preparation stages is likely to determine if a PPP project progresses, and is often more valued by the regulatory authorities and social participants, hence resulting in the higher corresponding indexes.

Figure 4–5 shows the indexes of provincial units at various stages of disclosure in due time. Unlike the case in immediate disclosure, the information disclosure in due time at identification stage does not appear to be as comprehensive as in preparation and procurement stages. This may be attributed to the identification stage requiring two important PDF files, namely the "Two Assessments" (value-for-money assessment and financial affordability assessment). The Research Group strictly reviewed the two files, and there were many projects with no disclosure or false disclosure, consequently contributing to a generally low index of each province at this stage.

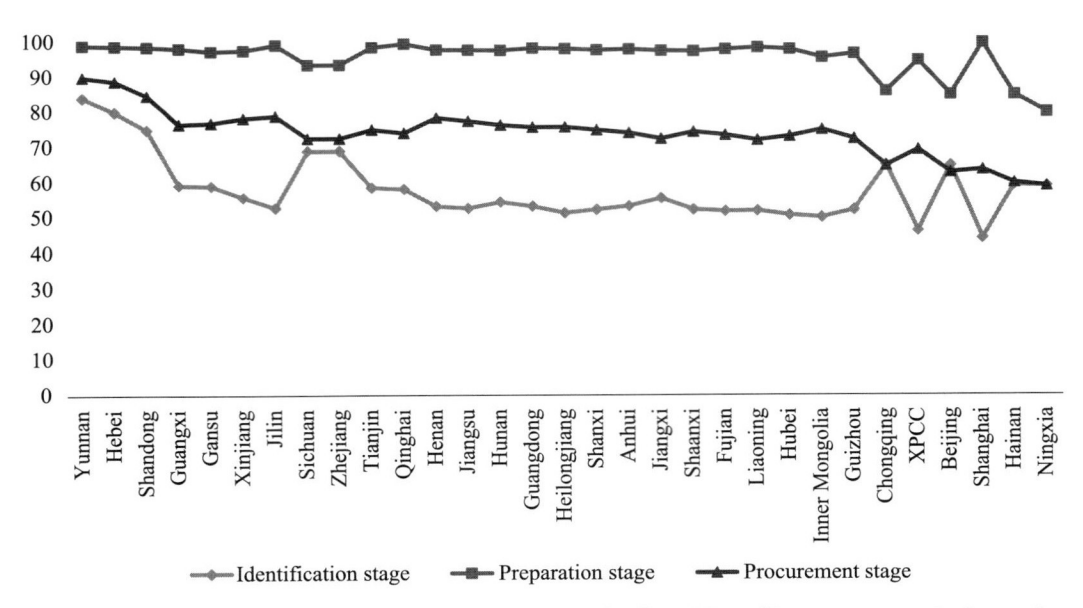

Figure 4–5 Provincial Distribution of Disclosure in Due Time Transparency Indexes by Stage in 2021

4.3 Analysis on Provincial Transparency Indexes of "Two Assessments and One Program"

The "Two Assessments and One Program" refer to the "value-for-money assessment report and approval documents by the competent industry authority

Ranking	Transparency index of disclosure in due time	Identification stage	Preparation stage	Procurement stage
26	Chongqing	Fujian	Sichuan	XPCC
27	XPCC	Heilongjiang	Zhejiang	Chongqing
28	Beijing	Hubei	Chongqing	Shanghai
29	Shanghai	Inner Mongolia	Beijing	Beijing
30	Hainan	XPCC	Hainan	Hainan
31	Ningxia	Shanghai	Ningxia	Ningxia

The last five on the list were occupied by Ningxia, Hainan, Shanghai, Beijing, and XPCC. According to Table 4–3, Beijing, Shanghai, Ningxia and Hainan also performed poorly in immediate disclosure (see the previous analysis), ranking among the last on the list. It indicates that their PPP information disclosure approaches are in need of improvement.

Figure 4–4 consolidates the indexes of provincial units at each stage of immediate disclosure and disclosure in due time. The comparison highlights that the disclosure of information at identification and preparation stages was more complete, while the indexes at procurement and implementation stages were generally lower. Such results are basically in line

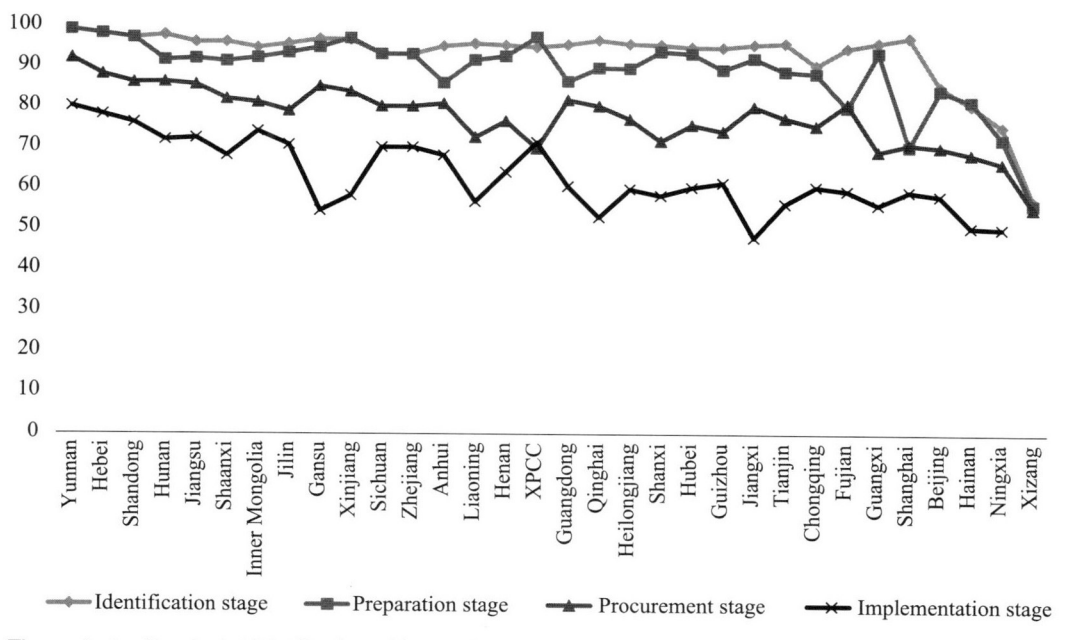

Figure 4–4　Provincial Distribution of Immediate Disclosure Transparency Indexes by Stage in 2021

4 Provincial Rankings and Analysis | 69

Table 4–5 Provincial Rankings of Disclosure in Due Time Index and Sub-index at Each Stage in 2021

Ranking	Transparency index of disclosure in due time	Identification stage	Preparation stage	Procurement stage
1	Yunnan	Yunnan	Shanghai	Yunnan
2	Hebei	Hebei	Qinghai	Hebei
3	Shandong	Shandong	Jilin	Shandong
4	Guangxi	Sichuan	Yunnan	Jilin
5	Gansu	Zhejiang	Hebei	Henan
6	Xinjiang	Chongqing	Shandong	Xinjiang
7	Jilin	Beijing	Liaoning	Jiangsu
8	Sichuan	Guangxi	Tianjin	Gansu
9	Zhejiang	Hainan	Guangdong	Guangxi
10	Tianjin	Gansu	Heilongjiang	Hunan
11	Qinghai	Ningxia	Guangxi	Heilongjiang
12	Henan	Tianjin	Fujian	Guangdong
13	Jiangsu	Qinghai	Anhui	Inner Mongolia
14	Hunan	Xinjiang	Hubei	Tianjin
15	Guangdong	Jiangxi	Shanxi	Shanxi
16	Heilongjiang	Hunan	Henan	Shaanxi
17	Shanxi	Anhui	Jiangsu	Anhui
18	Anhui	Henan	Hunan	Qinghai
19	Jiangxi	Guangdong	Jiangxi	Fujian
20	Shaanxi	Jilin	Xinjiang	Hubei
21	Fujian	Jiangsu	Shaanxi	Sichuan
22	Liaoning	Shanxi	Gansu	Zhejiang
23	Hubei	Shaanxi	Guizhou	Guizhou
24	Inner Mongolia	Guizhou	Inner Mongolia	Jiangxi
25	Guizhou	Liaoning	XPCC	Liaoning

(continued)

Province	Total quantity	Preparation stage	Procurement stage	Implementation stage
Hunan	363	4	33	326
Liaoning	280	42	126	112
Shaanxi	275	13	57	205
Inner Mongolia	274	12	41	221
Jilin	165	14	28	123
Gansu	148	3	32	113
Heilongjiang	127	6	40	81
Hainan	98	5	14	79
Beijing	77	1	5	71
Chongqing	75	2	28	45
Tianjin	71	2	11	58
Ningxia	47	2	6	39
Qinghai	42	2	11	29
XPCC	18	2	6	10
Shanghai	7	0	4	3
Xizang	3	1	2	0

4.2.2 Disclosure in Due Time

Table 4–5 shows the list of the top 10 provinces for the 2021 PPP project disclosure in due time index and sub-indexes at each stage. Hebei and Yunnan performed well at all stages. In particular, Hebei ranked second at both identification and procurement stages. Thanks to its outstanding performance in the identification stage, Shandong ranked No.3 in the disclosure in due time index ranking. Since the information disclosure in procurement stage was of the highest importance (according to the calculation results of the expert decision matrix, the weight of procurement stage was 0.45), Hebei and Yunnan occupied the first and second places in terms of disclosure in due time with a high score in procurement stage.

methods in Chapter 3, whereby the procurement and implementation stage weighting were "consolidated" into the preparation and identification stages. If a province does not have many PPP projects at preparation stage, its slight inadequacies at procurement and implementation stages may adversely affect the final general transparency index. For better clarification, Table 4–4 shows the distribution of PPP projects by stage in each province. It is easy to find out that Jiangsu had a significantly higher proportion of projects at the preparation stage than Gansu. It should also be noted that the purpose of highlighting the distribution difference in stages is to explain the results and possible reasons. It does not imply project companies should deliberately slow down the progress of PPP projects to raise the index.

Table 4–4 Quantity of PPP Projects by Stage in Each Province in 2021

Province	Total quantity	Preparation stage	Procurement stage	Implementation stage
Henan	841	71	239	531
Shandong	768	30	135	603
Guizhou	576	65	169	342
Sichuan	560	10	98	452
Guangdong	560	21	71	468
Zhejiang	513	13	49	451
Jiangxi	495	22	59	414
Anhui	488	12	39	437
Yunnan	485	14	91	380
Hebei	458	18	86	354
Shanxi	447	53	170	224
Hubei	436	30	116	290
Xinjiang	403	12	33	358
Jiangsu	392	10	57	325
Guangxi	379	20	145	214
Fujian	368	12	31	325

(continued)

Ranking	Transparency index of immediate disclosure	Identification stage	Preparation stage	Procurement stage	Implementation stage
26	Fujian	Sichuan	Anhui	Shanghai	Guangxi
27	Guangxi	Zhejiang	Beijing	Beijing	Gansu
28	Shanghai	Chongqing	Hainan	XPCC	Qinghai
29	Beijing	Beijing	Fujian	Guangxi	Hainan
30	Hainan	Hainan	Ningxia	Hainan	Ningxia
31	Ningxia	Fujian	Shanghai	Ningxia	Jiangxi
32	Xizang	Xizang	Xizang	Xizang	Xizang

  Yunnan, Hebei and Shandong performed well and consistently across all stages. Yunnan and Hebei ranked high in all the stages of identification, preparation, procurement and implementation, which earned them No.1 and No.2 in the general ranking of immediate disclosure index. Hunan delivered desirable results in the identification, procurement and implementation stages, but ranked No.18 in the preparation stage, resulting in its sixth place in the overall ranking. Better disclosure at the preparation stage is expected to improve the province's overall ranking. Xinjiang ranked high in the identification, preparation and procurement phases, but its poorer performance in the execution stage lowered its place in the general immediate disclosure index ranking.

  Xizang, Ningxia, Hainan, Beijing, and Shanghai occupied the last five places in the ranking. In particular, Shanghai ranked No.4 in the identification stage, but its poor performance during other stages lowered its overall ranking. Yunnan came in first in all the four stages, which led to its ranking at the top of the list.

  Jiangsu did not rank high in any stage, but it eventually occupied the fifth place in the overall ranking of immediate disclosure index. In contrast, Gansu ranked higher than Jiangsu in the identification, procurement, and execution stages, but it fell behind the latter in the general ranking. This implies the impact of the distribution of PPP projects in different stages on the final results. Where a province has a higher percentage of PPP projects in preparation stage and does a good job in disclosure, then the province can easily achieve a high score. This is partly due to the calculation

Table 4–3   Provincial Rankings of Immediate Disclosure Index and Sub-index at Each Stage in 2021

Ranking	Transparency index of immediate disclosure	Identification stage	Preparation stage	Procurement stage	Implementation stage
1	Yunnan	Yunnan	Yunnan	Yunnan	Yunnan
2	Hebei	Hebei	Hebei	Hebei	Hebei
3	Shandong	Hunan	XPCC	Hunan	Shandong
4	Hunan	Shanghai	Shandong	Shandong	Inner Mongolia
5	Jiangsu	Shandong	Xinjiang	Jiangsu	Jiangsu
6	Shaanxi	Gansu	Gansu	Gansu	Hunan
7	Inner Mongolia	Xinjiang	Shanxi	Xinjiang	XPCC
8	Jilin	Qinghai	Guangxi	Shaanxi	Jilin
9	Gansu	Shaanxi	Jilin	Guangdong	Sichuan
10	Xinjiang	Jiangsu	Hubei	Inner Mongolia	Zhejiang
11	Sichuan	Guangxi	Sichuan	Anhui	Anhui
12	Zhejiang	Tianjin	Zhejiang	Fujian	Shaanxi
13	Anhui	Jilin	Henan	Qinghai	Henan
14	Liaoning	Liaoning	Inner Mongolia	Sichuan	Guizhou
15	Henan	Heilongjiang	Jiangxi	Jiangxi	Guangdong
16	XPCC	Jiangxi	Jiangsu	Jilin	Chongqing
17	Guangdong	Guangdong	Liaoning	Tianjin	Hubei
18	Qinghai	Shanxi	Hunan	Heilongjiang	Heilongjiang
19	Heilongjiang	Henan	Shaanxi	Zhejiang	Fujian
20	Shanxi	Anhui	Qinghai	Henan	Shanghai
21	Hubei	XPCC	Heilongjiang	Hubei	Xinjiang
22	Guizhou	Hubei	Guizhou	Chongqing	Shanxi
23	Jiangxi	Inner Mongolia	Tianjin	Guizhou	Beijing
24	Tianjin	Guizhou	Chongqing	Liaoning	Liaoning
25	Chongqing	Fujian	Guangdong	Shanxi	Tianjin

(continued)

Ranking	Transparency index of immediate disclosure in 2021	Variance from 2020	Transparency index of disclosure in due time in 2021	Variance from 2020
9	Gansu	+2	Zhejiang	+15
10	Xinjiang	0	Tianjin	+9
11	Sichuan	+4	Qinghai	−3
12	Zhejiang	+9	Henan	−6
13	Anhui	−1	Jiangsu	−3
14	Liaoning	−1	Hunan	−2
15	Henan	−1	Guangdong	−4
16	Xinjiang	+4	Heilongjiang	−3
17	Guangdong	−1	Shanxi	−1
18	Qinghai	−1	Anhui	−4
19	Heilongjiang	+5	Jiangxi	+2
20	Shanxi	−1	Shaanxi	−5
21	Hubei	−3	Fujian	−3
22	Guizhou	+1	Liaoning	+3
23	Jiangxi	+4	Hubei	−3
24	Tianjin	+1	Inner Mongolia	−2
25	Chongqing	−3	Guizhou	−2
26	Fujian	0	Chongqing	+1
27	Guangxi	+3	XPCC	−1
28	Shanghai	+3	Beijing	0
29	Beijing	0	Shanghai	0
30	Hainan	+2	Hainan	0
31	Ningxia	−3	Ningxia	0
32	Xizang	−31		

Table 4–3 shows the provincial rankings of 2021 PPP project immediate disclosure index, and the sub-indexes of all stages in immediate disclosure.

4.2 Analysis on Provincial Index by Stage

4.2.1 Immediate Disclosure

The following is the analysis over the results of information disclosure by provinces in each stage of immediate disclosure and disclosure in due time. Table 4–2 shows the provincial rankings of 2021 PPP project immediate disclosure index and disclosure in due time index, as well as the variance from the previous year. As for immediate disclosure, Yunnan, Hebei, Shandong, Hunan and Jiangsu ranked as top five, while Xizang, Ningxia, Hainan, Beijing and Shanghai were in the last five places. Zhejiang presented the largest surge in the provincial ranking of immediate disclosure index, leaping from No.21 in 2020 to No.9 in 2021. The province recording the most significant decline were Xizang, dropping by 31 places from the previous year to No.32. As for disclosure in due time, Yunnan, Hebei, Shandong, Guangxi and Gansu ranked as top five, while Ningxia, Hainan, Shanghai, Beijing and XPCC were in the last five places. Zhejiang showed the largest rise in the provincial ranking of disclosure in due time index, from No.24 in 2020 to No.9 in 2021. Henan recorded the most significant decline of 6 places from the previous year to No.12.

Table 4–2 Provincial Rankings of Immediate Disclosure Index and Disclosure in Due Time Index

Ranking	Transparency index of immediate disclosure in 2021	Variance from 2020	Transparency index of disclosure in due time in 2021	Variance from 2020
1	Yunnan	+1	Yunnan	+1
2	Hebei	+4	Hebei	−1
3	Shandong	+1	Shandong	+2
4	Hunan	−1	Guangxi	+3
5	Jiangsu	0	Gansu	+4
6	Shaanxi	+1	Xinjiang	−2
7	Inner Mongolia	+1	Jilin	−4
8	Jilin	+1	Sichuan	+9

(continued)

rationale is that some provinces manage larger numbers of PPP projects, which may increase the difficulty in supervision and information disclosure, which in turn may result in a lower PPP transparency index. Therefore, in order to examine the relationship between the quantity of PPP projects managed in each region and its PPP market transparency, Figure 4–3 maps provincial PPP transparency indexes and project quantities. It indicates that the quantity of PPP projects does not have a significant negative relationship with the provincial PPP market transparency index, but instead shows certain positive correlation. In the statistical sense, the speculation that "a region is managing too many PPP projects, so it scores low in the information transparency" does not seem to hold true.

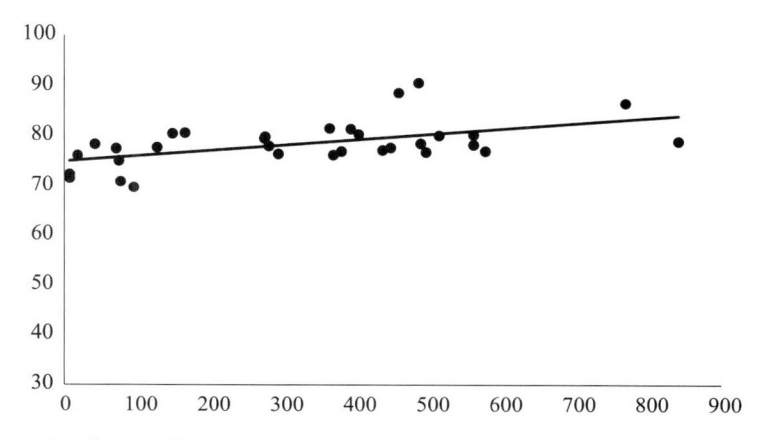

Figure 4–3 Scatter Diagram of Provincial PPP Project Quantity and PPP Market Transparency Index

Another doubt is that for the provinces with few PPP projects, which is deemed statistically insignificant, whether it is necessary to include them in the national ranking. In this Report, no provincial-level units with too few projects were deleted. Instead, all were included in the rankings in order to thoroughly and objectively reflect the PPP information disclosure work done by all provinces. This is because it is hard to define a scope for sample size, for which different readers might have different standards. Instead, they're free to intentionally omit the provinces they believe are operating few projects, and such omission doesn't affect the relative rankings of other provinces. Apart from that, it is also worthy of probing why the number of projects in a region is positively correlated with the region's PPP market transparency index. One possible reason is that in regions with a large number of PPP projects, their competent authorities tend to arrange more management personnel or dedicated persons in charge.

disclosure is higher than that for disclosure in due time (0.61 versus 0.39), it is more likely for the provinces that perform better in immediate disclosure to rank higher in the list of general index. For example, excluding Xizang, the top five provinces with the highest immediate disclosure index were also the top five in the ranking of general index. However, there still existed some differences in the provincial rankings of disclosure in due time index and immediate disclosure index. The No.4 in the ranking of immediate disclosure index Hunan ranked No.14 in terms of disclosure in due time, indicating that the province did do well in immediate disclosure, but less desirable in disclosure in due time. Another example is Hainan, which ranked last in terms of immediate disclosure, and the second from bottom in disclosure in due time, indicating that the province needs to put more efforts on both categories of disclosure. The gap between the two lists further indicates that each region has its own advantages and disadvantages in disclosing the information of PPP projects, and it is necessary for them to learn from each other, so that the overall transparency of PPP projects will come to a higher stage.

Comparison between the data in 2021 and 2020 shows no obvious trends of cross-phase changes in both immediate disclosure and disclosure in due time indexes. That is, all provinces delivered a steady performance with slight changes in terms of PPP project information disclosure. As for immediate disclosure, there are 17 provinces showing increase in index and 15 decline. Concerning the immediate disclosure index, the largest improvement came from Ningxia, the score of which climbed from 66.33 in 2020 to 88.14 in 2021, followed by Gansu, Jiangsu and Hunan; while the largest drop was delivered by Anhui, from 82.31 in 2020 to 78.42 in 2021. As for disclosure in due time, there are 27 provinces showing increase and 4 decrease. The largest increase in the disclosure in due time index was in Ningxia, rising from 62.45 in 2020 to 67.82 in 2021. Tianjin recorded the smallest increase in the same category, from 74.30 in 2020 to 74.54 in 2021, representing a growth of 0.24 points only. The disclosure in due time index decreased the most in Yunnan, from 86.80 in 2020 to 79.267 in 2021. On the whole, the transparency index of disclosure in due time in most provinces showed an upward trend, indicating the increasing effort in management.

4.1.3 Relationship between Transparency Index and Project Quantity

During index compilation, some experts and representatives from local finance departments suggested quantitative factors should also be taken into consideration. The

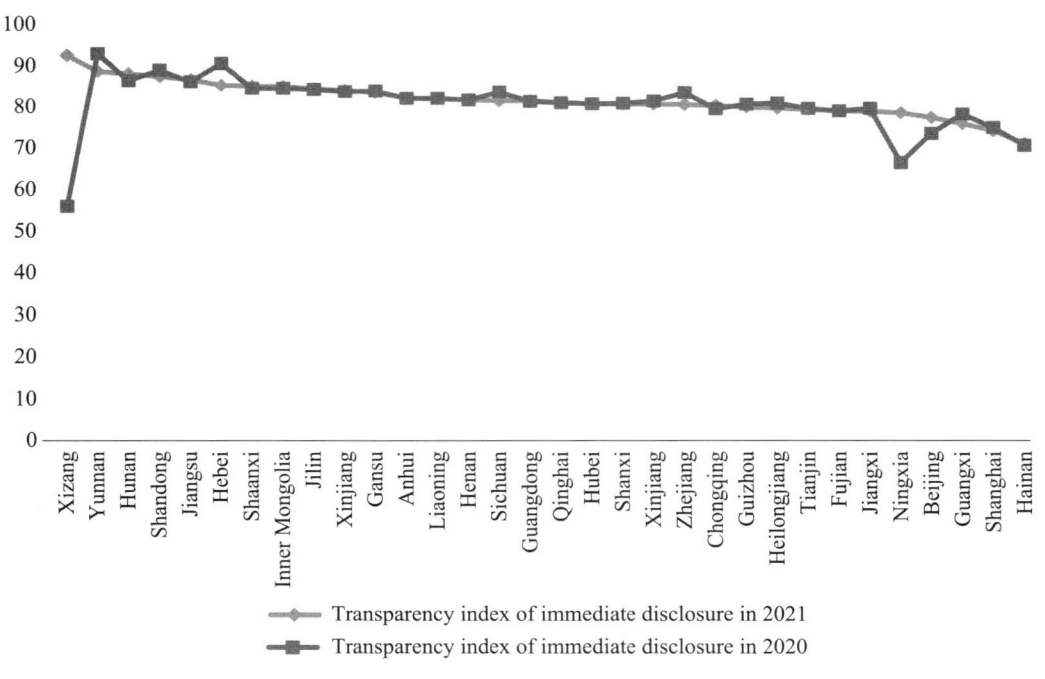

Figure 4-1   PPP Immediate Disclosure Index in 2020 and 2021 by Province

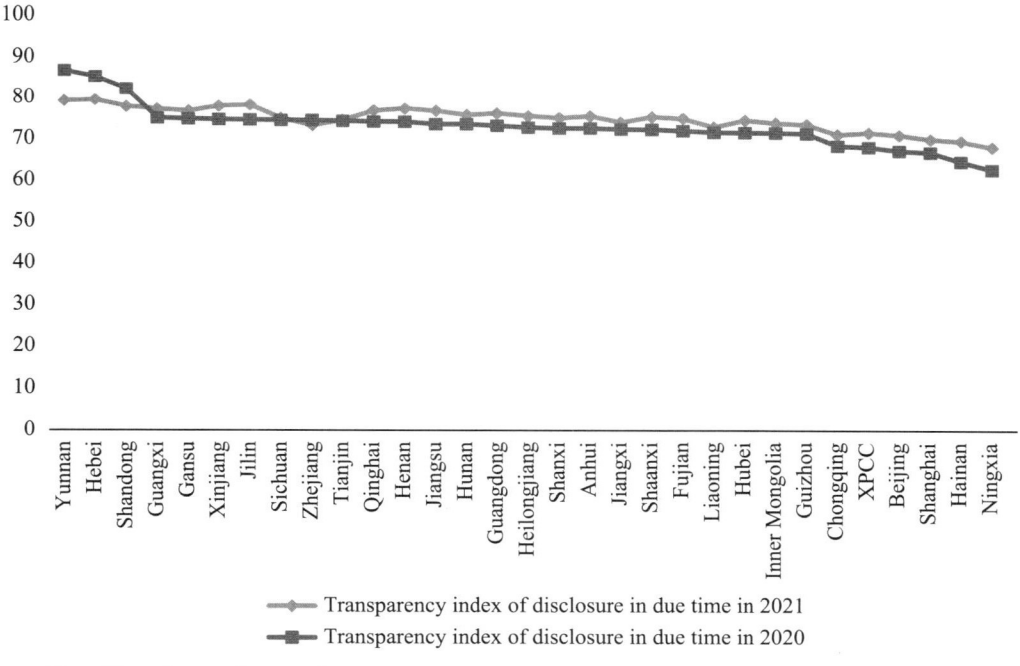

Note: Note: Among them, as there were no projects subject to disclosure in due time in Xizang, Xizang did not participate in the corresponding ranking.

Figure 4-2   PPP Disclosure in Due Time Index in 2020 and 2021 by Province

Province	Year 2021 Project quantity	Year 2021 Transparency index	Ranking in 2021	Variance from last year	Year 2020 Project quantity	Year 2020 Transparency index
Liaoning	273	77.97	17	0	406	78.22
Heilongjiang	125	77.67	18	+1	293	78.17
Shanxi	441	77.60	19	−3	103	78.47
Tianjin	71	77.48	20	+1	55	77.45
Hubei	435	77.11	21	−3	419	78.22
Guizhou	571	76.90	22	+1	507	77.17
Guangxi	372	76.89	23	+4	57	76.40
Jiangxi	484	76.70	24	+1	529	76.91
Fujian	368	76.15	25	−3	241	77.35
XPCC	18	76.13	26	−2	418	77.05
Chongqing	73	75.05	27	−1	16	76.56
Shanghai	7	71.60	28	+2	7	72.40
Beijing	77	70.92	29	−1	69	74.73
Hainan	98	68.16	30	+1	95	69.76
Ningxia	46	64.82	31	−2	43	73.83
Xizang	3	56.02	32	0	3	56.45

Notes: ① The projects contained in this table refer to the 10 175 PPP projects subject to immediate disclosure. The 7 598 PPP projects subject to disclosure in due time are a subset of it; ② "+" indicates rise in ranking, and "−" indicates drop in ranking, the same below.

4.1.2 Provincial Rankings of Immediate Disclosure and Disclosure in Due Time

Figure 4–1 and Figure 4–2 show the distribution of immediate disclosure indexes and disclosure in due time indexes of all provinces in 2020 and 2021. The results show:

First, disclosure in due time index of each province was generally higher than the immediate disclosure index. This finding is consistent with that in Chapter 3, which implies again that all provinces have done a poorer job in immediate disclosure than in disclosure in due time on PPP projects.

Second, while the provincial rankings of general transparency index, disclosure in due time index, and immediate disclosure index were generally consistent, it is important to qualify the impact of weightings on the results. As the weight allocated for immediate relatively poorly, occupying the last five places in the ranking. Comparing with the 2020 ranking, we found that the province that made the greatest progress in PPP project information disclosure was Zhejiang Province (79.94), rising by 10 places from the previous year to be among the top 10 in 2021. The provinces with a large decline in the ranking include Shaanxi, Inner Mongolia, Guangdong, Shanxi, Hubei, and Fujian, all of which dropped by 3 places. Their indexes decreased from 81.25, 80.61, 79.30, 78.47, 78.22 and 77.35 in 2020 to 79.78, 79.46, 78.15, 77.60, 77.11 and 76.15 in 2020, respectively. Despite the minor decline, due to the small index gap between provinces, these provinces ranked only No.11, No.12, No.16, No.21 and No.25 in 2021. Prominently, provinces such as Sichuan, Guangxi and Gansu ascended in the ranking compared with the previous year.

Table 4–1 Provincial PPP Market Transparency Index and Ranking in 2021

Province	Year 2021 Project quantity	Year 2021 Transparency index	Ranking in 2021	Variance from last year	Year 2020 Project quantity	Year 2020 Transparency index
Yunnan	485	90.55	1	0	495	84.98
Hebei	455	88.54	2	+1	734	82.99
Shandong	760	86.39	3	−1	434	83.72
Hunan	363	81.43	4	0	160	82.69
Jiangsu	392	81.27	5	0	386	82.63
Jilin	165	80.54	6	0	376	81.82
Gansu	145	80.39	7	+3	786	80.52
Xinjiang	402	80.24	8	−1	389	81.71
Sichuan	559	80.07	9	+6	552	78.99
Zhejiang	513	79.94	10	+10	359	77.60
Shaanxi	275	79.78	11	−3	278	81.25
Inner Mongolia	274	79.46	12	−3	123	80.61
Henan	838	78.76	13	−2	42	79.91
Anhui	487	78.39	14	−2	474	79.65
Qinghai	42	78.29	15	−1	262	79.22
Guangdong	559	78.15	16	−3	551	79.30

(continued)

4.1 Analysis on General Provincial Index

4.1.1 Provincial Ranking

The previous Chapter provides the 2021 national PPP market transparency index, while this Chapter will focus on provincial results. The calculation of the transparency index for each province was based on arithmetic average of the immediate disclosure index and the disclosure in time index for each province and multiplied by the weightings outlined in Chapter 2. (Based on the findings outlined in Chapter 2, the weight of immediate disclosure was 0.61, and the weight of disclosure in due time was 0.39). Table 4–1 shows the number of PPP projects and the transparency indexes of the 32 provincial-level units (provinces, municipalities, autonomous regions, and Xinjiang Production and Construction Corps, the same below) in 2021. From it the Research Group have come up with the following conclusions:

First, in 2021 the overall PPP market information transparency index at the provincial level rose steadily from 2020. The transparency index of most provinces was above 70, including 9 provinces with an index of over 80. In particular, Yunnan Province obtained more than 90 points — the first time for a provincial PPP market transparency index to reach 90 over the past five years since the Research Group started this project.

Second, compared with 2020, provincial PPP market transparency indexes were further differentiated. The transparency indexes of the top three provinces and the following provinces clearly demonstrated divergent trends: in 2021, most provinces scored similarly — if not slightly lower — compared with 2020. However, the top three provinces' scores increased by about 3~5 points, gradually expanding the gap with the rest.

Third, in specific, the top five in transparency ranking were Yunnan Province (90.55), Hebei Province (88.54), Shandong Province (86.39), Hunan Province (81.43) and Jiangsu Province (81.27). Xizang, Ningxia, Hainan, Beijing, and Shanghai performed

4

Provincial Rankings and Analysis

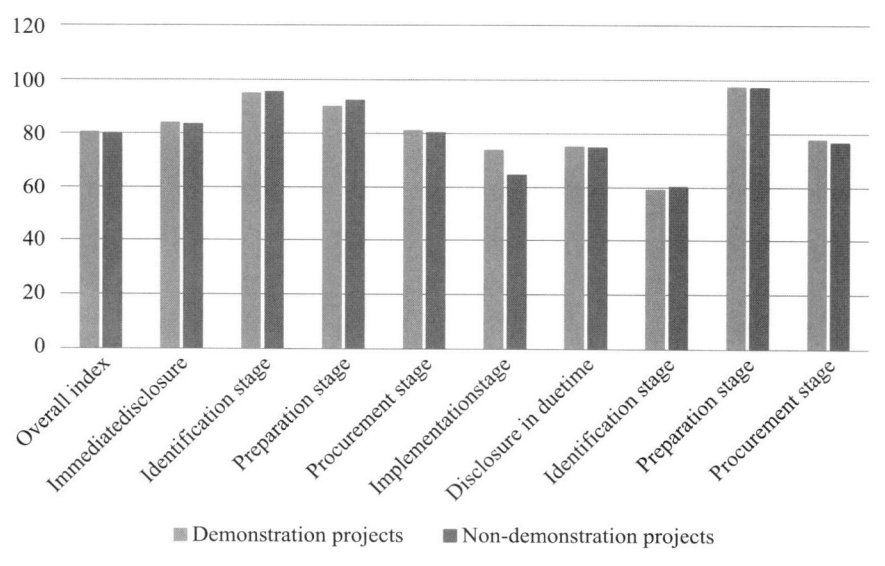

3.3.2 Transparency Indexes of Demonstration Projects and Non-demonstration Projects

As for demonstration and non-demonstration projects, as shown by Figure 3–5, the index gap between demonstration projects and non-demonstration ones in 2021 was not significant, with the general index of the former slightly higher than that of the latter. This conclusion is similar to those reached in previous reports. According to the evaluation results in the past three years, the overall index of demonstration projects increased from 77.19 in 2019 to 78.9 in 2020, and then to 79.92 in 2021 — indicating a moderate growth rate; likewise, the overall index of non-demonstration projects grew from 76.01 in 2019 to 78.23 in 2020, and then 80.34 in 2021 — a minor increase as well. This indicates that the variable "whether it is a demonstration project", as time goes by, is increasingly ungrounded to justify the difference in transparency indexes between projects.

Figure 3–5 Transparency Indexes of Demonstration Projects and Non-demonstration Projects in 2021

3.3.1 PPP Transparency Index by Sector

Let's first take a look at the PPP market transparency indexes in different industries. Figure 3–4 examines the PPP market transparency by sector. Although some differences were noted, they were not substantial. The highest transparency index was 81.7 for the water conservancy sector, and the lowest was 78.4 for the social security sector, showing a gap of only 3.3 points. Upon analysis on the immediate disclosure index and the disclosure in due time index by industry, as well as the sub-indexes at different stages, findings are similar. Therefore, generally PPP projects in different sectors showed no significant heterogeneity in information disclosure requirements and practices. It also means the existing rules and regulations for the disclosure of PPP project information are generally applicable to all sectors. Since PPP projects in different sectors are often managed and supervised by authorities with expertise in the respective industries, the above results also indicated that these authorities have managed PPP project information disclosure in a similar manner. Furthermore, Figure 3–4 shows that all the industries made improvement in the transparency index in 2021 compared with 2020.

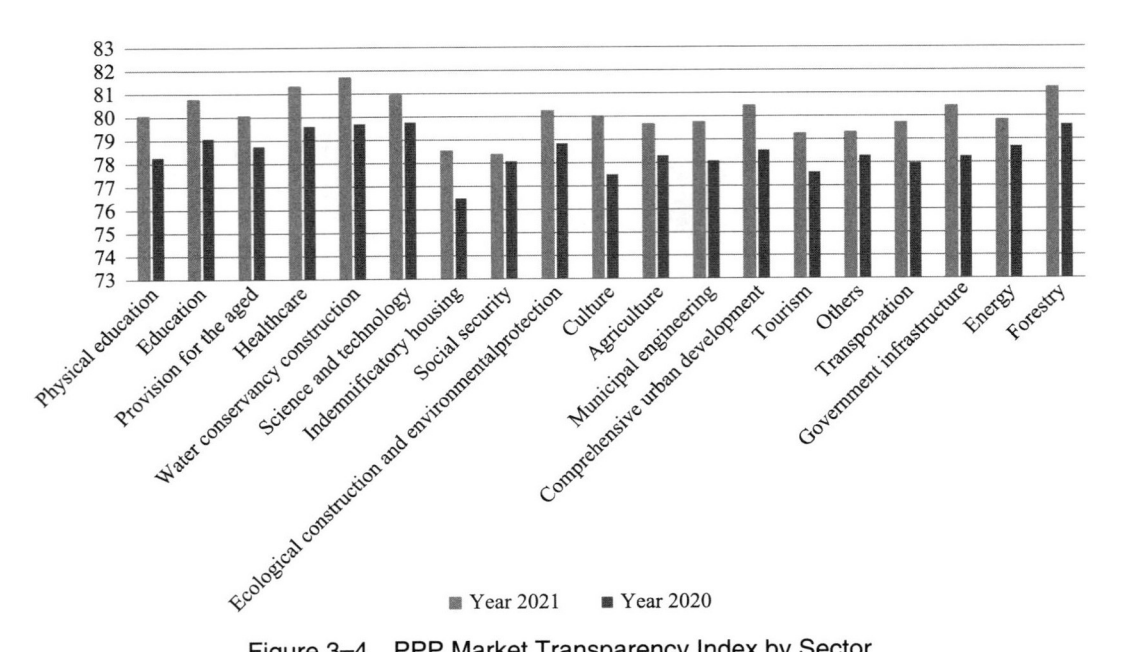

Figure 3–4 PPP Market Transparency Index by Sector

Also the immediate disclosure index and the disclosure in due time index, were synthesized for the national PPP market transparency index based on the weights of immediate disclosure index and disclosure in due time index calculated by AHP. The conclusion is, **by the end of December 2021, the national PPP market transparency index was 80.01 (83.27×0.61+74.90×0.39), slightly higher than 2020 at 78.15. This is also the first time that the national average score has reached 80 since the Research Group started this project.** Figure 3-3 shows the national PPP market transparency index, immediate disclosure index, disclosure in due time index, and the average transparency sub-index by stage.

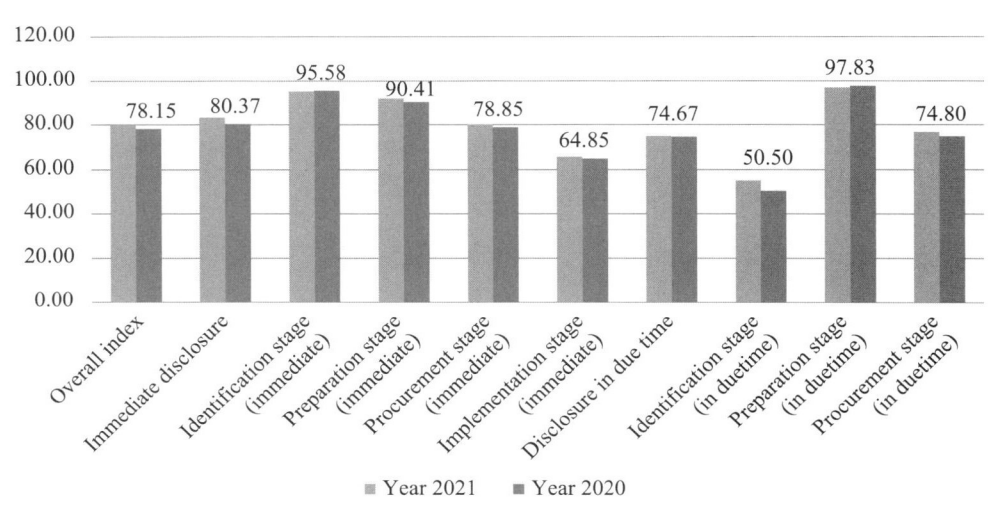

Figure 3-3 National PPP Market Transparency Index and Sub-index by Stage

3.3 Heterogeneity Analysis of National General Index

Based on the analysis above, the national PPP market transparency index was calculated based on the average transparency index of around 10 200 PPP projects across China. As discussed previously, the average transparency may have masked the heterogeneity between individual projects. Therefore, in order to offer a more in-depth and intuitive display of the transparency of the national PPP market, in this section, the analysis needs to focus on different perspectives, such as industry sector, type, etc. A more detailed discussion at the provincial and municipal levels will also be provided in the following two Chapters.

several core reports such as value-for-money assessment report and financial affordability reports. Only after these shortcomings are addressed will the index of disclosure in due time increase greatly. Compared with 2020, information disclosure in due time in the stages of identification, preparation and procurement was slightly better in 2021.

Table 3–4　Disclosure In Due Time Indexes at Different Stages

Stage	Year 2021			
	Minimum value	25 percentile	75 percentile	Maximum value
Identification stage	−51.97	51.97	69.10	100
Preparation stage	0	98.50	100	100
Procurement stage	3.81	72.70	84.80	94.16

Stage	Year 2020			
	Minimum value	25 percentile	75 percentile	Maximum value
Identification stage	−51.97	43.97	54.97	100
Preparation stage	0	100	100	100
Procurement stage	0	70.42	84.78	94.12

3.2.2　General Index

With transparency index at each stage, the Research Group synthesized the immediate disclosure index and disclosure in due time index based on the weights of the sub-index at each stage obtained by AHP as explained in the Chapter 2. Table 3–5 shows the general indexes of immediate disclosure and disclosure in due time. It shows that the mean values of immediate disclosure index and disclosure in due time index were 83.27 and 74.90 respectively. Compared with 2020, the two indicators in 2021 basically remained stable, with slight increase.

Table 3–5　Immediate Disclosure and Disclosure in Due Time Indexes

Index	Year 2021			Year 2020		
	Sample size	Mean value	Standard deviation	Sample size	Mean value	Standard deviation
Transparency index of immediate disclosure	10 175	83.27	10.72	9 962	80.37	8.57
Transparency index of disclosure in due time	7 598	74.90	7.38	5 801	74.67	3.02

Stage	Year 2020			
	Minimum value	25 percentile	75 percentile	Maximum value
Identification stage	66.26	94.27	100	100
Preparation stage	−17.43	83.33	100	100
Procurement stage	0	76.71	88.36	100
Implementation stage	0	53.91	90.43	100

Table 3–3 shows the disclosure in due time sub-indexes at different stages. Out of the 7 598 assessment objects, the average score was 55.13 at the identification stage, 97.15 at the preparation stage, and 76.80 at the procurement stage. Disclosure was poorer at the identification stage relative to the preparation stage. One explanation for this could be that the information required at the identification stage includes value-for-money assessment report, financial affordability assessment report and some other core documents, and a number of projects failed to properly disclose these documents. Comparison of performance in disclosure in due time between 2020 and 2021 shows that the average indexes at the preparation stage in the two years didn't vary much, while the average indexes of both the identification and procurement stages in 2021 were higher than those in 2020.

Table 3–3 Disclosure in Due Time Indexes at Different Stages

Stage	Year 2021			Year 2020		
	Sample size	Mean value	Standard deviation	Sample size	Mean value	Standard deviation
Identification stage	7 598	55.13	14.97	5 801	50.50	13.71
Preparation stage	7 598	97.15	5.66	5 801	97.83	6.86
Procurement stage	7 598	76.80	9.61	5 801	74.80	11.01

Table 3–4 presents the distribution of the transparency indexes of disclosure in due time at each stage, including minimum and maximum values, upper quartile and lower quartile. It shows that in terms of disclosure in due time, most projects did a better job in the preparation and procurement stages than in the identification stage. Therefore, if action is to be taken to improve the overall transparency of PPP projects concerning disclosure in due time, the focus should be on the compliant and complete disclosure of

Table 3-2 shows the distribution of transparency indexes assessed by stage, noting that negative scores are also possible where false or erroneous documents were published, while conversely projects with strong information disclosure has the potential to score 100 points. The Research Group paid attention to these "abnormal" projects and dealt with them specifically, in a bid to urge responsible departments to make up for shortcomings as soon as possible, and promote standardized management of PPP projects. However, we are more concerned with the information disclosure performance of most projects, since it represents the information transparency across the entire PPP market. Therefore, Figure 3-2 also highlights scores at the 75 and 25 percentiles. A comparison of immediate disclosure indexes at different stages between 2021 and 2020 shows: Few differences were seen in immediate disclosure at identification stage between 2020 and 2021, as the 25 and 75 percentiles in 2021 were 94.28 and 97.13, and those in 2020 were 94.27 and 100. As for preparation and procurement stages, the immediate disclosure in 2021 showed a significant improvement compared with 2020, since the 25 percentile of immediate disclosure in preparation and procurement stages in 2021 were 91.67 and 80.10, respectively — higher than the 83.33 and 76.71 in 2020. Finally, at implementation stage, the 25 percentile of immediate disclosure at implementation stage in 2021 was 61.74, which was higher than the 53.91 in 2020, indicating better immediate information disclosure work in the implementation stage. The 75 percentiles of immediate disclosure at the implementation stage in 2021 and 2020 were similar. In general, the conclusions made based on careful examination of the index distribution are basically consistent with the information provided by Table 3-1. Immediate disclosure in the identification and preparation stages in 2021 was slightly better than that in 2020.

Table 3-2 Immediate Disclosure Indexes at Different Stages

Stage	Year 2021			
	Minimum value	25 percentile	75 percentile	Maximum value
Identification stage	57.00	94.28	97.13	100
Preparation stage	−16.67	91.67	100	100
Procurement stage	0	80.10	89.07	100
Implementation stage	0	61.74	88.87	100

(continued)

Then, the total score of disclosure in due time at the identification stage was 16.667 points. Suppose a project was given 1 (complete disclosure), 1 (complete disclosure), 0.5 (partial disclosure), 0.5 (partial disclosure), 0 (no disclosure), and −1 (false disclosure) in the six fields at identification stage, then the project's score at the stage was (1×3+1×3+0.5×2.333+0.5×2.667+0×2.667+(-1)×3)/16.667×100=33. 33 was the sub-index of the project for disclosure in due time. In the same way, the sub-indexes of immediate disclosure and disclosure in due time at each stage were produced.

Table 3-1 summarizes the sub-indexes of immediate disclosure at different stages. Of the 10 175 immediate disclosure samples, the average scores were 95.30 at the identification stage, 92.00 at the preparation stage, 80.24 at the procurement stage, and 65.63 at the implementation stage. The results demonstrate that immediate information disclosure at the identification and preparation stages was generally satisfactory, yet poorer at the procurement and implementation stages. From the perspective of management mechanism, most of the information required to be disclosed at the identification and preparation stages must be submitted before PPP projects are included into the database. Due to the rigorous review by competent authorities for database entry, the indexes were generally higher. While after coming to the procurement and implementation stages, project progress wouldn't be hindered by the failure to upload information to the PPP Integrated Information Platform in time as required. As the information disclosure at these stages was not under proper regulation, lower indexes were seen. Compared with 2020, the indexes at the preparation, procurement and implementation stages all showed increase, while the index at the implementation stage remained roughly the same.

Table 3-1 Immediate Disclosure Indexes at Different Stages

Stage	Year 2021 Sample size	Year 2021 Mean value	Year 2021 Standard deviation	Year 2020 Sample size	Year 2020 Mean value	Year 2020 Standard deviation
Identification stage	10 175	95.30	3.70	9 662	95.58	3.30
Preparation stage	10 175	92.00	13.22	9 662	90.41	16.61
Procurement stage	9 715	80.24	18.28	8 866	78.85	23.24
Implementation stage	7 683	65.63	26.50	6 978	64.85	32.15

Year 2021

- "Forged" disclosure, 12, 0%
- No disclosure, 9, 0%
- Partial disclosure, 1 024, 14%
- Complete disclosure, 6 553, 86%

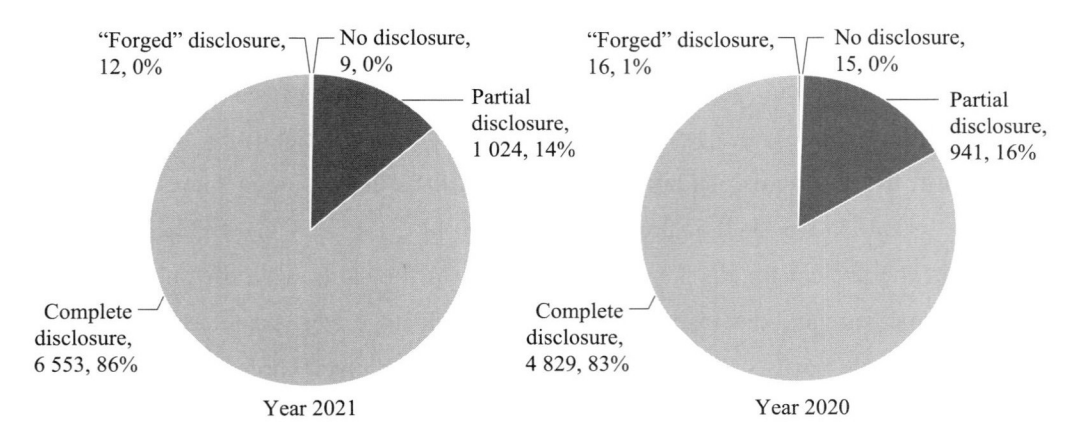

Year 2020

- "Forged" disclosure, 16, 1%
- No disclosure, 15, 0%
- Partial disclosure, 941, 16%
- Complete disclosure, 4 829, 83%

Figure 3-2　Disclosure of Value-for-money Assessment Report and Attachment

Once the scores were assigned, the final score of each field was determined by multiplying the score by the weighting (relative importance) determined through expert scoring (as outlined in Chapter 2).

3.2　Calculation of National General Index

3.2.1　Index Synthesis

With the score of each index, the Research Group would calculate the score of a PPP project at a certain stage (standardized to be a percentage out of 100), which is the sub-index at the stage. Take the disclosure in due time index at identification stage as an example: the stage contains six information items: "value-for-money assessment report and approval documents by the competent industry authority and the finance industry at the same level", "financial affordability report and approval documents by the finance department at the same level", "proposals for new or renovated or expanded projects and approval documents" and "feasibility study report or fund application report or report for project approval, and approval documents by competent authority; assets appraisal report with respect to the stocked public assets", "design documents and approval documents", and "asset evaluation report with respect to the stocked public assets or equity, and various programs and others (if applicable) that may be involved in the transfer of stocked assets or equity". The six fields scored 3 points, 3 points, 2.333 points, 2.667 points, 2.667 points and 3 points respectively in expert scoring.

authenticity. The remaining 37 fields were obtained directly from the website and were assigned "1" if the field recorded disclosed information or "0" if there was no information disclosed in the field. For the manually read fields, a more detailed scoring system was applied: "1" point was allocated for complete disclosure, "0.5" points for partial disclosure, "0" points for no disclosure, and "−1" points for false or erroneous disclosure (e.g. if there is a blank PDF file).

Standard definitions were developed to define Partial and False Disclosure, to support consistency in the points allocation. Partial disclosure was defined as a field which contained multiple items of information, but only part of which had been disclosed. For example, if the field "value-for-money qualitative assessment indicators and weights, scoring standards, scoring results" included only the scoring standards or results, then 0.5 point would be assigned. Similarly, the value-for-money assessment report and financial affordability assessment report requires the disclosure of the "value-for-money assessment report and approval documents by the competent industry authority and the finance industry at the same level" as well as the "financial affordability report and approval documents by the finance department at the same level". Some projects only disclosed the value-for-money assessment report and the financial affordability assessment report, but no approval documents, or vice versa. In these instances, a score of 0.5 was assigned too. False disclosure with a penalty of "−1" primarily applies to those circumstances where the uploaded PDF file was blank, or erroneous, or the information contained did not match with the field. It should be noted that in a very small number of cases some PDF files without appropriate documents lodged were not penalized. In these cases there were justifiable reasons (e.g. the project commenced before policies took effect) and under such circumstance, it was not assessed as false disclosure, and therefore no penalty was awarded, to avoid any unfair assessment.

Here we take the "value-for-money assessment report and approval documents by the competent industry authority and the finance industry at the same level" in disclosure in due time as an example to introduce our manual data collection. As shown in Figure 3-2, among the 7 598 samples subject to disclosure in due time, 6 553 completely disclosed the "value-for-money assessment report and approval documents by the competent industry authority and the finance industry at the same level", 1 024 made partial disclosure, 9 no disclosure, and 12 disclosed false or wrong documents. From 2020 to 2021, the complete disclosure rate under this index rose from 83% to 86%, the false disclosure rate dropped from 1% to 0.16%, and the non-disclosure rate from 0.26% to 0.12%.

3.1 Introduction to Sample Data

3.1.1 Sample Overview

As previously outlined, the Index System was classified into two groupings: the immediate disclosure index and the disclosure in due time index. Among them, the immediate disclosure index included 10 175 projects, an increase of 213 compared from 2020; the disclosure in due time index involved 7 598 projects, representing an increase of 1 797 compared with the previous year. Furthermore, among the total 10 175 samples in 2021, 460, 2 032 and 7 683 projects were at the stages of preparation, procurement, and implementation, respectively. As can be seen from Figure 3–1, compared with 2020, the proportion of samples in the implementation and procurement stages to the overall sample size in 2021 increased slightly, while the proportion of samples still in preparation stage declined.

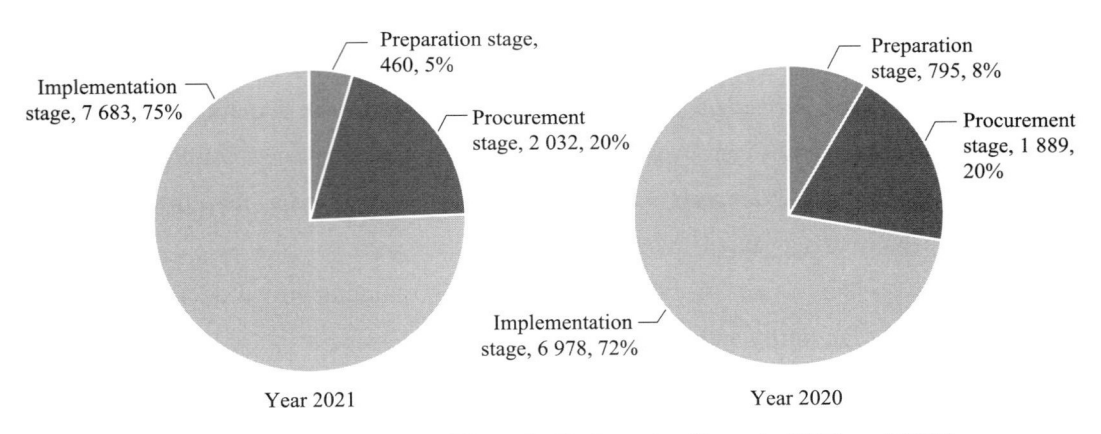

Figure 3–1   Distribution of Sample Projects by Stage in 2020 and 2021

3.1.2 Index Methodology

Chapter 2 highlights the Index System which consists of a total of 68 index fields, based on the CPPPC website, of which 31 were manually read from the website to verify

3

Primary Results and Overall Analysis

any information required by the Research Group, or it has disclosed some information, which was yet offset by certain forged disclosure. Of course, such circumstances were rare, especially upon the synthesis of a number of fields.

It needs to be emphasized that when the general index was calculated, some projects did not cover all five stages, in order to ensure index stability, weighting normalization was used to ensure the consistency of relative weights. For example, for immediate disclosure index, the weights of identification, preparation, procurement, and implementation stages were 0.19, 0.19, 0.40, and 0.22, respectively. But for a project with only the first three stages, the weights were:

Identification stage=0.19/(0.19+0.19+0.40)=0.244
Preparation stage=0.19/(0.19+0.19+0.40)=0.244
Procurement stage=0.40/(0.19+0.19+0.40)=0.512

2.2.4　Indicator Synthesis

In multi-index assessment, synthesis refers to the integration of assessment values of different fields on different aspects of a subject through a certain formula to produce a holistic assessment. There are many mathematical methods that can be used for synthesis. Common synthesis models are weighted arithmetic mean, weighted geometric mean, and their combination. All three have respective features and applicable occasions, with no absolute advantages or disadvantages. After comprehensively comparing the three methods, the Research Group chose weighted arithmetic mean, the formula of which is as follows:

$$d = \sum_{i=1}^{n} w_i d_i$$

Wherein, d is the general index, w_i is the normalized weight of each assessment index, d_i is the assessment score of single index, and n is the number of assessment indexes. Synthesis is based on a bottom-to-top layer-by-layer sequence. First, calculate the indexes on each hierarchy, and then weigh and consolidate the indexes to obtain the general index (see Chapter 4 for detailed calculation process).

Specifically, the disclosure status of each field from the website was firstly acquired and then given a score (a total of four scores, namely, 1 represents disclosure and no obvious forging; 0 represents no disclosure; 0.5 represents partial disclosure; −1 stands for "forged" disclosure). Subsequently, the scores of these fields were consolidated by the expert scoring method or coefficient of variation to calculate the scoring average (percentage system) at a certain stage (for example, disclosure in due time at identification stage). Then weights were generated by Analytic Hierarchy Process, and sub-indexes at different stages were synthesized into immediate disclosure index or disclosure in due time index. Finally, the immediate disclosure index or disclosure in due time index was weighted to obtain the PPP market transparency index.

It should be noted that based on the Index System and calculation methods, theoretically, a project's general transparency index (or staged index) may reach 100 points, indicating that the project has correctly and completely disclosed the information required by the Research Group; the lowest score can be negative, indicating that the project has disclosed much false information. 0 indicates that the project has not disclosed

Table 2–6 Expert Scoring Results on Specific Fields of Disclosure in Due Time

Stage	Specific field	Score	Weight
Identification stage	Value-for-money assessment report and approval documents	3.000	18.0
	Financial affordability assessment report and approval documents	3.000	18.0
	Proposals for new or renovated or expanded projects and approval documents	2.333	14.0
	Feasibility study report	2.667	16.0
	Design documents and approval documents	2.677	16.1
	Assets appraisal report with respect to the stocked public assets or equities	3.000	18.0
Preparation stage	Completion time of value-for-money assessment	1.556	33.3
	Completion time of financial affordability assessment	1.556	33.3
	Project implementation program as examined and approved and amendments thereto	1.556	33.3
Procurement stage	Prequalification: announcement time	1.778	5.5
	Prequalification: prequalification time	1.667	5.2
	Procurement: announcement time	1.889	5.9
	Procurement results: time of review on response documents	1.556	4.8
	Procurement results: time of negotiation about confirmation	1.889	5.9
	Procurement results: time of government review	1.778	5.5
	Procurement results: time of contract signing	1.778	5.5
	Procurement results: time of contract announcement	1.889	5.9
	Procurement results: media for contract announcement	1.444	4.5
	Project investment amount specified in contract	2.556	8.0
	Procurement documents	2.889	9.0
	Concluding observations with respect to prequalification, and the list of prequalification experts	2.111	6.6
	Concluding observations with respect to response documents, and the list of review experts	2.111	6.6
	List of the working group of negotiation about confirmation	1.222	3.8
	Appendixes to PPP project contracts	2.556	8.0
	Responsibility confirmation documents for expenditure by the government at the same level	3.000	9.3

Stage	Specific Field	Score	Weight
Preparation stage	Approval time of implementation program by the government at the same level	1.727	14.4
	Authorization documents of the people's government at the same level to implementing agencies, that is, the contracting parties of PPP project contracts	2.000	16.7
	Government's approval documents with respect to implementation program	2.091	17.4
Procurement stage	Prequalification announcements (including prequalification application documents)	2.364	11.2
	Announcement of pre-bid winners and transaction results, the announcement of the bid-winning and transaction results and the letter of acceptance	2.545	12.1
	Review opinions on proposed PPP contract by the competent industry authority at the same level	1.909	9.1
	Review opinions on proposed PPP contract by the finance department at the same level	2.000	9.5
	Review opinions on proposed PPP contract by the legal department at the same level	1.909	9.1
	Whether people's government at the same level has approved the proposed PPP contract	2.455	11.6
	Date of approval	2.455	11.6
	Review opinions by the people's government at the same level on incorporating the government's financial expenditure liability which spans two years into the mid-term financial plan	2.727	12.9
	Date of review	2.727	12.9
Implementation stage	Name of project company	1.636	15.6
	Establishment time of project company	1.545	14.8
	Registered capital of project company	1.818	17.4
	Economic nature of project company	1.455	13.9
	Subscription by shareholders	2.000	19.1
	Authorization by the people's government at the same level to government's investment representatives	2.000	19.1

Table 2–5 Expert Scoring Results on Specific Fields of Immediate Disclosure

Stage	Specific Field	Score	Weight
Identification stage	Total investment	2.455	5.52
	Partnership duration	2.273	5.11
	Secondary industries	1.091	2.45
	Operation mode	2.182	4.91
	Return mechanism	2.909	6.54
	Time of project initiation	1.636	3.68
	Type of initiation	1.455	3.27
	Name of initiator	1.182	2.66
	Project profile	2.000	4.50
	Contact person of project	1.455	3.27
	Contact number of project	1.455	3.27
	Contact person of financial affairs	1.455	3.27
	Contact number of financial affairs	1.455	3.27
	Land use area of project	2.000	4.50
	Proposed development year	2.000	4.50
	Selection of the mode of purchasing social capital	2.455	5.52
	Description of implementation program	2.364	5.32
	Cooperation scope (identification)	2.182	4.91
	Value-for-money qualitative assessment indicators and weights, scoring standards, scoring results	2.545	5.72
	Conclusions on whether value-for-money assessment passes or not (including opinions of the finance departments)	2.636	5.93
	Financial expenditure liabilities of the project and those of the PPP projects implemented and to be implemented in the year and annual budget arrangements, and the ratio of expenditure for all the PPP projects out of the budget in each year in the expenditure of the general public budget	2.818	6.34
	Conclusions on whether the financial affordability assessment passes or not	2.455	5.52
Preparation stage	Proposed investment value of social capital	2.182	18.2
	Proposed government investment value	2.273	18.9
	Name of government approving implementation program	1.727	14.4

(continued)

the table of weights calculated based on the decision matrixes provided by experts. For immediate disclosure, the weights of the sub-indexes at identification, preparation, procurement, and implementation stages were 0.19, 0.19, 0.40, and 0.22; regarding disclosure in due time, the weights of the sub-indexes at identification, preparation, procurement stages were 0.25, 0.30 and 0.45; and when being consolidated into the general index of PPP market transparency, the weights of the two disclosure modes were 0.61 and 0.39 respectively.

Table 2–4 Table of Weights Based on Decision Matrixes by Experts

Transparency index of immediate disclosure		Transparency index of disclosure in due time		General index	
Stage	Weight	Stage	Weight	Sub-index	Weight
Identification stage	0.19	Identification stage	0.25	Disclosure in due time	0.39
Preparation stage	0.19	Preparation stage	0.30	Immediate disclosure	0.61
Procurement stage	0.40	Procurement stage	0.45	—	—
Implementation stage	0.22	—	—	—	—

2.2.3 Weight Calculation Method

After the weighting of each middle hierarchy on upper hierarchy was finalized through AHP, it was also required to determine the weighting of the bottom hierarchy (that is, each specific field) on upper hierarchy. In this regard, the Research Group applied the experts scoring method.

Based on the discussion above, especially the "principle of significance", the Research Group scored the specific fields by means of expert scoring, giving them certain weights. The fields were divided into "common", "important" and "especially important", corresponding to 1 point, 2 points, and 3 points respectively. The higher the point is, the more significant the field is. 11 experts from college, government, business, and consulting were invited for scoring. Table 2–5 and Table 2–6 show the results of expert scoring. It needs to be further noted that the scores of the above indicators were compared with each other within a certain stage, rather than directly compared among all. To clarify this, the Research Group also listed the specific weights corresponding to the scores in each stage in Table 2–5 and Table 2–6.

obtain the eigenvector of the decision matrix. With the maximum eigenvalue of the reciprocal matrix, the corresponding eigenvector can be obtained and then normalized to be the weight vector.

$$CW = \lambda_{max} W$$

Step 4, consistency check. Firstly, calculate the consistency index CI of the $n \times n$ decision matrix.

$$CI = \frac{\lambda_{max} - n}{n-1}$$

Secondly, calculate the average random consistency index RI. 1) Randomly select numbers from 1–9 and their reciprocals to form a $n \times n$ positive reciprocal matrix and calculate its maximum eigenvalue. 2) Repeat 1 000 times to obtain the maximum eigenvalues of 1 000 random positive reciprocal matrices, and calculate the mean value of the 1 000 maximum eigenvalues. 3) Obtain the average random consistency index RI.

$$RI = \frac{k-n}{n-1}$$

Finally, calculate the consistency ratio CR and check consistency.

$$CR = \frac{CI}{RI}$$

When $CR<0.1$, it is generally considered that the inconsistency degree of matrix A is within tolerance range, and its eigenvector can be used as a weight vector. Otherwise, the decision matrix needs to be modified (repeat Steps 2 and 3) until $CR<0.1$.

Step 5, calculate the weight vector. By normalizing the eigenvector corresponding to the maximum eigenvalue of the decision matrix that has passed consistency check, the weight of the factor on the factors of upper hierarchy can be obtained.

Accordingly, the Research Group invited 11 representatives from universities and colleges (3), government (3), corporate partners (3) and intermediary consulting (2) to fill in the three decision matrices, then calculated the weights of each stage through the AHP described above, and finally obtained the mean values of the weights assigned by these experts. Appendix I shows the decision matrix survey for experts. Table 2–4 shows disclosure index), and the disclosure in due time decision matrix (to judge the relative importance of sub-indexes at identification, preparation, and procurement stages when compiling the disclosure in due time index).

In general, to compare the influence of n factors $c_1, c_2, ..., c_n$ on the factors on upper hierarchy, the decision matrix requires that the relative importance of two factors on the factors on upper hierarchy be compared each time, and the relative importance is usually expressed in values of 1–9. Value is assigned to each factor that constitutes the decision matrix c_{ij} (the meaning of the values is shown in Table 2–3, which is usually assigned by experienced experts). All comparison results constitute "paired comparison matrix", also called "positive reciprocal matrix".

Table 2–3 Meaning of Decision Matrix Scale

Scale c_{ij}	Definition	Meaning
1	Equally important	The impact of c_i is the same as that of c_j
3	Slightly more important	The impact of c_i is slightly stronger than that of c_j
5	Relatively more important	The impact of c_i is stronger than that of c_j
7	More important	The impact of c_i is obviously stronger than that of c_j
9	Extremely more important	The impact of c_i is absolutely stronger than that of c_j
2, 4, 6, 8	Middle value of two adjacent scales	The impact ratio of c_i to c_j is between two adjacent scales
1/2, ..., 1/9	Reciprocal	The impact ratio of c_i to c_j is the reciprocal of the a_{ij} above

$$C = \begin{pmatrix} c_{11} & c_{12} & \cdots & c_{1n} \\ c_{21} & c_{22} & \cdots & c_{2n} \\ \vdots & \vdots & \vdots & \vdots \\ c_{n1} & c_{n2} & \cdots & c_{nn} \end{pmatrix}$$

$C = (c_{ij})_{n \times n}$, $c_{ij} > 0$, $c_{ji} = \dfrac{1}{c_{ij}}$, $c_{ii} = 1$.

If the positive reciprocal matrix C meets $c_{ij} \times c_{jk} = c_{ik}$, then C is called complete consistency matrix.

Step 3, calculate the maximum eigenvalue of decision matrix and its eigenvector. Determining the weight of each index with decision matrix is actually to

Group utilized expert scoring method.[①]

2.2.2 Analytic Hierarchy Process

Analytic Hierarchy Process (AHP) is a comprehensive assessment method for system analysis and decision making, which can quantify qualitative problems in a relatively rational manner. The main feature of AHP is that by building a hierarchical structure, it converts judgments into the importance comparison between two factors, thereby transforming qualitative decision into quantitative decision, which is easier to justify.

In an AHP model construct, a decision matrix is formed through investigation and judgment. When the decision matrix passes consistency check, it is accepted to calculate the weight of each index; if the consistency check fails, the element values of the decision matrix need adjustment until it passes the consistency check. Specifically, the steps of AHP are as follows:

Step 1, establish a hierarchical model. Upon the in-depth analysis on the factors that affect PPP information transparency, subdivide the factors into several hierarchies according to their subordination relationship. The top is target hierarchy, the middle is rule hierarchy, and the specific fields are at the lowest. The hierarchical model for this Report is shown in Figure 2-1.

Step 2, build a decision matrix. Construct a decision matrix to compare the relative importance of two specific fields. As the schematic diagram of the PPP project transparency hierarchy in this Report shows, there are two classified indexes. Therefore, three decision matrixes were built, namely the general index decision matrix (to judge the relative importance of immediate disclosure index and disclosure in due time index when compiling the general index of PPP market transparency), the immediate disclosure index decision matrix (to judge the relative importance of sub-indexes at identification, preparation, procurement, and implementation stages when compiling the immediate

---

[①] The Research Group used the coefficient of variation method when calculating the weight of each specific indicator on the upper-rule hierarchy. It turned out that the results obtained by the coefficient of variation were in high consistency with those obtained by expert scoring. The decision to choose expert scoring method was made given that the method could better reflect the views on indicator importance of different sectors of the society, including industry authorities, university scholars, and social capital owners, rather than relying solely on the statistical characteristics of indicators. This makes it easier for each locality to locate problems in PPP information disclosure and make improvements in a targeted manner.

contained in the No.1 Document), if a project has disclosed corresponding information, it wins scores in the assessment, no matter the work is done well or poorly. For example, the PDF files of financial affordability report, as key information, were verified by the Research Group manually one by one, and at the same time, experts may assign a higher score to them. These are the factors considered in the assessment. As to whether a financial affordability assessment report is normative, scientific, has sufficient argument and reliable conclusion, etc., is not the research subject of this Report. Because logically speaking, even if the financial sustainability report is unstandardized or poor in quality, as long as the responsible party chooses to disclose the report in a real and public manner, it wins scores under the assessment process used. Of course, the Research Group may go beyond "information transparency assessment" in the future and conduct special assessments on the standardization of PPP work in a certain region or field reflected by these important reports.

2.2 Calculating Methodology

2.2.1 Introduction to Calculating Methodology

For multi-index assessment, weights directly affect the results. There are many ways to determine weights. According to different sources of raw data, they can be roughly divided into two categories: subjective weighting and objective weighting. Subjective weighting is to obtain results by experts based on subjective judgments, such as Delphi method, AHP (Analytic Hierarchy Process), expert scoring method, etc., which invites authoritative experts to compare the importance among different fields, but the approach compromises objectivity. Objective weighting is to obtain results based on the numerical calculations of fields. It does not rely on subjective judgments, so it has strong objectivity, but cannot necessarily reflect the importance relations among different fields, nor can it necessarily satisfy the requirements of decision makers. Representatives of objective weighting are principal components analysis and coefficient of variation. Both subjective and objective weightings have their advantages and disadvantages. In calculating the weights of the fields of each rule hierarchy on the upper-hierarchy targets, the Research Group used subjective weighting — AHP; when calculating the weights of specific fields on the upper-rule hierarchy, the Research

Primary index	Specific field	Remarks
Preparation stage	Completion time of value-for-money assessment	
	Completion time of financial affordability assessment	
	Project implementation program as examined and approved and amendments thereto	
Procurement stage	Prequalification: announcement time	
	Prequalification: prequalification time	
	Procurement: announcement time	
	Procurement results: time of review on response documents	
	Procurement results: time of negotiation about confirmation	
	Procurement results: time of government review	
	Procurement results: time of contract signing	
	Procurement results: time of contract announcement	
	Procurement results: media for contract announcement	
	Project investment amount specified in contract	
	Procurement documents	
	Concluding observations with respect to prequalification, and the list of prequalification experts	
	Concluding observations with respect to response documents, and the list of review experts	
	List of the working group of negotiation about confirmation	
	Signed PPP project contracts	
	Government's responsibility confirmation documents for the expenditure of the project or the update or adjustment documents of the people's congress at the same level (or the NPC Standing Committee) including the financial expenditure liability of the project into budgets which span two years	

2.1.4 Explanatory Notes to Other Core Issues

This Report assesses whether information disclosure is in place, rather than the "quality" of the information disclosure. Therefore, the Research Group has assessed the information disclosure of PPP projects, including completeness and importance, etc., but apart from obvious forging, the assessment does not touch upon the "quality" of specific content. Specifically, for a field (i.e., a defined information disclosure obligation

Primary index	Specific field	Remarks
Procurement stage	Prequalification announcements (including prequalification application documents)	
	Announcement of pre-bid winners and transaction results, the announcement of the bid-winning and transaction results and the letter of acceptance	
	Review opinions on proposed PPP contract by the competent industry authority at the same level	
	Review opinions on proposed PPP contract by the finance department at the same level	
	Review opinions on proposed PPP contract by the legal department at the same level	
	Whether people's government at the same level has approved the proposed PPP contract	
	Date of approval	
	Review opinions by the people's government at the same level on incorporating the government's financial expenditure liability which spans two years into the mid-term financial plan	
	Date of review	
Implementation stage	Name of project company	
	Establishment time of project company	
	Registered capital of project company	
	Economic nature of project company	
	Subscription by shareholders	
	Authorization by the people's government at the same level to government's investment representatives	

Table 2–2　Index System for Disclosure in Due Time

Primary index	Specific field	Remarks
Identification stage	Value-for-money assessment report and approval documents	
	Financial affordability assessment report and approval documents	
	Proposals for new or renovated or expanded projects and approval documents	
	Feasibility study report	
	Design documents and approval documents	
	Assets appraisal report with respect to the stocked public assets or equities	

(continued)

Table 2–1 Index System for Immediate Disclosure

Primary index	Specific field	Remarks
Identification stage	Total investment	
	Partnership duration	
	Secondary industries	
	Operation mode	
	Return mechanism	
	Time of project initiation	
	Type of initiation	
	Name of initiator	
	Project profile	
	Contact person of project	
	Contact number of project	
	Contact person of financial affairs	
	Contact number of financial affairs	
	Land use area of project	
	Proposed development year	
	Selection of the mode of purchasing social capital	
	Description of implementation program	
	Cooperation scope (identification)	
	Value-for-money qualitative assessment indicators and weights, scoring standards, scoring results	
	Conclusions on whether value-for-money assessment passes or not (including opinions of the finance departments)	
	Financial expenditure liabilities of the project and those of the PPP projects implemented and to be implemented in the year and annual budget arrangements, and the ratio of expenditure for all the PPP projects out of the budget in each year in the expenditure of the general public budget	
	Conclusions on whether the financial affordability assessment passes or not	
Preparation stage	Proposed investment value of social capital	
	Proposed government investment value	
	Name of government approving implementation program	
	Approval time of implementation program by the government at the same level	
	Authorization documents of the people's government at the same level to implementing agencies, that is, the contracting parties of PPP project contracts	
	Government's approval documents with respect to implementation program	

(continued)

projects, some projects contain information for both immediate disclosure and disclosure in due time, and some contain information for immediate disclosure only, so they cannot be assessed under the same framework. Therefore, for the transparency of individual projects, the PPP information transparency index includes two independent fields — one on immediate disclosure, the other on disclosure in due time. Considering that it is necessary to assess the transparency of the PPP market at regional and industry levels eventually, the Research Group used the analytic hierarchy process to weigh the index on immediate disclosure and the index on disclosure in due time, thus calculating a general index.

Both the index on immediate disclosure and the index on disclosure in due time include two levels — staged index and specific index. PPP projects are generally divided into five stages: identification stage, preparation stage, procurement stage, implementation stage, and transfer stage. However, there are no PPP projects having entered transfer stage in China, so it was not covered by both indexes. In addition, due to the lack of appropriate index fields on disclosure in due time, the corresponding index didn't contain the information at implementation stage either. Therefore, in the end the index on immediate disclosure included four stages: identification, preparation, procurement, and implementation; the index on disclosure in due time included three stages: identification, preparation, and procurement.

The hierarchy diagram of our final index system is shown in Figure 2-1. The specific index systems for immediate disclosure and disclosure in due time are shown in Table 2-1 and Table 2-2 respectively.

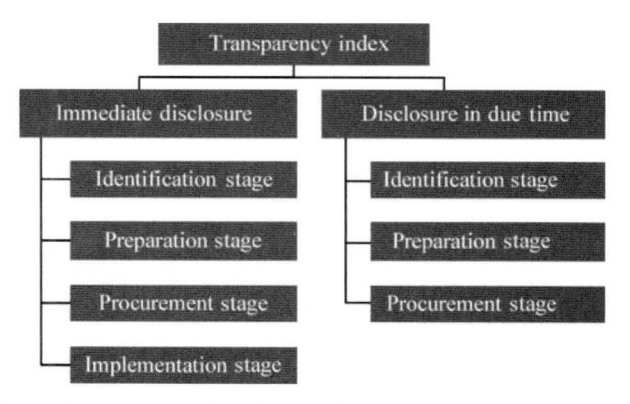

Figure 2-1 Hierarchy of PPP Transparency Index System

Among the 68 fields, some fields needed to be acquired from PDF files. However, after reading them through, the Research Group found that there were a number of "forged" samples: for some projects, PDF attachments corresponding to the selected fields were uploaded, but they turned out to be blank or false. This is because the system has stipulated mandatory materials. If the PDF files are not uploaded, the project cannot enter the database or proceed with subsequent steps. As a result, some project teams chose to upload false or blank files. In order to identify and reduce such acts in the future and ensure robust accuracy and fairness, the Research Group conducted meticulous manual verification of all the PDF files of all projects and "punished" the "false uploads". Specifically, for the fields related to PDF files, the scoring rules are as follows: if a true file is uploaded, it scores 1; if there is no upload, scores 0; if a fake file is uploaded, scores −1. In case of inadequate fields in an uploaded file, the Research Group marked it with 0.5.

2.1.3 Construction of Index System

The No.1 Document requires that certain specified information in PPP projects should be immediately disclosed, and the remainder disclosed in "due time". The requirements on immediate disclosure were easy to identify and process, but those on disclosure in "due time" were quite difficult, because the Research Group had to define "due time". However, as per the No.1 Document, "disclosure in due time" mostly refers to "disclosure within six months after entering into the implementation stage". Therefore, the Research Group decided to follow the approach applied in the previous years, that is, to select the projects that had entered the implementation stage by the end of June 2021 for assessment. For those projects, if they had not disclosed corresponding information as of December 31, 2021, the Research Group would conclude that they failed to disclose relevant information "in due time", and as a result, performed poorly in terms of "disclosure in due time".

Adopting such an approach led to a gap between the research samples for immediate disclosure and those for disclosure in due time. Specifically, as of the end of December 2021, the total number of samples entering the Management Database was 10 175, all of which could be used as assessment samples for immediate disclosure; however, there were only 7 598 projects having entered the implementation stage by the end of June 2021 and could be used for the assessment on disclosure in due time. For individual projects in the Management Database of the MOF's PPP Integrated Information Platform as of December 31, 2021, the No.1 Document of 2017 is still used as the primary basis for designing the Index System in this year's Report. And the No.110 Document and its annexes will be used as the assessment basis for years to come.

(2) Data sources. According to the requirements of the China Public Private Partnerships Center, all local PPP projects must be included and published on the PPP Integrated Information Platform set up on the homepage of the CPPPC website. For the consistency of data sources, the Research Group has chosen the PPP Integrated Information Platform as the main source. Therefore, in this Report, the main basis for index design is the No.1 Document, and the primary data source is the PPP Integrated Information Platform.

(3) Assessment object. On November 10, 2017, the General Office of the Ministry of Finance issued the *Circular on Regulating Project Database of the National PPP Integrated Information Platform*, which requires the establishment of Project Reserve List and Project Management Database on the basis of the Project Database. The document defines that "the Project Reserve List corresponds to the identification stage, which incorporates the candidate projects that local government departments have the intention to adopt the PPP model, but have not completed the value-for-money assessment and the financial affordability assessment; and the Project Management Database covers the stages of preparation, procurement, implementation, and transfer". In conjunction with the policy advices of competent departments, the Research Group has limited the assessment object to projects that have at least commenced the preparation stage, that is, projects that have been entered into the Project Management Database. That is, a total of 10 175 samples were eventually selected as analysis objects, an increase from the previous year.

(4) Method of acquisition. The Research Group mainly acquired the data available on the website of CPPPC[①], and referred to the requirements in the No.1 Document to select and acquire the source data before categorization. Upon analysis by the Research Group, a total of 68 index fields were determined. The Research Group extracted them one by one, by directly reading and downloading PDF files from the CPPPC website.

---

① CPPPC has also provided some data directly to the Research Group, for which the Research Group would like to show gratitude.

the objective and exogenous reasons that lead to discrepancies in the results in various regions and industries.

(6) Principle of common time-point. This Research Group has assessed the disclosure of all project information in the Management Database on the MOF's PPP Integrated Information Platform as of December 31, 2021, which falls into the concept of inventory, that is, what is assessed is the accumulative information disclosure status of all PPP projects before this time point. Restricted by data availability, the assessment did not address the dynamic characteristics such as the specific time of disclosure. For example, some indicators involved disclosure in due time, so theoretically, in addition to whether or not information was disclosed, the Research Group should have assessed the timeliness of such disclosure, which is an important assessment basis as well. However, as the Research Group could not obtain detailed information such as the specific time point of disclosure, such information has not been included in the Index System this time.

2.1.2 Design Basis for Index System

(1) Design basis. To assess information disclosure in PPP market, the primary basis is the relevant policies promulgated by the MOF and/or the China Public Private Partnerships Center (CPPPC). On January 23, 2017, the MOF promulgated the No.1 Document. This is the main operating guide for local competent authorities to disclose information on PPP projects. Therefore, the rules in the No.1 Document are the essential basis for the design of the PPP Market Transparency Index System. The Index System designed by the Research Group aligns with the requirements of the No.1 Document. In principle, the information not required by the No.1 Document is not included into the Index System, for the sake of fairness to all regions.

It should be noted that, as introduced in Chapter 1, on December 16, 2021 the MOF issued the No.110 Document. Compared with the preceding ones, the new policy on PPP information disclosure management has expanded the scope of responsible parties, increased the information to be disclosed, and specified information disclosure methods (from immediate disclosure and disclosure in due time to voluntary disclosure and disclosure upon application) and time limits, alongside the establishment of a proper supervision mechanism and a proper dynamic adjustment mechanism. However, given that the policy took effect on January 1, 2022 and the assessment this time covers all the

(2) Principle of commonality and comparability of available information. Since the transparency assessment covers every PPP project, which may contain unique information, the Research Group has selected the indicators that apply to all the project samples for the sake of comparability. Those inapplicable to all projects, such as "design documents and approval documents", "government's authorization documents (if any) for the adjustment and updates at the project procurement stage", "increase or decrease of the capital", etc., were not included in the Index System. However, the Research Group has provided some policy suggestions at the end of the Report on the administration measures for improving the disclosure of such information.

(3) Principle of continuity for on-going measurement of transparency. Since this is the fourth time we assess the transparency of PPP market, the Index System is required to not only reflect the progress made by China in PPP project information disclosure in 2021, but also seamlessly link with the systems in the previous three years, so that the index continuity will be maintained with consideration of potential future changes. In other words, the Index System shall have strong dynamic adaptability. The Research Group hopes that the information disclosure status of China's PPP market can be continuously assessed longitudinally through long-term tracking.

(4) Principle of significance in weighting scores. While the selection of indicators should be as comprehensive as possible, the selection should also be able to distinguish relative importance for transparency. For some particularly important indexes, as many fields as possible shall be selected. At the same time, the Research Group has set high scores for more important information and low scores for less important information through an expert survey. For example, the scores assigned to value-for-money assessment and financial affordability assessment might be higher than those to basic project information.

(5) Principle of impartiality. As an assessment report on policy effectiveness, this China PPP Market Transparency Report is expected to have certain impacts on regions and projects upon release. Therefore, the Research Group considers that this Report must adhere to the principle of fairness and impartiality, treat all projects equally and elaborate on each and every achievement and problem. It is necessary to truthfully present the objective conditions of information disclosure in different regions and different types of PPP projects, and at the same time, make as clear as possible

2.1 Construction of Index System

2.1.1 Basic Principles of Index System

The legitimacy of the Index System is directly related to the quality of the steps taken in index preparation and the validity of the interpretation of assessment results. To this end, the Index System established must reflect all factors that affect the transparency of PPP information in an objective, reasonable and comprehensive manner, and also take into account the availability and reliability of data. To establish a reliable PPP Market Transparency Assessment Index System, the Research Group defined key principles that should underpin the construction of an Index System. These key principles are hierarchy, commonality, continuity, as well as significance, impartiality and time-point.

(1) Principle of hierarchy within the Index System. Hierarchy refers to the multiplicity of levels within the Index System itself. Due to the multiple levels that PPP information covers based on PPP project life-cycles, the Index System must also be composed of a multi-level structure to reflect the features of each level in the PPP project life-cycle. At the same time, all the elements are linked to each other to form an organic whole, which is to reflect the full picture of PPP market transparency from the projects at different stages and levels. Specifically, with reference to the spirit of related administration measures, the Index System for PPP Market Transparency can be divided into three levels, namely, the overall index, a secondary index based on the five phases of PPP projects, and underlying specific index for tasks within each phase of a PPP project. Therefore, the transparency index can be classified into a general index and then sub-indexes at identification, preparation, procurement, implementation, and transfer stages. Of course, given that different projects may be at different stages (i.e., phases in the project cycle), not every individual project's transparency index covers all the five stages.

Index System and Calculating Methodology

Ranking by the cumulative number of projects, the top three in the Management Database were BOT (7 995), others (997) and TOT+BOT (399), together accounting for 92.3% of the total number in the Project Database. By the cumulative investment value, the top three in the Management Database were BOT (RMB 13 trillion), others (RMB 2.0 trillion), and TOT+BOT (RMB 407.6 billion). The number and investment value of projects in the Management Database by operation mode by the end of 2021 are shown in Figure 1–11.

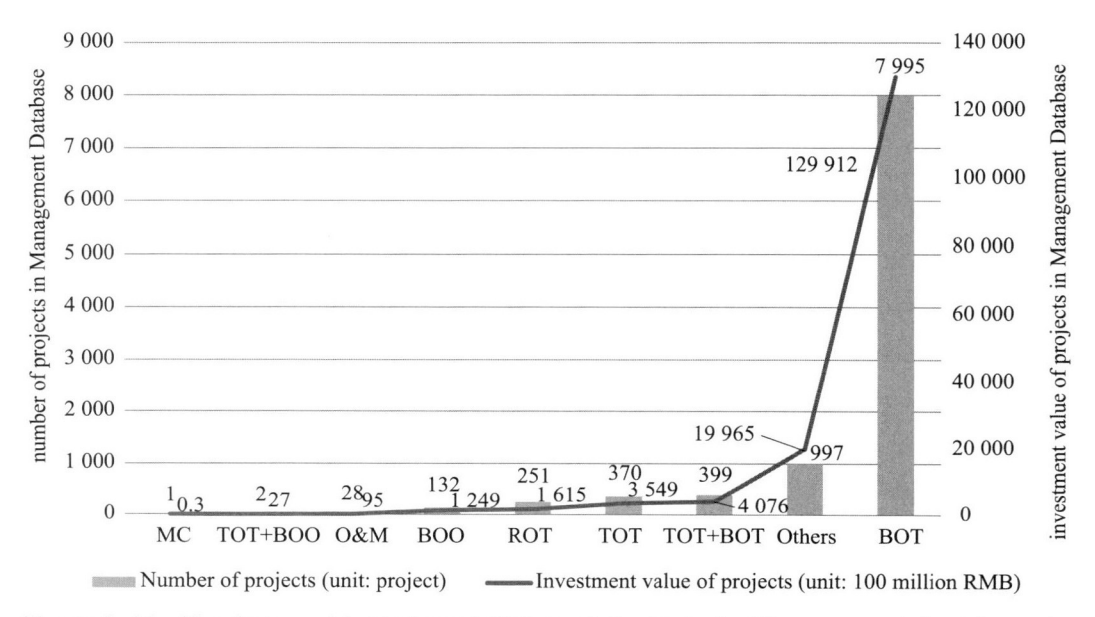

Figure 1–11 Number and Investment Value of Projects in Management Database by Operation Mode by the End of 2021

1.5.6　Proportion of Green and Low-carbon Projects

Proportion of green and low-carbon projects increased steadily Among the newly-increased projects in the Project Database in 2021, there were 373 green and low-carbon projects, with a total investment value of RMB 345.7 billion, accounting for 55.3% and 26.8%, respectively. 53 of them have been implemented, representing an implementation rate of 14.2%. As of the end of 2021, there were 5 881 green and low-carbon projects in the Project Database, accounting for 57.8%; and they contributed to a cumulative investment value of RMB 5.7 trillion, accounting for 35.4%, of which 4 315 have been implemented, with an implementation rate of 73.4%.

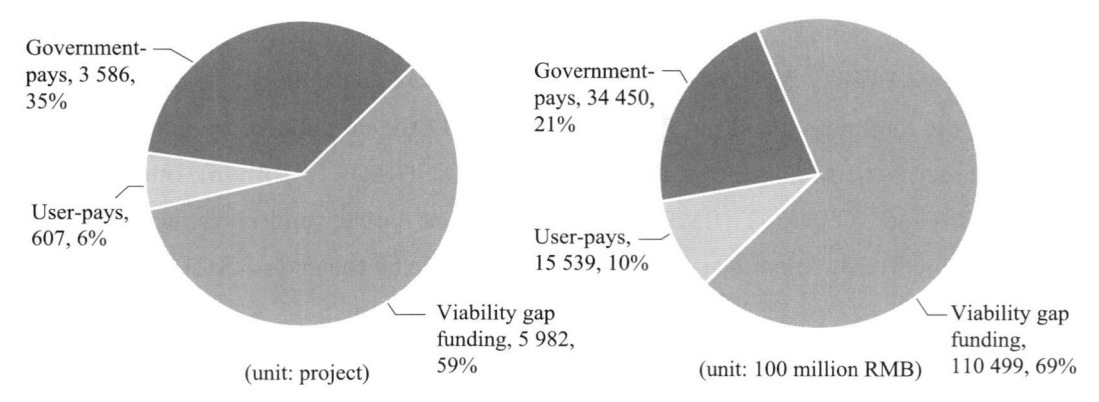

Figure 1-9 Number and Investment Value of Projects in Management Database by Payment Mechanism at the End of 2021

1.5.5 Distribution of Projects in Management Database by Operation Mode

In 2021, the top three operation modes with most newly-added projects in the Management Database were BOT (526), others (67) and TOT (33); while the top three in terms of the investment value were BOT (RMB 1.1208 trillion), others (RMB 91 billion), and TOT+BOT (RMB 30.6 billion). See Figure 1-10 for the number and investment value of new projects in the Database by operation mode in 2021.

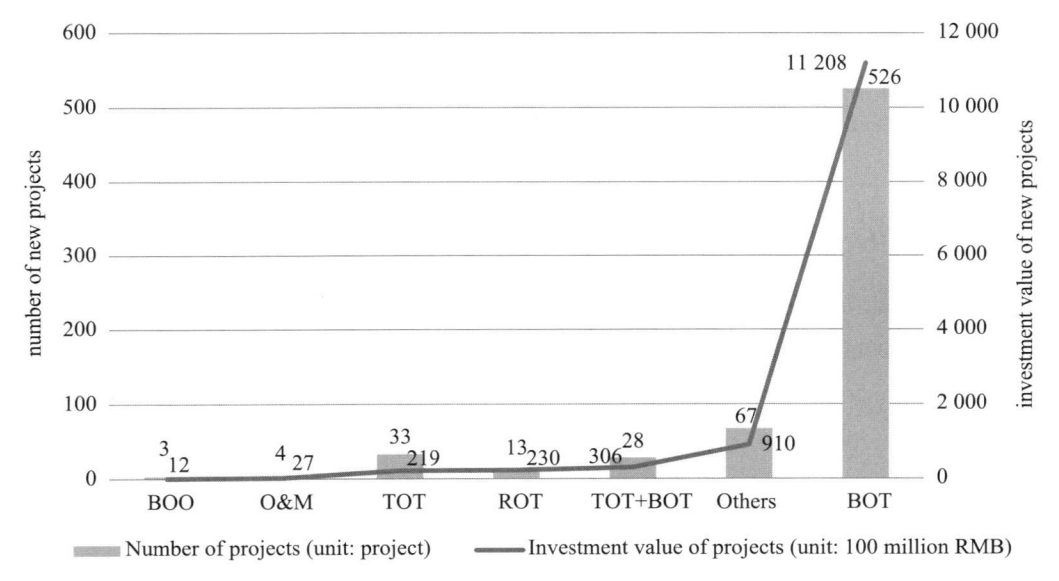

Figure 1-10 Number and Investment Value of Projects in Management Database by Operation Mode in 2021

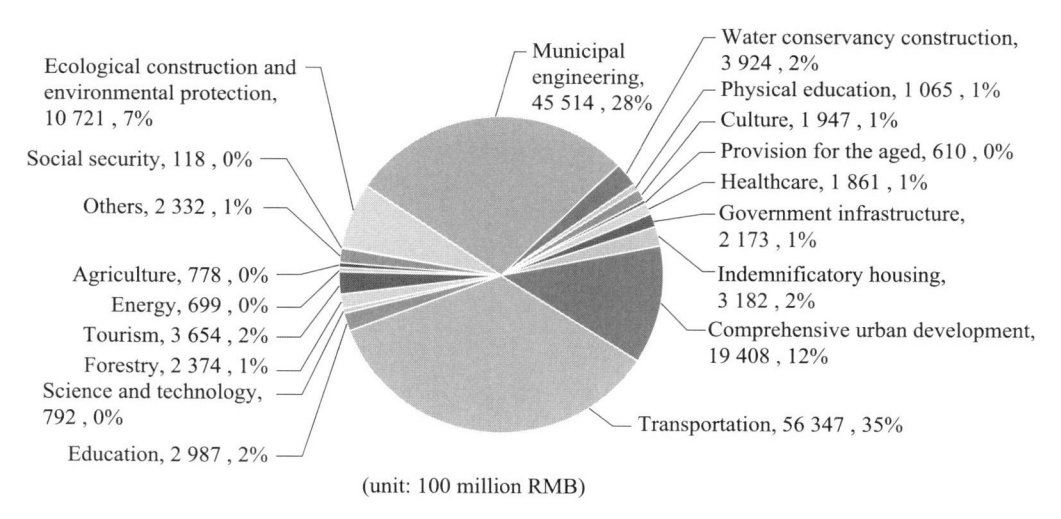

Pie chart labels (unit: 100 million RMB):
- Municipal engineering, 45 514, 28%
- Water conservancy construction, 3 924, 2%
- Physical education, 1 065, 1%
- Culture, 1 947, 1%
- Provision for the aged, 610, 0%
- Healthcare, 1 861, 1%
- Government infrastructure, 2 173, 1%
- Indemnificatory housing, 3 182, 2%
- Comprehensive urban development, 19 408, 12%
- Transportation, 56 347, 35%
- Education, 2 987, 2%
- Science and technology, 792, 0%
- Forestry, 2 374, 1%
- Tourism, 3 654, 2%
- Energy, 699, 0%
- Agriculture, 778, 0%
- Others, 2 332, 1%
- Social security, 118, 0%
- Ecological construction and environmental protection, 10 721, 7%

Figure 1–8 Investment Value of Projects in Management Database at the End of 2021 by Industry

Environmental Protection (RMB 1.1 trillion) and Water Conservancy (RMB 392.4 billion), accounting for 84.7% of the total.

1.5.4 Distribution of Projects in Management Database by Payment Mechanism

Divided by the three return mechanisms, in 2021 alone there were 44 user-pays projects with an investment value of RMB 208.8 billion, accounting for 16.2% of the total investment value delivered by new projects in the Database; 467 viability gap funding (that is, payment by both government and market) projects with an investment value of RMB 945.3 billion, accounting for 73.2% of the total; and 163 government-pays projects, with a net decrease of RMB 136.9 billion in investment value, accounting for 10.6% of the total.

As of the end of 2021, there were a total of 607 user-pays projects with an investment value of RMB 1.6 trillion, accounting for 6.0% and 9.7% of the total in the Management Database respectively; 5 982 viability gap funding projects with an investment value of RMB 11.0 trillion, accounting for 58.8% and 68.9% of the total; and 3 586 government-pays projects with an investment value of RMB 3.4 trillion, accounting for 35.2% and 21.5% of the total (see Figure 1–9).

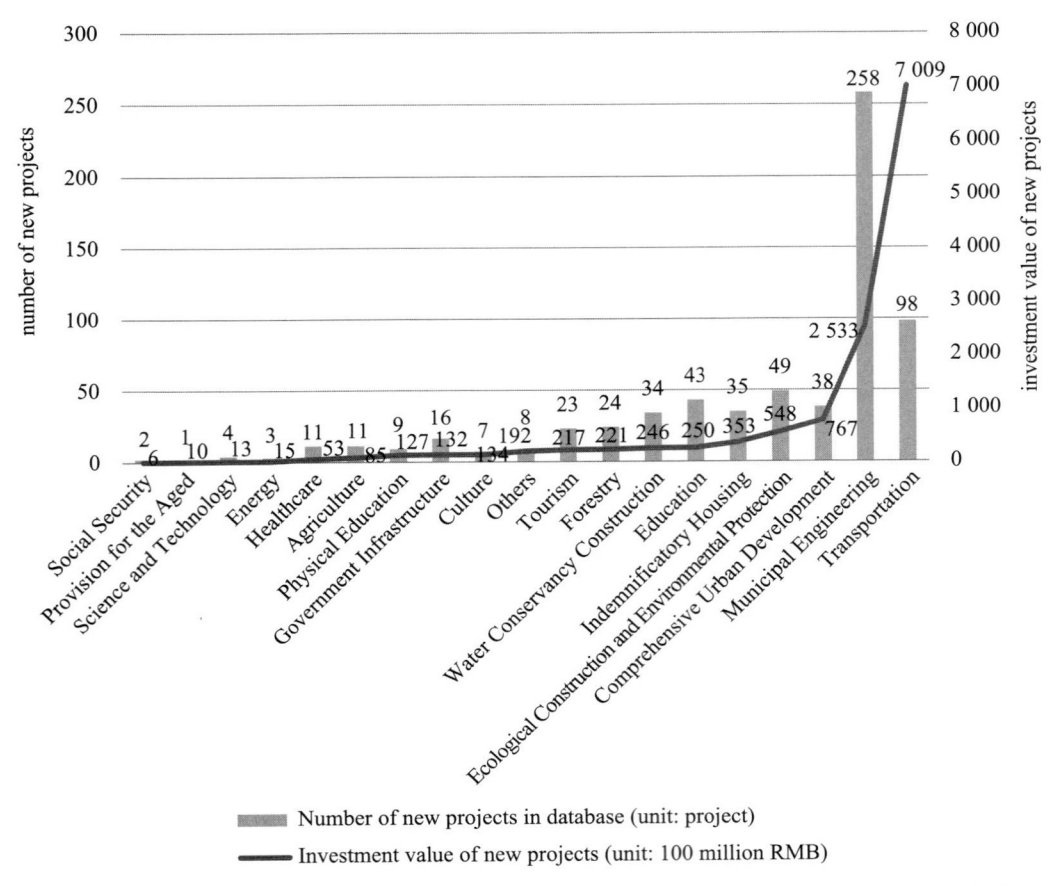

Figure 1-6 Number and Investment Value of Projects in Management Database by Industry in 2021

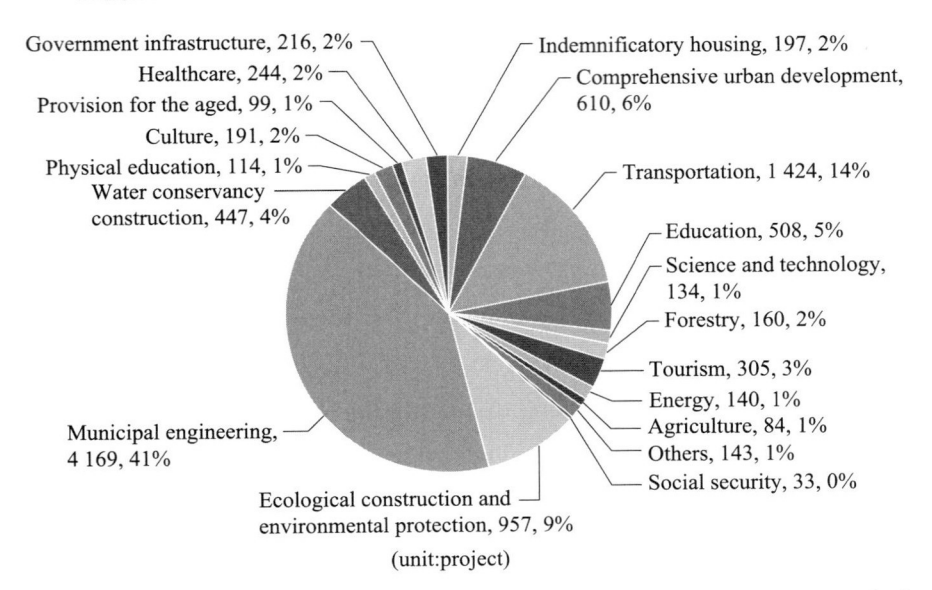

Figure 1-7 Number of Projects in Management Database at the End of 2021 by Industry

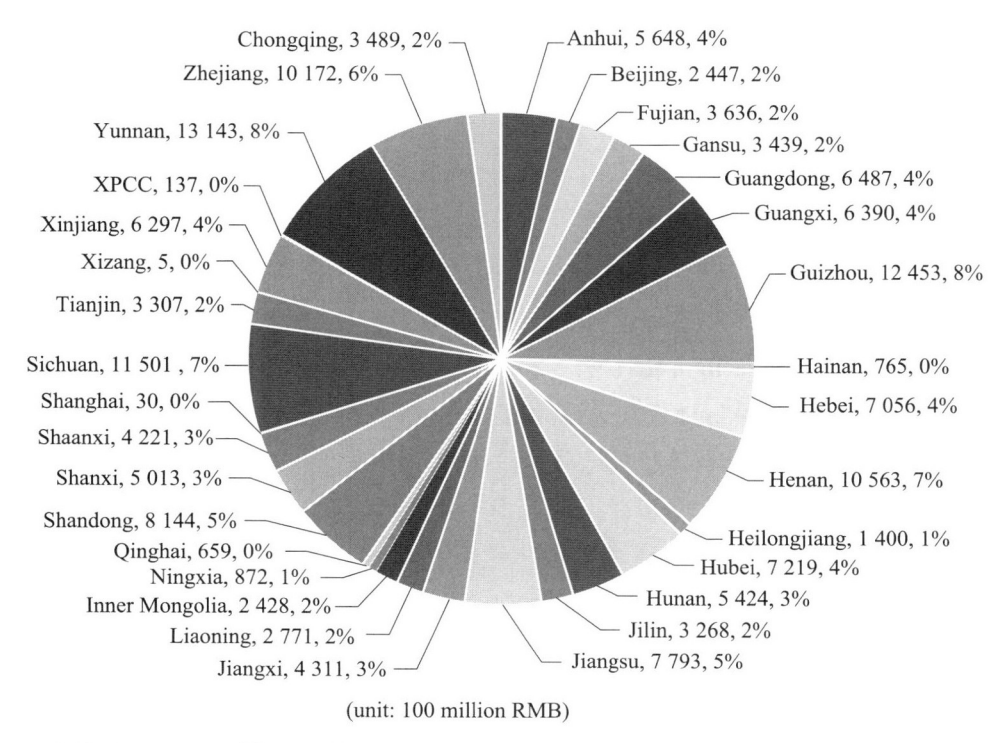

Chongqing, 3 489, 2%
Zhejiang, 10 172, 6%
Yunnan, 13 143, 8%
XPCC, 137, 0%
Xinjiang, 6 297, 4%
Xizang, 5, 0%
Tianjin, 3 307, 2%
Sichuan, 11 501, 7%
Shanghai, 30, 0%
Shaanxi, 4 221, 3%
Shanxi, 5 013, 3%
Shandong, 8 144, 5%
Qinghai, 659, 0%
Ningxia, 872, 1%
Inner Mongolia, 2 428, 2%
Liaoning, 2 771, 2%
Jiangxi, 4 311, 3%
Anhui, 5 648, 4%
Beijing, 2 447, 2%
Fujian, 3 636, 2%
Gansu, 3 439, 2%
Guangdong, 6 487, 4%
Guangxi, 6 390, 4%
Guizhou, 12 453, 8%
Hainan, 765, 0%
Hebei, 7 056, 4%
Henan, 10 563, 7%
Heilongjiang, 1 400, 1%
Hubei, 7 219, 4%
Hunan, 5 424, 3%
Jilin, 3 268, 2%
Jiangsu, 7 793, 5%

(unit: 100 million RMB)

Figure 1-5   Investment Value of Projects in Management Database at the End of 2021 by Region

(43 projects) and Comprehensive Urban Development (38 projects); and the top five industries in terms of the investment value of newly-increased projects were Transportation (RMB 700.9 billion), Municipal Engineering (RMB 253.3 billion), Comprehensive Urban Development (RMB 76.7 billion), Ecological Construction and Environmental Protection (RMB 54.8 billion) and Indemnificatory Housing (RMB 35.3 billion). See Figure 1-6 for the number and investment value of new projects in the Database by region in 2021.

By the end of 2021, the cumulative number and investment value of PPP projects in the Management Database by industry are shown in Figure 1-7 and Figure 1-8. In specific, the top five industries with most projects in the Management Database were Municipal Engineering (4 169 projects), Transportation (1 424 projects), Ecological Construction and Environmental Protection (957 projects), Comprehensive Urban Development (610 projects) and Education (508 projects), together accounting for 75.4% of the total; and the top five industries in terms of the investment value of projects were Transportation (RMB 5.6 trillion), Municipal Engineering (RMB 4.6 trillion), Comprehensive Urban Development (RMB 1.9 trillion), Ecological Construction and

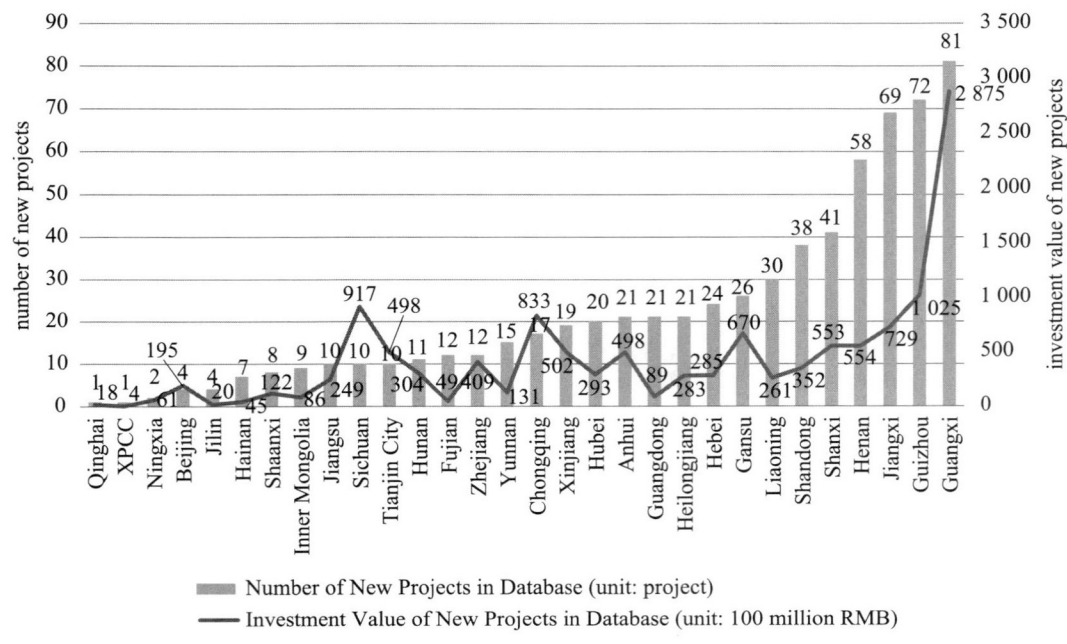

Figure 1-3   Number and Investment Value of Projects in Management Database by Region in 2021

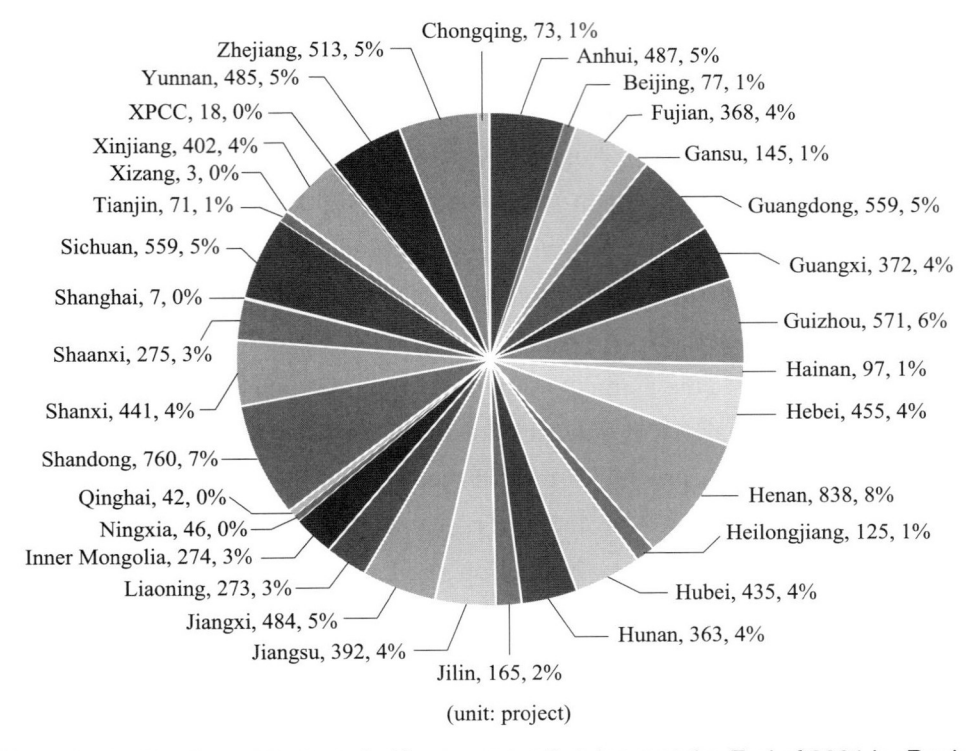

Figure 1-4   Number of Projects in Management Database at the End of 2021 by Region

In 2021, the PPP market's focus shifted from quantity and speed to quality. Throughout the year, 674 new projects were included in the Project Management Database, a year-on-year decrease of 324 or 32.5%. They contributed to an investment value of RMB 1.3 trillion, dropping by RMB 0.3 trillion or 18.8% year-on-year. Due to the change in investment value caused by the structural adjustment to inventory projects in the Management Database, the difference obtained from the investment value of newly-increased projects minus that of the removed projects was not the same as the net investment value increased.

The net increase of projects for the year recorded 251 (that is, the number of new projects in the Database at the end of 2021 minus that at the end of 2020), a year-on-year drop of 233 or 48.1%.

1.5.2 Distribution of Projects in Management Database by Region

In 2021, the top five provinces with most projects included into the Database were Guangxi (81 projects), Guizhou (72 projects), Jiangxi (69 projects), Henan (58 projects), and Shanxi (41 projects); the top five provinces in terms of investment value of newly-increased projects were Guangxi (RMB 287.5 billion), Guizhou (RMB 102.5 billion), Sichuan (RMB 91.7 billion), Chongqing (RMB 83.3 billion), and Jiangxi (RMB 72.9 billion). See Figure 1-3 for the number and investment value of new projects in the Database by region in 2021.

In terms of the total number of projects in the Database by the end of 2021, the top five provinces were Henan with 838 projects, Shandong (including Qingdao) 760, Guizhou 571, Guangdong 559, and Sichuan 559, together accounting for 32.3% of the total. Sorted by the total investment value, the top five were Yunnan with RMB 1.3 trillion, Guizhou RMB 1.2 trillion, Sichuan RMB 1.2 trillion, Henan RMB 1.1 trillion, and Zhejiang RMB 1.0 trillion, accounting for 36.0% of the total. By region, the number and investment value of total projects in the Management Database at the end of 2021 are shown in Figures 1-4 and Figure 1-5.

1.5.3 Distribution of Projects in Management Database by Industry

In 2021, the top five industries with most new projects included to the Management Database were Municipal Engineering (258 projects), Transportation (98 projects), Ecological Construction and Environmental Protection (49 projects), Education

Partnership (PPP) Integrated Information Platform (Cai Jin [2015] No.166), the MOF has developed the Public-Private Partnership (PPP) Integrated Information Platform and Project Library. The assessment of PPP project information disclosure in this Report is based on the data available on the Information Platform. In this section, with reference to such data, an overview of the PPP market in China is provided below.

1.5.1 Overview and Stages Distribution in National Project Management Database

As of the end of 2021, the Project Management Database included a total of 10 175 projects, an increase of 251, or 2.5% over the same period last year; the investment value totaled RMB 16 trillion, growing by RMB 0.8 trillion, or 5.3% year-on-year; these projects covered 31 provinces and Xinjiang Corps, and 19 industries. A total of 7 683 projects were implemented, with an investment value of RMB 12.8 trillion, and an implementation rate of 75.5%, rising by 4.0 percentage points from the end of 2020. A total of 4 804 projects with an investment value of RMB 7.65 trillion were started, representing an operating rate of 62.5%, 2.3 percentage points higher than that at the end of 2020. 460, 2 032, and 7 683 projects in the Project Management Database were at preparation, procurement, and implementation phases respectively, with investment values of RMB 555 billion, RMB 2.7 trillion, and RMB 12.8 trillion, respectively (see Figure 1-2). There are no projects in the transfer stage.

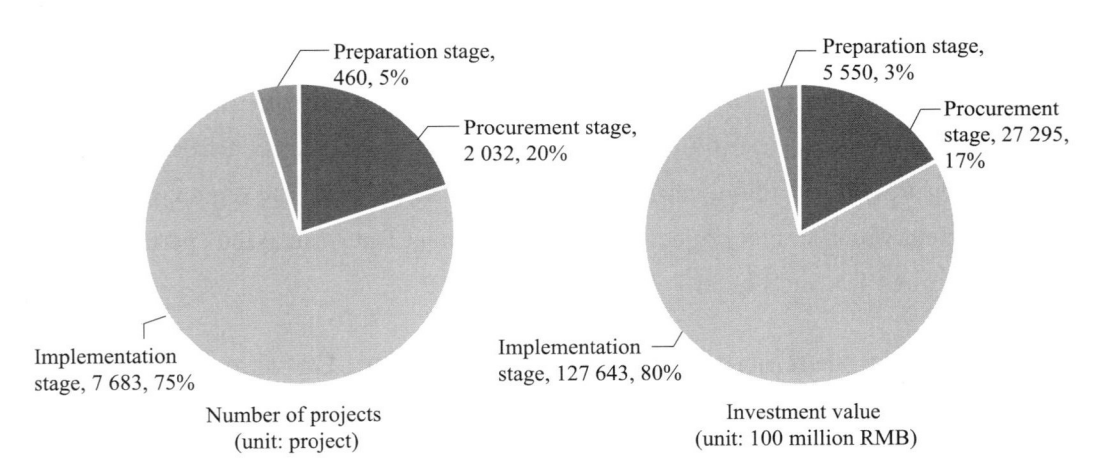

Figure 1-2 Management Database Projects in Each Stage in 2021

World Bank has evaluated the PPP policies and regulations in 140 economies from four dimensions: preparation of PPPs, procurement of PPPs, PPP contract management and unsolicited proposals (USPs) for PPPs. The report noted that China has established a basic PPP institutional framework, standardized the operation methods on key stages such as the value-for-money evaluation report and the financial affordability assessment report, and formulated a system for publicizing important information such as procurement documents and project progress, thus having created a favorable policy environment. In specific, China scored 80 points in Procurement of PPPs (average score of high-income economies, 73; average score of upper-middle-income economies, 62), ranking among the top in the world; 81 points in Contract Management (average score of high-income economies, 64; average score of upper-middle-income economies, 64); 54 points in Preparation (average score of high-income economies, 50; average score of upper-middle-income economies, 44); and 50 points in USP (average score of high-income economies, 63; average score of upper-middle-income economies, 60). Information disclosure is a critical approach for improving the state's governance system and modern governance capacity, as well as an effective measure to enhance government management. Strengthening PPP information disclosure is key to practicing new development ideas, comprehensively deepening reforms, and modernizing the state's governance capabilities, all while contributing to the establishment of an institutionalized, regulated and standardized PPP model for high-quality development.

The achievements and experience gained in disclosing PPP market information needs summary. At the same time, it is also necessary to analyze the content waiting for further improvement. The purpose of this Report is to summarize the disclosure work of the PPP market and analyze its strengths and deficiencies through index preparation. The rigorous and fair assessment on market transparency depends on scientific assessment methods. As for this Report, such a principle is articulated by the design of the PPP market transparency index system and index preparation methods, which is the topic of Chapter 2.

1.5 Overview of PPP Information Disclosure in China

Pursuant to the *Circular on Regulating the Operation of the Public-Private*

According to statistics, as of the end of December 2021, the PPP Integrated Information Platform included 10,239 projects and 360 PPP intermediaries. Websites, WeChat accounts, etc. have become the authoritative publishing platforms for PPP news.

IV. Sound measures for the administration of PPP information disclosure have been developed. In January 2017, the Finance Department of MOF released the No.1 Document, which clarifies the responsible parties of the PPP project information disclosure, and details disclosure content, time limit and methods to ensure timely and full disclosure of key information such as the basic information, implementation program, evaluation and assessment report, procurement documents, project contracts and other information of the PPP projects to be included in the database, for the purpose of standardized project implementation. On March 31, 2020, the MOF released the *Guideline for PPP Project Performance Management*, proposing a complete appraisal system for PPP performance. While clarifying who to take accountability, the document has also incorporated truthfulness, openness, transparency and quality into specific assessment rules. The Guideline is expected to more accurately and effectively improve the quality of information disclosure. On December 16, 2021, the MOF published the No.110 Document. Compared with the preceding ones, the new policy on PPP information disclosure management has expanded the scope of responsible parties, increased the information to be disclosed, and specified information disclosure methods (from immediate disclosure and disclosure in due time to voluntary disclosure and disclosure upon application) and time limits, alongside the establishment of a proper supervision mechanism and a proper dynamic adjustment mechanism. This is of great significance to furthering the standardized management and high-quality development of PPP projects. On November 11, 2022, the MOF issued the *Circular on Further Promoting the Standardized Development and Transparent Operation of Public-Private Partnership*, providing a specific operation guideline for PPP projects from four aspects: performing proper preliminary project demonstration, promoting standardized project operation, prohibiting hidden debt risks, and ensuring transparent project operation. The document is instrumental to driving the PPP model's high-quality development, better leveraging social capital, and establishing a unified national market, as well as a new development pattern of dual circulation.

PPP information disclosure has played a positive role in the China's PPP development. The Benchmarking Infrastructure Development 2020 released by the information that runs through the finance departments at all levels of "state-province-city-county" has been built up. Second, two platforms — information disclosure and online management, have been set up to publish PPP policies and regulations, news, share knowledge, and enable information tracking & management; and three functions: project management, transaction matchmaking, and information service are offered. Finally, four core application databases, i.e., Project Database, Expert Library, Institution Library and Data Bank are built: Project Database is used to collect and manage key information of PPP projects across the country; Expert Library and Institution Library are designed for the collection and management of the information on experts, consulting agencies, private capital, financial institutions and other parties involved; Data Bank collects and manages PPP related policies and regulations, work updates, guidebooks, training materials and best practices.

II. An information disclosure mechanism has been set up. It clarifies the accountability for information disclosure of PPP projects, the information to be disclosed and specific requirements at each stage, specifies the management of Expert Library and Institution Library, and publishes requirements for information disclosure by PPP experts and consulting organizations.

III. The PPP information disclosure system has been innovated. The information on the addition and removal of PPP projects is disclosed on a monthly basis, and overall PPP project information statistics and release are carried out on a quarterly basis. PPP policies and work updates are published through multiple channels, including the "PPP column" on the official website of the Ministry of Finance, the Chinese and English websites of the China Public Private Partnerships Center (CPPPC), the WeChat public account "China PPP Center", the mobile application "China PPP Map" and other online media. So far, a PPP project information disclosure model featuring regularity, comprehensiveness and multiple approaches has been established in China. Thanks to the care, support and joint efforts of all stakeholders, PPP information disclosure has achieved positive results. Project Database, Institution Library and Expert Library are gaining greater social influence and recognition, and have become useful tools for strengthening project management, advancing project connection, and promoting project implementation. The Project Database Quarterly Report is regarded as the "CSI 300 Index" in the PPP market. Financial institutions have even opened up a "green channel" for the credit support granted to demonstration projects that have done a better job in information disclosure.

Sixth, build up national image and demonstrate national confidence in political system. Many countries use PPPs for the delivery of infrastructure and services, which attracts the participation of multiple international organizations. After years of exploration and consideration of options, China has developed its own model and style of PPP projects, and has made innovations in many aspects of PPP models. Accordingly, the summary and analysis of PPP market transparency is important in the shaping of an open and efficient image of the Chinese government as well as increasing its influence and participation in the international PPP market. Moreover, as infrastructure is also an important component of the Belt and Road Initiative, promoting PPP standardization through information disclosure helps China's PPP model to spread in the countries and regions along the Belt and Road, demonstrating China's soft power while exporting products and technologies.

1.4 Development of PPP Information Disclosure in China

Since the initiation of PPP projects in 2013, as deployed by the CPC Central Committee and the State Council, the Ministry of Finance has issued the No.1 Document, the *Circular on Regulating Project Database of the National PPP Integrated Information Platform* (Cai Ban Jin [2017] No.92), the *Circular on Further Regulating the Project Information Management of the National PPP Integrated Information Platform* (Cai Zheng Qi Han [2018] No.2), the *Circular on Amending and Issuing the Measures for the Administration of Information Disclosure for Public-Private Partnership Integrated Information Platform* (Cai Jin [2021] No.110, hereinafter referred to as **the No.110 Document**), and the *Circular on Further Promoting the Standardized Development and Transparent Operation of Public-Private Partnership* (Cai Jin [2022] No.119), among other documents. And the Ministry of Finance is responsible for planning and implementing the PPP reform and promoting the information disclosure of PPP projects.

I. The National PPP Integrated Information Platform has been established. In 2015, under the guidance of the national "Internet+" action plan, the MOF established the PPP Integrated Information Platform — a PPP information network covering all regions of the country and 19 sectors, encompassing all stages of project implementation, and serving all market players. First, a channel for the collection and management of PPP project and consumers. Finally, sound information disclosure will also help resolve local debt and financial risks.

Fourth, raise governance level and build a new public management model. PPP is a market-oriented and socialized management model for the provision of public goods and services. It aims to, via reforms and innovations, break monopolies, introduce competition mechanisms, utilize market's professional and innovation capabilities, increase public goods and services and improve their provision, in order to satisfy the growing demands of people for diverse public goods and services. Therefore, it is of great practical significance to improve governance and build a new public management model. Early in the 1980s and 1990s, China began to experiment with public-private partnerships in the field of infrastructure construction. However, due to the absence of institutional construction, the projects faced "variation and distortion". To solve such problems, in this round of PPP promotion, the competent department of the industry started with institutional construction by formulating a system in line with the concept of "top-level design + supporting policies + operating guidelines", covering the life cycle of PPP. Adequate information disclosure is an integral part of the system, where competent authorities could take PPP information disclosure as a means to urging local governments and all relevant parties to participate in PPP projects in a more regulated manner, thereby jointly promoting the continuous improvement of the new public management model.

Fifth, promote PPP development and propel comprehensive reform deepening. Promoting PPPs in the provision of public infrastructure and services is a key task in the delivery of reform. It is also an important measure for advancing structural reform at the supply side, and an important means for implementing innovation-driven development and developing the new economy. Driving the development of PPP market fully reflects the core spirit of law-based governance, giving play to the decisive role of market in resource allocation, and better exerting the function of the government. The development of PPP market has promoted reform of the administrative system, the financial system, and the investment & financing systems. Therefore, the standardized development of PPP market brought about by its improved transparency is also of great value to other reforms. At present, China's PPP market is in a leading position in terms of disclosure work among similar government affairs, and even in the whole world. In-depth assessment, analysis and summary of achievements and experience in PPP market's information disclosure can enlighten other reforms.

1.3 Necessity and Significance of PPP Information Disclosure

First, improve business environment and encourage private capital to participate in public services. PPPs by nature are generally long term with the social capital providers (including private capital providers) often investing large sums of money over extended time period before any returns can be realized. Successful PPPs rely in part on the integrity of Government and the equity of the partnership arrangements. Therefore, improving the market transparency of the PPP processes can support greater participation in PPP projects, encourage competition which drives value and has the potential to create a fairer and more equal market environment. At the same time, improved PPP market transparency will also help improve the partnering spirit between the government and enterprises, assist to eradicate corruption, and maintain a clean and efficient government image.

Second, promote social harmony and enhance public awareness and confidence. The adoption of PPP for the provision of public infrastructure and services is closely aligned to the interests of the public. PPP projects are usually infrastructure, goods and services provided for the general public, and therefore, the construction, operation and quality of which directly affects them. Additionally, PPP projects are ultimately paid by either taxpayers or end users. Therefore, strengthening the disclosure of PPP information will help the public to understand and supervise the PPP market and PPP projects in a more convenient manner, facilitate the understanding and cooperation of the public, and create a harmonious atmosphere for the progress of related work.

Third, improve supply efficiency and enhance performance management over public goods. PPP projects are mostly applied to infrastructure and other public goods and services. They are generally characterized by detailed information, frequently technical in nature and with complex pricing structures. Strengthening information disclosure will help professionals in various fields make scientific and rigorous appraisal concerning issues such as pricing benchmarks, financial affordability, and charging standards in PPP projects, for the scientific pricing of public goods and services. At the same time, higher PPP market transparency alleviates information asymmetry during the construction and operation of public goods, eliminates insider trading, realizes the maintenance and appreciation of state-owned assets, and safeguards the rights and interests of taxpayers information transparency of PPP intermediaries, which is introduced in a separate chapter.

PPP is a market-oriented public service provision mechanism that requires the management means and service capabilities compatible with marketization, of which improved PPP market transparency is a critical component. PPP information disclosure in China has improved over the last three years following the systematic promotion of the PPP Integrated Information Platform. It has become an essential tool for local governments to strengthen project management, promote project connection, and facilitate project implementation. At present, China is accelerating the disclosure of PPP project information and government service information, with an aim to continuously improving PPP management transparency.

In January 2017, the Finance Department of MOF released the *Circular on Issuing the Interim Measures for Administration of Information Disclosure for Public-Private Partnership Integrated Information Platform* (Cai Jin [2017] No.1, hereinafter referred to as **the No.1 Document**). The document further clarifies the responsible parties of the PPP project information disclosure, details disclosure content, time limit and methods to ensure timely and full disclosure of key information such as the basic information, implementation program, evaluation and assessment report, procurement documents, project contracts and other information of the PPP projects to be included in the database. It also requires disclosure priority of demonstration projects to ensure that projects operate in a transparent manner, strengthen government supervision and social supervision, and promote project implementation. Therefore, this document also serves as the major basis for the Report to evaluate China's PPP market transparency: PPP projects that more completely meet the information disclosure requirements of the No.1 Document are projects which will be assessed as projects with high information transparency, and where projects fail to disclose information as required by the No.1 Document, they will be assessed as projects with low information transparency. Moreover, for the purpose of objective and fair assessment, all information beyond the scope of the No.1 Document is not included in the assessment scope in this Report. The reason is that data used by the Research Group comes from the Integrated Information Platform of the China Public Private Partnerships Center, which was designed mainly based on capturing the information disclosure requirements detailed in the No.1 Document.

In November 2017, the Ministry of Finance issued the *Circular on Regulating Project Database of the National PPP Integrated Information Platform* (Cai Ban Jin (2017) No.92), which further optimizes the process management of PPP projects by implementing classification management, classifying the project database into Project Reserve List and Project Management Database according to the stage of each project. Projects in the Project Reserve List shall focus on project incubation and promotion; while those in the Project Management Database are subject to strict supervision and life cycle management. The Project Reserve List corresponds to the identification phase, and incorporates the candidate projects to which local government departments have the intention to apply the PPP model, but considering their uncompleted value-for-money evaluation and financial affordability assessment, they cannot be called PPP projects in the strict sense; the Project Management Database covers the stages of preparation, procurement, implementation, and transfer, and incorporates the PPP projects subject to life cycle management in accordance with related management measures.

1.2 Concept of PPP Market Transparency

Information transparency refers to the degree of information disclosure of a market, company or project. For the purposes of this Report, transparency of PPP market refers to the degree of information disclosure of PPP projects by responsible parties (competent authorities, government-authorized partners, corporate partners, intermediaries, etc.). In theory, information disclosure across the PPP market also covers the disclosure of project management methods, policy documents, and the information of all project participants. Existing PPP expert database, institution library, etc. also contains mass data, but due to data availability and other reasons, the PPP market transparency in this Report refers only to the degree of information disclosure of PPP projects, and transparency indexes of all kinds are compiled on this basis. Horizontally, we constructed transparency indexes by province, city, and industry. Vertically, our indexes were divided into overall transparency index, transparency index of immediate disclosure, transparency index of disclosure in due time, and phased index. Besides PPP projects, this Report has also incorporated the capital covers private capital, foreign capital, state-owned enterprise capital, etc.

For the purposes of this Report, PPP refers to the provision of public products or services (usually infrastructure and public services) through a co-operative partnership between government and social capital. The government generally follows a competitive tendering model to select a social capital partner with optimal investment, financing, operation and management capabilities. The partnership is contracted so that the social capital partner provides public infrastructure and services and the government pays consideration to the social capital partner based on the performance and delivery evaluation of the contracted public infrastructure and/or services. Specifically, in this PPP model, the social capital partner can take charge of project design, construction, operation and maintenance of the infrastructure and the delivery of services as well as assuming commercial and financial risks, for a commensurate investment return (within a contract which clearly specifies the delivery obligations of the social capital partner). The government in turn supervises the quality and pricing of public services and infrastructure, protects the interests of consumers to ensure the maximization of public interests, and bears policy and legal risks. PPPs worldwide have evolved to cover most public infrastructure and/or service areas, including transportation, energy, water conservancy, water utilities and other economic infrastructure, as well as technology, environmental protection, education, culture, sports, health, tourism, social welfare and other social infrastructure.

1.1.2 PPP Operating Procedure

The *Guidelines for the Public-Private Partnerships Model* issued by the Ministry of Finance on November 2014 stipulate the operating standards for the life cycle of PPP projects, incorporating the stages of design, financing, construction, operation, maintenance, and termination & transfer. The operating procedure can be divided into five stages: identification, preparation, procurement, implementation and transfer of project (See Figure 1–1). The separation of the five stages is a crucial intermediate step in the compilation of PPP market transparency indexes.

Identification stage → Preparation stage → Procurement stage → Implementation stage → Transfer stage

Figure 1–1 Operating Procedure of PPP Projects

1.1 Basic Concept and Operating Procedure of PPP

1.1.1 PPP Definitions

Definitions of Public-Private Partnerships (PPPs) differ from international organizations and different governments, however they generally involve the use of private capital and in some cases, other forms of social capital in the investment and operation of infrastructure and public utility projects. The Asian Development Bank describes PPPs as a range of possible relationships among public and private sectors in the context of infrastructure and other services. The United Nations Development Programme, also refers it to the partnership between government, for-profit companies and non-for-profit organizations regarding certain infrastructure and services projects. Typically, government does not transfer the project responsibility wholly to the private sector. Instead, the parties involved in the cooperation share responsibility and financing risks. The European Commission refers it to the partnership between public sector and private sector, with the aim of providing public projects or services traditionally provided by public sector. The World Bank also provides a definition of PPPs as long-term contracts between the private sector and a government entity regarding the provision of public infrastructure assets or services, in which the private sector bears material risks and management and delivery responsibility. The Chinese government has adopted a specific definition for the PPP model incorporating a long-term benefit and risk sharing partnership established by the government through franchising, reasonable pricing, financial subsidies and other agreed revenue sharing rules disclosed in advance, to introduce social capital to the investment and operation of public infrastructure projects such as urban utility, thus enhancing capacity of supplying public goods and services and improving supply efficiency. The main difference between the Chinese government's definition and those by other international organizations and governments relates to the use of the word "social capital" in addition to the word "private capital". In China, social

1

Introduction

5 Municipal Rankings and Analysis

5.1 Municipal Distribution of PPP Projects ·· 77
5.2 Municipal PPP Market Transparency Index ································· 78
5.3 Analysis on Municipal Transparency Indexes of "Two Assessments and One Program" ·· 86
5.4 Analysis of Social and Economic Benefits of PPP Information Transparency ··· 89

6 Report Summary and Outlook

6.1 Report Summary ··· 95
6.2 Policy Suggestions ·· 97
6.3 Outlook ··· 99

Appendix I   Determination Matrix Survey for Experts ············· 101

Appendix II   Interim Measures for the Administration of Information Disclosure for Public-Private Partnership Integrated Information Platform ··· 103

Appendix III   Measures for the Administration of Information Disclosure for Public-Private Partnership Integrated Information Platform ··· 118

Appendix IV   List of PPP Information Disclosure and Regulatory Management Systems ·· 125

Appendix V   Ranking of Cities with Over 30 Projects in PPP Market Transparency Index ··· 128

Postscript ··· 134

Contents

1 Introduction

1.1 Basic Concept and Operating Procedure of PPP ·············· 3
1.2 Concept of PPP Market Transparency ·············· 5
1.3 Necessity and Significance of PPP Information Disclosure ·············· 7
1.4 Development of PPP Information Disclosure in China ·············· 9
1.5 Overview of PPP Information Disclosure in China ·············· 12

2 Index System and Calculating Methodology

2.1 Construction of Index System ·············· 23
2.2 Calculating Methodology ·············· 32

3 Primary Results and Overall Analysis

3.1 Introduction to Sample Data ·············· 45
3.2 Calculation of National General Index ·············· 47
3.3 Heterogeneity Analysis of National General Index ·············· 52

4 Provincial Rankings and Analysis

4.1 Analysis on General Provincial Index ·············· 57
4.2 Analysis on Provincial Index by Stage ·············· 63
4.3 Analysis on Provincial Transparency Indexes of "Two Assessments and One Program" ·············· 71

Province (90.55), Hebei Province (88.54), Shandong Province (86.39), Hunan Province (81.43) and Jiangsu Province (81.27).

Third, most cities delivered PPP market transparency indexes higher than those in 2020. The Research Group selected 53 cities that managed a relatively large number of PPP projects (>50 projects in the Management Database) for more detailed analysis. Comparison with the indexes in 2020 shows that most cities above the prefecture level scored higher in 2021 than in 2020. Among them, the largest increase was delivered by Rizhao of Shandong, the 2021 overall score of which increased by 21.79 points compared to 2020, followed by Weifang of Shandong, with increase of 20.53 points from 2020. However, there were also several cities recording lower scores in 2021 than in 2020, represented by Guiyang of Guizhou and Xining of Guangxi — the two saw the greatest drop in overall score, which was 2.67 and 2.19, respectively.

Fourth, information transparency helps increase the engagement of social capital and the implementation rate of projects. On average, cities with higher PPP information transparency showed a larger share of private capital contributions, as well as a shorter project launch cycle (measured by the interval between the time of contract signing and the time of project launch).

During the preparation of this Report and the analysis behind it, the Research Group has also reached some policy recommendations for the further improvement of the information disclosure of PPP projects, together with a preliminary plan for next year's report. We hope to further enhance the information transparency in the PPP market by refining the system of PPP information disclosure and standardized management, thereby facilitating the better and more sustainable development of the entire PPP market.

adjustment mechanism; on November 11, 2022, the Ministry released the *Circular on Further Promoting the Standardized Development and Transparent Operation of Public-Private Partnership*, providing a specific operation guideline for PPP projects from four aspects: performing proper preliminary project demonstration, promoting standardized project operation, prohibiting hidden debt risks, and ensuring transparent project operation.

Against this backdrop, the Research Group of PPP Research Center at the Shanghai University of Finance and Economics (SUFE), following the evaluation of the information disclosure of PPP projects in the past four years, carried out a detailed assessment on the latest status as of December 31, 2021. The Research Group assessed in detail the information disclosure work of 10 175 projects included into MOF's PPP Project Management Database as of the end of 2021, and compiled a set of "2021 China PPP Market Transparency Index", which incorporates 68 index fields and is divided into transparency index of immediate disclosure, transparency index of disclosure in due time, and transparency sub-indexes at each stage, i.e., identification, preparation, procurement, and implementation. Regarding the synthesis of indexes, the Research Group adopted an approach combining analytic hierarchy process (AHP) and expert scoring: for specific indexes, different scores were set according to the importance determined by selected experts; and for the synthesis of sub-indexes, the Research Group adopted AHP, a method commonly used in the compilation of similar indexes, thus guaranteeing the reliability of the index preparation method. In the end, through the statistical analysis of final results, the Research Group obtained the following findings:

First, the overall national PPP market transparency index 2021 was 80.01, a slight improvement from 2020. This is also the first time that the national average index has reached 80 since the Research Group started this project. Further analysis on heterogeneity shows no obvious difference in the transparency indexes between industries or between demonstration and non-demonstration projects.

Second, the overall PPP market information transparency index at the provincial level rose steadily, yet with a larger gap between different provinces. The transparency indexes of the top three provinces and the following provinces clearly demonstrated divergent trends: in 2021, most provinces scored similarly — if not slightly lower — compared with 2020. However, the top three provinces' scores increased by about 3~5 points, gradually expanding the gap with the rest. The top five provinces are Yunnan

Abstract

PPPs is the acronym for Public-Private Partnerships. At present, China's PPP model is not only a means of market-oriented investment and financing by government, but also has become a comprehensive and systematic market and social reform on the provision of public infrastructure and services. Therefore, all stakeholders (both internal and external) have high expectations for the further development and implementation of PPP, hoping it could play a key role in leading the reform of public finance system and assisting the public sector in deepening reforms. In this context, standardized arrangements for the management of PPP projects is particularly important, in which the timely and complete information disclosure of PPP projects serves as the basis. Since 2017, the Ministry of Finance (MOF) has introduced a number of key documents to continuously reinforce management over the information disclosure of PPP projects: in early 2017, the Ministry released the *Interim Measures for the Administration of Information Disclosure for Public-Private Partnership Integrated Information Platform*, which details all the requirements for PPP project information disclosure; on March 31, 2020, the Ministry released the *Guideline for PPP Project Performance Management* to establish a complete PPP performance management system, identify responsible parties, and include the authenticity, openness, transparency, and quality of information into specific assessment rules; on December 16, 2021, the Ministry amended and released the *Measures for the Administration of Information Disclosure for Public-Private Partnership Integrated Information Platform*, which expands the scope of responsible parties, increases the information to be disclosed, specifies how and when information disclosure should be completed, and establishes a sound supervision mechanism and a sound dynamic

2021
China PPP Market Transparency Report

Research Group

Fang Fang **Zong Qingqing** **Shi Cheng**

2021
China PPP Market Transparency Report

PPP Research Center
Shanghai University of Finance and Economics

Shanghai University of Finance and Economics Press